The Toughest Peace Corps Job

Letters from Somalia, 1969

by
JIM DOUGLAS

PORTLAND • OREGON
INKWATERPRESS.COM

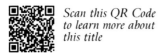
Scan this QR Code to learn more about this title

Publisher: Inkwater Press | www.inkwaterpress.com

Paperback ISBN-13 978-1-62901-327-5 | ISBN-10 1-62901-327-7
Hardback ISBN-13 978-1-62901-328-2 | ISBN-10 1-62901-328-5
Kindle ISBN-13 978-1-62901-329-9 | ISBN-10 1-62901-329-3

Printed in the U.S.A.

1 3 5 7 9 10 8 6 4 2

Dedication

To the Somalia 8s, a motley and honorable bunch that supported each other during our once-in-a-lifetime experience in Somalia and that has supported each other since.

To Bill Thompson, without whom our time in Somalia would have felt even more thankless and frustrating.

To Fadumo Jama Ali Wignot, who made life in Mogadishu both more pleasant and unpredictable.

And especially to Sasha, who has heard the stories for forty-five years and still seems able to withhold judgment and love me in spite of them.

Acknowledgments

Thanks to 8s John Marks, for providing access to his archives and photos and for vetting facts and making editorial suggestions; Gilles Stockton, for sharing his recollections, making editorial suggestions, and providing an update on recent Somali history; Bob Bonnewell, for sharing his detailed recollections and photos; Randy Meyers, for his photos and analysis; John Jimison, for his photo and sharing his reaction to the preface; Duane Nosbisch and Don Gregg, for their thoughts on the preface; and Baker Morrow, published author several times over, for his encouragement.

Thanks to Bill Thompson for his input and encouragement, reminding me just how difficult our time in Somalia actually was.

In Seattle, thanks to Jim Oswald and Alan Waugh for critiquing an early draft and encouraging me. Thanks to Alan for preparing the maps that help locate the places I describe. Particular thanks to Rosette Royale for sampling the manuscript and constructively telling me the author comes across as "an ass." Thanks to Peter McKee for his photos of the objects from the Somali bush.

And, finally, thanks to my wife, Sasha Harmon, who has provided support, editorial improvement, and unvarnished criticism, and helped me to keep my aspirations realistic. I couldn't have done this project without her.

Contents

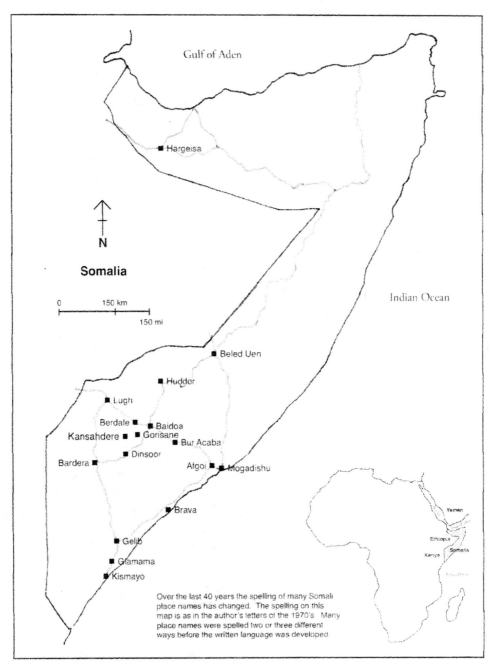

Gulf of Aden

N

Somalia

0   150 km

150 mi

Indian Ocean

Hargeisa

Beled Uen

Huddor

Lugh

Berdale ■ ■ Baidoa

Kansahdere ■ ■ Gorisane

Bardera ■

Dinsoor

Bur Acaba

Afgoi ■ Mogadishu

Brava

Gelib

Giamama

Kismayo

Over the last 40 years the spelling of many Somali place names has changed. The spelling on this map is as in the author's letters of the 1970's Many place names were spelled two or three different ways before the written language was developed

Yemen

Ethiopia

Kenya   Somalia

Map by Alan Waugh

Preface

ASTER SOMALIA'S SUPREME REVOLUTIONARY COUNCIL KICKED the Peace Corps out of the country in December 1969, we volunteers were told Peace Corps had a ranking of country assignments. Somalia was tied for 80th—least desirable—with Chad. We knew this was bogus. We had met volunteers from Chad and they had it much better. Somalia had been the hardest Peace Corps assignment in the world.

We should not have been surprised. Early in our training, Felix Knauth, the director of Peace Corps/Somalia, told us he had asked for "the best group of volunteers ever assembled," because we would have "the toughest Peace Corps job ever to be done." He may have been right—at least about the latter. I have never heard of a more difficult Peace Corps experience. Good intentions proved to be insufficient to overcome dramatic differences in culture.

I served as a Peace Corps Volunteer (PCV) in Somalia from November 13, 1968, until December 26, 1969. For the first six months, I was in an agriculture and rural development program, stationed in two villages in the Somali bush, living among people whose lives had been touched very little by modernity. I then moved into the capital city, Mogadishu (called Mog), to work in sports and recreation. In October 1969 the president was assassinated and the military took over, installing a government with a socialist and pro-Soviet orientation. Two months later—the day after Christmas—the new government expelled us.

1

Since that time, I have carried vivid memories of my thirteen months in Somalia. I sporadically kept a journal and made carbon copies of my letters home, and when I discovered them in 2013, the idea for this book began to grow. The experiences I describe—as crude and unreflective as my descriptions frequently are—form the basis for my memories of my time in the Peace Corps. Rereading what I wrote more than 45 years ago has prompted me to consider in a more mature manner the challenges people from very different cultures and conditions have in trying to understand each other. I hope this collection will stir a similar reaction in the reader.

Somalia

Somalia lies on the eastern Horn of Africa. Shaped like a number "7," it is the size of Texas and has 2,500 miles of coastline along the Indian Ocean and Gulf of Aden. Much of the country is arid scrubland, a rocky expanse with thorn bushes and an occasional acacia tree. In 1969 there were only 700 miles of all-weather road. Seventy percent of the population was nomadic, with herds of camels and a largely subsistence, or non-cash, economy. There was virtually no industry. The language was unwritten and, we were told, one of the hardest languages in the world for an English-speaker to learn. In 1969 most Americans had never heard of Somalia and had little idea where it was. My college alumni publication said I was in "Samala."

Although the situation has improved more recently, news from Somalia for much of the previous three decades was disastrous, concerning drought, famine, pirates, civil war, a lack of recognized government, and terrorism, including al-Shabaab's ongoing violent attempts to impose its particular brand of conservative Islam. Although far from simple, conditions in 1969 were better; the country did not start to fall apart politically until 1991, when the president/dictator who had ruled since the 1969 coup was deposed and numerous clan warlords began fighting for what little spoils the country could provide.

Plunging into Somali culture was a difficult task for a young middle-class American. Most rural Somalis had had no prior contact with white people. More than 99% of Somalis were (and are) Muslim. Although Islam there was moderate compared with the current wave of radicalism, the country was still very conservative socially. Volunteers had Somali friends, but most people regarded us as infidels who were damned to hell and worthy of little regard. The Peace Corps driver, a Somali man who we all liked and who had genuine affection for us, was saddened that we PCVs would all eventually burn in hell. I remember shaking hands with a woman who put her hand inside her clothing so that her skin would not contact mine. People sometimes followed us, calling us names, including "*gaal*" or "white infidel"—a word we heard very frequently. On a few occasions, kids threw rocks at us. We were definitely outsiders.

Somalis come from a proud nomadic culture. They are very direct, expressing exactly what is on their minds. The Somali language is guttural and spoken loudly. The norm for conversation is often confrontational, which to the uninitiated seems harsh and unpleasant. We had to adjust to a culture where people frequently responded with "*abaha wass*" (literally "fuck your father") when they disagreed with someone, even a stranger. It was a new experience to have a cute little kid come up to me, smile, and say, "*gaala, abaha wass*" ("white infidel, fuck your father"). I felt a sense of accomplishment when a guy hauling water in tins on the back of his donkey said something insulting to me, and I was able to respond, "Tell it to your donkey's asshole" ("*Damarka futadis ushek*").

A shrunken leg, a stammer, any peculiarity would give rise to a nickname that seemed insulting to a newcomer.* I was born with a cleft palate and have a nasal voice. It was common for Somalis to

---

* For more information, see "The Somali love of 'rude' nicknames" at www.bbc.com/news/magazine-26354143.

3

comment directly on my voice and call me by what seemed a rude name (*"san goleh,"* roughly translated as "nose-y"). At least it was better than the government minister in the 1980s who was commonly referred to as Goat Fucker.

The Peace Corps

Urging Americans, "Ask not what your country can do for you—ask what you can do for your country," President Kennedy established the Peace Corps by executive order in 1961. The Peace Corps Act declared the agency's purpose was "to promote world peace and friendship" by sending qualified young Americans "to help the peoples" of other countries. Over the years, more than 215,000 Americans have served in 139 countries. Peace Corps has been criticized by people at both ends of the political spectrum, and it is fair to see the agency as an element of U.S. foreign policy as much as a vehicle for good work overseas. A common aphorism provides that volunteers get more personally from their experiences than they contribute to the people they are serving.

Everyone in our PC training group was motivated by the desire to serve and to help "less fortunate" people in Somalia. Additionally, the Viet Nam War was in high gear, and the Peace Corps was an alternative to military service. All of us who went to Somalia were willing to take on the challenges presented by life in the bush. Many PCVs in many countries, then and now, have a very rewarding and fulfilling experience. In contrast, our time in Somalia, although unique and memorable, was far from satisfying or productive.

The Somalia 8s

In August 1968, less than two months after graduating from Stanford, I was one of twenty-one guys in their early- to mid-20s who reported for training on the Standing Rock Sioux Reservation, on the banks of the Missouri River, fifteen miles from Fort Yates, North Dakota. We were mostly from small towns. Some had not finished four years of college, choosing a Peace Corps adventure over continuing their education or being drafted to go to Viet Nam. We were the Somalia 8s—the eighth PC group to go to Somalia. Of the previous seven groups, six went as teachers and one built schools. We were the first group assigned to rural locations for agriculture and rural development.*

To prepare for the physical hardships expected in Somalia, we were in an isolated location and began training by working long hours constructing our own buildings out of plywood. As our training materials put it:

> The setting is decidedly isolated, and as such, reflects a characteristic of many of the Somali villages where Volunteers will be posted ... In order to emphasize the self-help concept which is the foundation of the Somalia 8 program, all living quarters, showers, and other facilities are to be constructed by the trainees.

After the first couple of weeks, we received instruction six hours a day in Somali language and culture, plus training in basic agriculture, such as raising chickens and working with young oxen. Three months after arrival, fifteen of us left for southern Somalia, most to be stationed in rural locations. Two others were "deselected," and four decided for different reasons that a two-year stint in Somalia was not for them.

Our experience was a debacle from the beginning—far from the

---

* Fellow 8 Bob Bonnewell recalls that we were told the plan for our group was hatched when Vice President Hubert Humphrey visited Somalia in January 1968. People in PC/Washington had substantial reservations about our program—so significant that the proposal was twice rejected by the program division. It was not until Mohamed Ibrahim Egal, the prime minister of Somalia, who happened to be in Washington at the time, put in his personal request that the program was finally approved.

classic feel good Peace Corps story. It was to be a very memorable thirteen months. We arrived in Mog shortly after the rainy season began. Because the roads were unpaved and therefore impassable, we were stuck there and missed the beginning of our first six-month long growing season. To occupy our time, the Peace Corps put us through a few more weeks of language training. Finally, after more than three hundred total hours of language instruction, two-thirds of us were sent to the sorghum-growing area in the Upper Juba region, where many people did not speak Somali. I was unable to even say "hello" in a language local people could understand.

Ten of us were assigned to the Upper Juba region.

- I, from Davis, California, and Stanford, was posted in Gorisane.
- Tim Gaudio, Santa Monica, California, and California Lutheran College, was also in Gorisane.
- John Marks, Westport, Connecticut, and Middlebury College, went to Kansahdere.
- Bob Bonnewell ("Bone"), Ottumwa, Iowa, and Iowa State University, was probably the most geographically isolated in Huddor.
- Dan Krall ("Kraw"), Cerro Gordo, Illinois, and Manchester College, was posted in Lugh.
- Don Gregg ("Fritz"), from Austin and University of Texas, was in Baidoa.
- Phil Lovdal, Southbury, Connecticut, and Waterbury State Technical College, was sent to Bardera.
- Duane Nosbisch, Ionia, Iowa, and University of Northern Iowa, was posted to Bur Acaba.
- Dave Zakem ("Zak"), Grand Rapids, Michigan, Michigan State University and a year teaching sixth grade in California, was in Berdale.
- Dave Zwink ("Zwinko"), Macksville, Kansas, and Kansas State College at Fort Hays, was in Dinsoor.

Five 8s were assigned to towns or cities farther south. Because it was easier to socialize there, either with educated Somalis or with other foreign workers, they had a somewhat more pleasant experience than the rest of us. *

- Baker Morrow ("Bakes"), Albuquerque, New Mexico, and University of New Mexico, worked briefly at an experimental farm near Mogadishu, and then taught English at the Training School for Animal Health Assistants in Mog.
- Randy Meyers, Northridge, California, and San Fernando Valley State, started as an acting veterinarian at the Livestock Management Department in Kismayo, on the coast, 325 miles south of Mog.
- Gilles Stockton, Grass Range, Montana, and Rocky Mountain College, was in Brava, a small town on the coast south of Mog.
- Bill Clumpner ("Clumps"), The Dalles, Oregon, and Oregon State University, was in Gelib.
- John Jimison, Granville, Ohio, and College of Wooster, was in Giamama.

Our assignment in the Upper Juba was to introduce ourselves (perhaps in a language no one understood), settle into village life, and figure out ways to work with local farmers to improve their production. We were to demonstrate some basic agricultural techniques: seed selection, planting in rows, thinning, cultivating, and— under optimal conditions—using animal power. Local farmers did

---

*   Several other people are also mentioned in the letters:
- Bill Thompson was assistant director of PC/Somalia and in charge of our program.
- Felix Knauth was director of PC/Somalia when we arrived.
- Leo Gallarano succeeded Felix as director.
- Rich Gallagher, from Lorraine, Ohio, was with the legendary 5s school construction group. Lacking in good sense, he returned to the country and quickly became an honorary 8.
- Finally, Fadumo Jama Ali was my girlfriend for much of the time I was in Mog.

not know we were coming and, apart from lip service, we had no support from the Ministry of Agriculture, such as access to vehicles or assistance from "counterparts" with whom we could collaborate. We learned much later that the minister himself had told PC/Somalia director Felix Knauth that, if Felix was so determined, he should go ahead and bring us over, but not to expect any support from him.* Our work was bound to fail, and Felix, on some level, must have known that. It was no wonder most of us had little success doing our "jobs."

After grumblings from the 8s, in mid-July 1969, PC/Washington sent program evaluator Dale Fritz on a tour of our posts. He concluded that the 8s were at least 20 years early, well ahead of the time local conditions might be receptive to and suitable for our program.**

My Experience

Initially, I was posted with Tim Gaudio in Gorisane, a village with a

---

* The minister's position allowed him to both receive and bestow significant perks. Labor jobs were created at research farms and demonstration plots run by the U.S., Soviets, Germans, mainland Chinese (called "Red" China at the time), Taiwanese, and Italians. The U.S. Agency for International Development sponsored educational trips and scholarships to the U.S. Other countries did the same thing. The minister's retort to Felix occurred when he learned that we 8s would be bringing none of these benefits for him to distribute as favors. (Thanks to Bob Bonnewell for this bit of history.)

** The September 8, 1972, issue of *Life Magazine* ran an article entitled "How a National Dream Grew Middle-Aged: Whatever Happened to the Peace Corps?" Interesting to the 8s was the statement, "'The agricultural program started in Somalia in the fall of 1968 is considered a complete failure,' another [Peace Corps] evaluation concluded. 'Volunteer plots produced less than the Somali farmers' plots and what was produced by the volunteers' plots was eaten by birds. In retrospect, it has been decided that what was needed in agriculture [in Somalia] was research.'" I don't know about the smaller yield or the birds (since there weren't many of us who actually produced much sorghum), but the 8s would all agree that our project was "a complete failure."

population of perhaps 300. No one there—particularly the nomads who passed through town by the hundreds with their camels—had ever spent time around a foreigner. If their reactions to us, as described in the letters, are puzzling, it is because they did not know how to relate to us. Understandably, we were a curiosity. Looking back, I can see that we had no better idea at the time how to relate to them.

Later, we came up with the analogy of "Martians." Suppose someone was to knock on your front door at home, say he was from Mars, and tell you he (it?) was on earth to help you learn something new. Certainly, language would be a barrier to communication. Also, you might well be skeptical that he could teach you anything that would improve your life. Finally, you would be very curious about him and perhaps not know how to treat him in a way he was accustomed to.

We were in the same relationship with people in the Somali bush. We weren't prepared for how they would react to us, how they would regard us. As you'll see in the letters, Tim put it, "This place [meaning us and the hut we lived in] is the biggest fucking freak show in town." As I wrote at the time, "We are not just the new people in town. We are the only freaks they've ever had the opportunity to stare at for any appreciable length of time." It was common for people to come in our hut and watch silently for two or three hours at a stretch as we read or wrote letters.

Our training materials stated:

[T]he general objective of these Volunteers is to leave some few Somalis better able to manage their environment to their advantage, or to leave some few Somalis less disposed to circumstances they now assume to be beyond their control. To achieve this objective there must develop a synthesis of attitude changes, both on the part of the Volunteers and of the Somalis with whom they will work. To achieve this synthesis, both Volunteers and Somalis will have to come as far as possible to know each other, to understand each other, and to respect each other.

No such synthesis occurred. I may be better able now to explain that failure than I was then, but when I wrote a summary of the reasons for the failure of the experiment to post volunteers in the bush, I said:

> The two cultures are so incredibly different and white men are so incredibly strange that the possibility of becoming anything but a freak in the eyes of the people is precluded. The people have heard of white guys, but the idea of one coming to live in their village makes no sense whatsoever. Because of his total strangeness, the white man is nothing but an object—to be laughed at, talked about, toyed with, *"baksheesh*ed" [that is, asked for stuff], and instructed concerning the benefits of planting in hills rather than rows. The things that the white man does, the things that he suggests, the things that he has, are so totally different from anything the local inhabitants have ever seen. The *gaal* [white infidel] does not fit into any framework known to the local people. Anything goes as far as relating to him and dealing with him are concerned.

But I'm getting ahead of myself. After six frustrating months in the bush, I talked my way into moving to Mogadishu to work in sports and recreation, a job I devised as I went along. I supervised recreation at the juvenile section of the prison and taught secondary school students to play basketball. Many of them had never held a ball before. I organized adult Somali basketball players to help coach the students and worked with the Interscholastic Sports Commission and the Somali Basketball Federation. I also played a lot of basketball, trying to model the fundamentals I was teaching the kids. Shortly before we were expelled from the country, I was asked to coach the national basketball team.

Basketball was new to Somalia in 1969, and it was a phenomenon. The prime location in Mog was a concrete outdoor court, lit by six bulbs at the corners and midcourt. Games were played at night because of the heat. There were no bleachers or seats, and big games drew well over a thousand people, all standing. It was frequently a wild experience, by any standard—sometimes with abuse and rocks coming from the crowd, but also in the final game before we departed, with hundreds of fans rooting for us over a team named for the revolution and stacked with the best local players.

My Letters

For much of my fourteen months in Somali, I had plenty of time on my hands—and a typewriter. I kept a journal sporadically and wrote dozens of detailed letters. I wrote one of my friends at the time, "I'm keeping carbons of all my letters, so that I can read them over in a couple years and see how my attitudes have changed—or warped as the case may be." Because my intention now is to describe the experience as I and the other 8s lived it, these letters and journal entries are by and large presented as I recorded them at the time.

Several years after returning home and getting on with life, I looked at these letters again. I was appalled at the sarcasm and immaturity of the person who wrote them. I was embarrassed by how infuriated I got from relatively small incidents. I am still mortified at my reactions. I couldn't believe I had shared such crude feelings with my friends and, to a lesser extent, my family. Years later I thought I had thrown the letters away because I was so chagrined by their tone. But a couple of years ago, they turned up at the bottom of a box with other papers and photos from long ago.

It is shocking to read the insulting and racially charged way I characterized people in Somalia, particularly during my time in the bush. Wogs. Savages. Really? I was 22 years old, a recent graduate from a prestigious university, and proud of not being a racist. What happened to me? In the following 45 years I have traveled a lot, including in Africa, and I have never had reactions toward others even remotely like those reflected in my letters.* In part, my interest in these letters now is to help myself understand why I had the reactions I had then. How could a person like me, a political progressive who went on to live a socially conscious life, have felt such negativity and anger in my youth? In publishing these letters, I suppose that, in a sense, I am "trying to come clean," facing how I reacted to Somalia.

I showed the letters to someone who commented, "The person who wrote this comes across as an ass." I have to agree with him. I wanted the most challenging post in Somalia, the most challenging country the Peace Corps had to offer. I got what I wanted, and I wasn't as prepared for it as I thought I was. The only way I can understand now the language I used then is to realize that the experience was so difficult and intense—and so dramatically different from anything I'd previously experienced or actually been prepared for—that I lost my social and moral bearings.

I wasn't "an ass"—at least in our culture—when I arrived in Somalia. But I'm sorry to say that the challenges of dealing with life in the Somali bush turned me into "an ass." Because of the intensity of the experience, I lost the ability to treat the Somali people with respect. I am not at all proud of it, but that's what happened.

When we left North Dakota, we all thought we were prepared for the hardships that awaited us in Somalia. I genuinely believed then—and I believe now—that I was prepared for much of what I encountered in the bush, specifically the physical hardships. The people who put on our training tried to prepare us for the cultural collision that awaited, but they were educated city Somalis and probably would have felt as out of their element as we did. We received no training in how to live in isolation among rural communities in the bush or how to understand the reactions we would get from people there. I was not prepared for life in a fishbowl 24 hours a day.

---

*   This subsequent travel has included volunteering with Earthwatch and Habitat for Humanity housing construction teams, frequently leading the latter. I have not been back to Somalia.

The other 8s had similar, but not identical, experiences. Some had a better time of it than others, but we all experienced frequent ups and downs. I suspect that Tim and I were in the most challenging situation, because Gorisane was so small and rural. The cultural differences were as great as they could possibly have been. The rhythm of life, the nature of our relationship with local people, and the content of most conversation were totally different from everything we were used to. We also had to deal with isolation and, sometimes in Gorisane, the fact that we ate less than a thousand calories a day. Creatures lived in our thatched roof, and camels and cows defecated outside our door. We suffered from dysentery.

In short, every second in the Somali bush was drastically different from every second at home. And most of those seconds involved challenges. In a tape to friends, I said that "being discouraged was a 24-hour-a-day deal." We joked about going home in a "wrap-around sport coat" (a strait jacket). Although not military combat or walking solo across the Congo, it was tough duty by any measure.

Particularly in the bush, the biggest problem involved our relationships with the local people. Everywhere we turned there was an impediment to feeling successful or satisfied, and frequently the cause was our clash with the way Somalis did things. We all knew some Somalis with whom we were friendly. But to most people in the bush—particularly the men—we were "Martians."

Cultures have traits that are admirable (at least in a foreigner's eyes) and traits that are not. A country the size of Somalia has a personality of its own, and the Somali personality was very different from ours. Somalis were and are a product of their harsh and hostile environment. In general, Somali people were argumentative and certain they were right in just about every conversation. This was true with us and with each other.

Surprisingly, to us, people in the bush were very xenophobic and ethnocentric, emphatically believing that they were superior to us and lived in the best country in the world.* Americans argu-ably have a national personality as well and frequently carry with them a feeling of superiority or arrogance. There must have been at least some of that in the mix, contributing to the frequent diffi-culty we had dealing with people.

In 1969 and more recently, other PCVs have encountered very different, more open, and friendlier "national personalities" in other African countries. People in Somalia were noticeably dif-ferent from the people I've met in subsequent travels to Ghana, Cameroon, Kenya, and Botswana. Somalis were harsh with each other, saw us as foreign infidels, and were harsh with us. By our cultural norms, their treatment of us was frequently scornful and derisive. They seemed insensitive and biased against us. Perhaps that partially explains what seems like our bias against them.**

I've also come to realize over the intervening years that we are not nearly as wise in our early twenties as we think we are.*** Our

---

* At the same time, they knew very little about the rest of that world. For example, it was common for people in the bush to have had no formal education and not to know there was an ocean that would prevent walking from Somalia to America.

** Fellow 8, Gilles Stockton, recently wrote with an additional possible expla-nation for the way Somali people treated us: "Nomadic peoples don't like to share. In his latest book, *The World Until Yesterday*, Jared Diamond discusses how societies came to govern themselves, starting from hunter/gather groups, evolving to chieftains [etc.]. In the hunter/gather societies of New Guinea, every person you do not know and live with is a potential enemy. The first instinct is to kill the person lest he kills you ... Being a hunter/gatherer is a state of extreme personal liberty but you are never secure, because neighboring hunter/gatherers might kill you any time you are not vigilant ... Somali culture in 1969 was still dominated by a kind of hybrid between hunter/gatherer and a very weak chiefdom. From their point of view, outsiders could only be there in order to take something away. The agro-pastoralists that we were supposed to work with were in a very insecure position. They had little political power in the Somali state ... The natural question [they] would be asking themselves is, 'What are these new *Meraican* invaders here to take away from us?'"

*** Additionally, 1969 was a very different time, and my thinking was a product of that time period. For example, Stanford was still known as the thinking and behavior are not as completely formed or as mature as we might think at the time. Young men sometimes say and do stupid things. There is a reason that psychologists now say the final stage of child development does not end until age 25.*

I'm certain that I lost my temper more times in the Peace Corps than in the rest of my life. Other Somali 8s behaved in ways they have never done since. We had many contentious interactions with Somalis, frequently because we thought we were being treated differently than a Somali would be. I wish now that I had been prepared not to take that behavior personally, even though it seemed very personal at the time.

Because the way I expressed myself in these letters and journal entries reflects the powerful reaction I and most of the 8s had to our experience, I have resisted the temptation to make myself look better by changing the language. The tone of the letters does, however, change significantly over time. The first weeks in the bush I was filled with enthusiasm and optimism. I remember we joked about fining ourselves every time we used the word "fantastic" to describe our situation.

Then the reality of our situation sank in—our inability to communicate and the Somalis' perception of us. Over time, my tone became more and more frustrated and irritated. At times, things seemed fine, but every turn for the worse was like picking at a scab. Finally, when the experiment in the bush failed and I moved into

---

Indians and had a song that included the line "Indians scalp [opponents] with a tomahawk."

* It is probably relevant to this point that in the early '70s the Peace Corps adopted a policy of "New Directions," moving from predominantly recruiting "A.B. generalists," like most of the 8s, to seeking out older volunteers who had more specific skills. The same article in *Life* cited earlier said "[The Peace Corps] has dropped every emphasis it once placed on its identification with the nation's youth for whose energies and willingness to serve it was originally created. The Peace Corps instead prefers to lay stress upon the quiet and handy technical skills of the elders it now recruits." It was a significant change, which recognized that 22-year-olds right out of college may not make the best PCVs.

Mog, my feelings of frustration moderated and my temper tantrums were less frequent. I still wrote some rude things about the country and its people, but I was much happier, my attitude was better, and I expressed myself in a more mature manner.

It is probably generally true that if you put young Americans— or young people from any country—in a very different culture under very trying circumstances, they will say and do some things they won't be proud of later. I encourage readers to put themselves in our situation. I have no doubt that any outsider who spent six months living under the same conditions in the Somali bush—at least one 22 years old, with a background similar to mine and no previous relevant experience—would also have been unsettled psychologically. This is not intended as an excuse, just my best attempt to understand my reaction and the way I expressed myself.

Technical Information

I have eliminated typos, reduced duplications, and done some editing to make things read more smoothly. The Somali language was unwritten in 1969. My spellings are phonetic and may differ from the same word or name written in the Somali script introduced in 1972. I have eliminated some but not all of the gratuitous profanity and sarcasm that adds nothing to the story, and I have altered slang that was peculiar to my crowd in college. I have deleted some conversations with friends that do not relate to my being in the Peace Corps. ("How was Christmas?") I have added some clarifying information in brackets and italics in order to help the reader understand the context. However—for better or worse— to a great extent, these letters and journal entries are as I wrote them. In Somalia. In 1969. Certainly, I have done little to conceal the attitudes I expressed at the time.

About endnotes: The excerpts from the letters are presented by subject rather than strictly chronologically. Each time the text changes from one letter or journal entry to another, the citation for the source document is included as an endnote at the end of the first sentence from the next document. In some cases, there are citations every few sentences. In others, the citations are pages apart.

I have included some photos, but they are an incomplete record of my experience. Taking photos would typically attract a crowd of people, many of whom were suspicious. We understood that in the bush some people were concerned that having their picture taken would steal their soul. In Mog, taking photos only added to people's suspicions that PCVs were spies. As a result of these factors, none of us took many photos while we were in Somalia.

After several months in the bush I wrote to a college friend regarding my experience, "I can't expect anyone at home to understand it. My reaction has seemed so strange when I think about it myself that I don't see how anyone who hasn't lived through the experience second-by-second could ever be expected to understand." More than 45 years later, I am publishing this because I hope that's not true. It's also an interesting story.

The Final Chapter

Somalia After We Left[*]

Any effort to understand what has happened in Somalia since 1969 must take into account the importance of the clan structure. There are four large clans, three of which are historically nomadic: Isaaq in the northwest, Hawiye in the center, and Darod in a large arc that starts in the north, runs to the west, and ends in the south. The fourth clan is a grouping of agro-pastoralist people between the Shabelle and Juba Rivers, where most of the 8s were posted, collectively known as the Digil Mirifle. Understanding contemporary Somali politics is further complicated by the fact millions of Somalis live in neighboring countries: in half of the area of Djibouti, a third of Ethiopia, and a quarter of Kenya. In addition to the four clans, there are dozens of sub-clans and hundreds of sub-sub-clans, among which alliances have constantly shifted. Unique to the countries in Africa, Somalia encompasses just one people, with one language (except in the Upper Juba) and one religion—but those people have a history of not being able to get along very well.

The leader of the Supreme Revolutionary Council when we were expelled was General Mohamed Siad Barre, nicknamed *Af Wayne*

---

[*]   This section is an edited version of a description written by fellow 8 Gilles Stockton.

(Big Mouth). His Marehan sub-clan of the Darod clan was well represented in the military and anchored his hold on power. His implementation of "scientific socialism" started well. For example, the new government created a written version of the Somali language and mobilized the population to learn to read and write it. However, a very serious drought in 1974 and a Somali invasion of Ethiopia in 1977 (which failed when the Soviets switched their support to Ethiopia) led the government into decline, and Siad Barre's rule became increasingly repressive. Curiously, the U.S. then became the main source of his international support.

In 1988, responding to rebel activity among the Isaaq clan in Somalia's northwest, the Somali air force bombed the major northern city of Hargeisa, killing tens of thousands of civilians. Full-scale civil war ensued, and in 1991 much of northern Somalia declared independence as the Republic of Somaliland. Civil war also broke out in central Somalia, and Hawiye militias drove Siad Barre's government out of Mogadishu in 1991. However, the Hawiye coalition was unable to establish a new government, and Hawiye sub-clans began to fight each other for supremacy. Chaos resulted, coupled with poor harvests, and hundreds of thousands died.

The international community responded with massive amounts of food aid, but distribution broke down when competing militias targeted relief efforts and confiscated maize, rice, and beans to resell on the open market—at a low price, but one which no one could afford. In December 1992 President Bush sent marines to Mogadishu to guard and coordinate the relief effort. The effort went well until the U.S. military was pulled into the conflict between the various clans and tasked to apprehend infamous warlord Mohamed Farrah Aidid. This culminated in the "Black Hawk down" incident of October 1993, in which 18 U.S. Rangers were killed. President Clinton recalled the U.S. military and left Somalia to sort out its own problems.

Media coverage in the years since has focused on chaos and lawlessness. However, Somaliland, Puntland, and to a lesser extent, the rest of Somalia have demonstrated remarkable resourceful-ness. Somaliland in the north was eventually able to form a func-tional government and maintain peace, in part by taxing livestock exports and distributing funds to sub-clans to buy off their militias. Although never recognized as an independent country, Somaliland has thrived economically, and many of the million exiles have returned and invested in their homeland.

People in the area east of Somaliland took a different road, declaring themselves Puntland, an autonomous administration of a future Somali federation. Its economy is also based on livestock exports, as well as remittances from the Somali diaspora, supple-mented by receipts from piracy. Continuing internal conflicts have hindered Puntland's stability and economic growth.

Somalia itself had the first and least expensive mobile phone system in Africa, all privately funded and managed. Although banks have not been able to reestablish themselves, an interna-tional money transfer system has thrived, linking the diaspora with even the smallest village in the middle of the most lawless area. A major import trade has also developed, bringing in signif-icant quantities of consumer goods. Finally, and remarkably, both Somalia and Somaliland have maintained independent currencies with very stable exchange rates against the dollar.

The international community has propped up a string of tran-sitional governments in southern Somalia and Mogadishu, in part by paying for security forces from other African countries. None have been particularly successful at establishing peace or essential services. The result has been a vacuum that radical Islamic move-ments have exploited. At times al-Shabaab militants occupied large areas of southern Somalia, while also terrorizing the citizens of Kenya and Uganda, but they have never succeeded in establishing an enduring government. The most recent Somali government has made gains against al-Shabaab and extended its authority over more territory. As of this writing, peace and economic recovery are slowly taking hold in southern Somalia. Perhaps the Somali people's long nightmare is coming to an end.

What Became of the 8s?

Tim, with whom I lived in Gorisane, was last seen in early 1970 in Dar es Salaam, on the coast of East Africa, getting on a small sailing dhow headed for Oman and India. He was never heard from again, and we and his parents assume he was killed or otherwise died at sea. Zak died of ALS several years ago. Some of the 8s have not been in close touch. Many of the rest of us, however, have had regular reunions, on two farms and at a nearby general store in Wisconsin, on a sheep and cattle ranch in Montana, in a back yard in Seattle, in Taos.

In August 2014 eight of us met to celebrate our 45th anniversary as PCVs. We stayed at a former convent that John Marks and his wife own in Wabasha, Minnesota, on the banks of the Mississippi River. After the group collected at the Minneapolis airport, our first stop was a combined tea shop, convenience store, and butcher shop—a gathering place for people in the city's large Somali immigrant community. Remarkably, Bob Bonnewell has retained the ability to speak a fair amount of Somali and paved our way with the appropriate and extensive greetings. Six or seven of us shared tea with a group of Somali men and talked about how it happened that we spent a year in Somalia a long time ago. From there we went to a Somali mall, where we attracted small crowds as we wove our way past stalls selling fabric, shoes, food, and cell phones. People were curious how Bob knew the language, and the Somalis expressed amazement—and amusement—that we had once lived in their homeland. Unlike many experiences in Somalia, our encounters were very friendly—just like every encounter I've had with Somalis in Seattle.

At least for some of us, culture shock after the Peace Corps was substantial, and the process of integrating back into American culture took months. Somewhere along the way, however, we rid ourselves of whatever animosity we felt as youth toward the Somali people. Whether we enjoyed every aspect of our time in Somalia, the experience has stayed with us. To slightly modify the comments made during our training by PC/Somalia director Felix Knauth: while our time in Somalia was not pleasant, we wouldn't have missed the experience for the world.*

Being in PC/Somalia was an experience that has had a major influence on our lives. Several of the 8s—John Marks, Gilles, Randy and Zak—worked in Africa off and on during their subsequent careers, employed by NGOs and U.S. government agencies, in an effort to better people's lives. John, Gilles, and Randy spent significant time in Somalia before it descended into chaos.

My life was certainly changed by my time in Somalia. As a result of interacting with the people and culture, I had a different and more informed view of the conditions facing most people in the world. People living in huts in Africa became more than images on TV. I also better understood developing countries and the imbalance of their relations with more powerful nations. I had a new perspective on the many shortcomings of the U.S. I now believe that my understanding of racism and sensitivity to it in the U.S. started by being on the receiving end in Somalia, where we were constantly being judged based on prejudice and stereotype. But that's another subject.

I was radicalized at Yale Law School, of all places, and rather than pursue a career in a big Wall Street firm like many of my classmates, I spent much of my life as a political activist. I decided to "serve the people," representing claimants for Social Security disability benefits. I hope I was doing my small part to make the world a better place for my mostly downtrodden clients. Additionally, I have devoted substantial time to volunteering. I was proud to be awarded the Washington State Bar Association's Community

---

* Felix told us, "The average departing volunteer has hated every minute of his [or her] 2 years but wouldn't have missed the experience for the world."

Service Award for 2012. My volunteer activities have included leading teams of Habitat for Humanity volunteers to remote locations in Africa and elsewhere. And I have gone to those places without once losing my temper or calling someone by an insulting name. Perhaps I did learn something by going to Somalia.

Jim Douglas
Seattle, WA
December, 2015

And on to my letters ...

The Bush—Gorisane

Training—and More Training—in Mogadishu

December 13, 1968 letter. I spent 3 truly incredibly mismanaged months in training in North Dakota, being prepared for this place by a bunch of anti-Peace Corps Somalis who haven't seen their homeland for years.[1]* We were on the Standing Rock Sioux Indian Reservation, living in plywood shacks on a hill overlooking the Missouri River. [Presumably to toughen us up for the challenges in Somalia, conditions weren't comfortable. When we arrived there was no electricity or hot water. We built our own cabins. One of our projects was to dig a ditch for a water line with picks and shovels—6 feet deep and about 30 yards long.] We were ostensibly being trained to work in agriculture in the southern part of Somalia. From my vantage point right now, I'm not sure that the training was particularly relevant. I imagine time will tell.

 ✍ *Early in training I wrote my family.*

Within the first week of training we'd been told that "Somali is supposed to be the most difficult language for an English-speaking person to learn."[2] Felix [Felix Knauth, Peace Corps/Somalia

---

* Numbered references are source refrences listed in the Endnotes section beginning on page 315. Starred references are footnotes.

director] told us that Somalia is "the most difficult PC country in the world."

[He] told us that he asked for "the best group of volunteers ever assembled" [because we would have] "the toughest Peace Corps job ever to be done." Whether or not he was telling us the truth we really ate it up. We are really taking a lot of pride in what we're doing, and I think rightfully so. We have accomplished a lot with very little to start with and will have even less to work with when we get to Somalia. We all accept the fact that life in Somalia will be unbearable, very uncomfortable and unpleasant—but I think we're all determined to do what we can. Felix says that the average departing volunteer has hated every minute of his 2 years but wouldn't have missed it for the world.

December 13 letter. We ended training on just about a completely sour note, with a considerable amount of friction within the staff and between the staff and the trainees—caused principally by poor planning on the part of the group contracted to run our training (an independent corporation of ex-PCVs) and the bunch of basically anti-PC Somali ex-patriots who made up our language staff.[3] A couple of the original group of 21 trainees were driven out by the negative BS that we were fed, and another couple were "deselected" (including just about the best friend I had in training). At the time, it seemed like the irrational powers above had split up one big family, but this feeling passed with the excitement of taking off for NYC and then Mogadishu.

We arrived November 13 in the capital, Mogadishu, usually called Mog ... Of the original group of 21 who started training, 15 are here now. [When we arrived] the rainy season still had the roads hopelessly messed up.[4] There are 2 rainy seasons, each about 2 ½ to 3 months, when transportation is just about impossible.

> *Perhaps the fact that our arrival was scheduled a couple of weeks after the start of the rainy season, when the roads*

*were impassable, was the first indication that our assign-
ment in Somalia would prove to be poorly planned.*

Because of the roads and because our language ability was not
the most fantastic, we spent two weeks, 8 hours day, on more language training in Mog. I now believe all that we were told about
the difficulty of the Somali language—not written, no grammar as
far as those who speak it are concerned, possessing sounds which
the human mouth and throat cannot possibly utter, etc. To say the
least, we were a damn unenthusiastic group, rationalizing our difficulty by being more or less pissed at having to stay in the big city,
away from our posts, for 3-plus weeks.

First Stop: Baidoa

*Finished with the additional training, nine of us traveled to
Baidoa, which was a small inland city 230 km (140 miles)
from Mogadishu. It was by far the largest town in the Upper
Juba region in southern Somalia. We were going to be stationed in the U. J., and the trip was a suitable introduction
to the Somali bush.*

The trip [from Mog to Baidoa] was very cool—actually pretty
exciting as far as danger of getting stuck was concerned, etc.[5] It
made for a very good introduction to the Somali bush. When the
roads are good, the 230 km [140 miles] to Baidoa is covered in
about 6 or 7 hours.[6] We left before the roads had dried up, and
everyone thought we were out of our minds for trying to get out
of town. But we showed them. We made the trip in only 2 days—
about 20 hours to go 140 miles.

In some spots the roads were not too bad, not too muddy. But
in others they were incredibly bad. We were travelling in an International Harvester pickup and a big IH Travel-All, both 4-wheel
drive, the latter having a winch on the front. The pickup, which
was loaded down with gas in drums (we have to take everything

with us that we would need for the trip) and all our stuff, never got stuck—although it did lose a gas tank in the struggle. The Travel-All also did quite well, considering all the bad things that had been predicted by those whom we told that we were actually going to Baidoa over those roads. It only got stuck twice and got a flat tire. Everyone was quite pleased at how things went.

We saw a lot of different types of birds—I'm going to have to get a book and find out a little about them. Several of the types are beautiful. We also saw dik-diks (very small antelope), lizards, and lots of domesticated camels, cattle, and goats.

The people in this area seem to be friendly, and, I think that, when the "white army"—which we must presently resemble as we stalk through town—disbands into individuals, things will be OK.

Mog will probably seem like a pretty good place to go back to after several months in the bush, with its cold beer, relatively good food, nice beach, etc. (Although the country is Muslim and very few people drink, Mog had an unlimited supply of cold beer.) But right now Mog just seems like a big city (250,000 people—at least 10 times bigger than any other city in the country). But Mog was kind of fun, and we really didn't realize what we were in for in the bush.

🖎 *We stayed with volunteer Jim Mikulski in Baidoa while we tried to get organized to settle into the bush.*

Mikulski has been working in ag here in Baidoa for the last 1 ½ years and has apparently been doing well at getting people to try new seeds and new techniques such as animal power, planting in rows, thinning—all things that the people here have a very hard time seeing the benefit of. Jim is recognized by all as the epitome of a successful ag volunteer. Except for Arabs (of which there are a few), the people have farmed for only about 100 years. (And even now, not too many of the people farm, guessing, maybe 15%.) Not much experience. Before that they were herdsmen, concerned only with keeping themselves and their camels alive. Now they understandably have a little trouble handling new techniques aimed at improving their crop yield. Most of them still think only in terms of subsistence.

All of us were really ready to leave Mog. Most of us were anxious to get on to what we will be doing for 2 years—eager to see what is in store. I personally seem to like what I see, although the psychological vacillations must rank as one of the foremost of PC/Somalia phenomena. One minute, "This is my country," the next minute, for no apparent reason, your mind will have flipped around 180 degrees, and you're sort of down in the dumps. Fortunately, the latter state of mind never lasts too long, and I don't expect any real problems, although some PCVs apparently do [have real problems].

I was just driven inside by a tremendous cloudburst, and now the corrugated iron roof of the larger of the two buildings is just being bombarded. It's incredible. It seems like we must have had ½ inch of rain in the last 5 minutes, if that's possible. It was good in one respect—a couple of guys are presently out in the rain taking showers, although we don't need any more rain as far as the roads are concerned.

✎   *We were all eager to get to our posts.*

Maybe I told you that I expected to be posted in Dijuma, a very small town that is extremely isolated because of the rains. The attraction was the job, which was almost totally construction (post office, municipal office, maybe a school). I was looking forward to the place, figuring that it would make for a total experience—unlike superficial Mog. As long as I'm to be here 2 years, I might as well get something out of it. But, in my first encounter with the Ministry of Agriculture, it was decided that Dijuma was a bad place for a volunteer to go, because the Agricultural Development Agency (ADA), who we are supposedly to work with, doesn't have anyone there. That was probably a good reason for me not to go there. [I also realize now that being that isolated during the rainy season would have made for an even more challenging situation than Gorisane, the village where I ended up going, proved to be.]

Instead, they want someone to go to one of several little farming villages near Baidoa, where quite a bit of progress has been made. Apparently, the people there are eager. At first I was disappointed, but Baidoa looks like a pretty good place—although I wouldn't want to be stationed here. It's too big, about 15,000, or so we're told. It will be good to be near other PCV's. Our entire group is going to lone posts, although there may be other volunteers [who are teachers] from earlier groups there.

Tomorrow we all leave for our posts. I'll be going with Mikulski to take Phil to Bardera, Zwink to Dinsoor, John Marks to Kansahdere, and then I'll get the guided tour of the place where I'm likely to end up. I can't remember the name. If it looks good, I'll come back to Baidoa, pick up my stuff, and head for my new home. I'm looking forward to it.

There is not much to add, and it's getting dark—no electricity—so this will have to close. Mail is going to have to be a sometime thing, since the service where I'll be will likely not be that good. I'll keep writing as things happen, and I'm sure you will share my news with everyone who's interested.

✎ *We were definitely in for more adventure travel.*

We made it to Dinsoor [where Dave Zwink will be posted] without any trouble.[7] The road was fine. When we got there, we discovered that there had been a little inter-tribal [this was more properly put, inter-clan] trouble over which group owned a certain bunch of harvestable corn. The tiff had resulted in 8 deaths in one group and 2 on the other (averaging the reports is a requirement). The police and regional governor were there trying to restore order, but, more importantly, to see to it that proper monetary retribution was made. For each member of the other group that is killed, the killing tribe has to pay 100 camels or 20,000 shillings—say $3,000. In this country that is an astronomical price. (Consider, for example, that the average rent our group will pay for houses in the bush towns will be $7 or $8 a month.) That was the biggest concern of the police, and probably justifiably so: to see to it that the blood money was paid. The police will, in effect, hold hostages until the money is handed over.

As we left Dinsoor for Bardera, we saw one of the "teams," as we so wittily chose to call them. They must have been the winners, for they looked to be in good spirits. Sometimes in these intertribal disputes, people use guns and pistols. But this group's weapons were knives, spears, bundles of pointed sticks, and, last but far from least, poison arrows—supposedly so deadly that, if one of the combatants is wounded in a limb, he will immediately cut it off. Death is supposed to come that quickly. They couldn't have seemed to care less about knocking us off—rather, they seemed to enjoy saying hello.

To move on with the saga—we left for Bardera, in spite of lots of advice to the contrary. We shouda stood in bed. What a horror movie! Things went OK for about $^1/_{10}$ of the way, say 8 km [5 miles]. Then disaster struck. We got hopelessly stuck in gross, gray mud—but we knew our trusty winch would save us. Well, the control lever broke and there we were. We'd have to dig our way under the Travel-All to see what was going in. Surprise, no shovel. We pushed, shoved, and dug around a little bit with a machete that we wouldn't even have had if the guy who got off in Dinsoor hadn't forgotten it. Finally, the driver-mechanic—Ali Jama, great guy—got to the winch control under the car, mired down in all this muck, and, after trying to adjust it for an hour or so, gave up and resorted to the crawl-under-the-car-flip-the-lever-crawl-out-etc technique. After about 4 hours of this—and just as the sun was completely disappearing—we finally got out of the hole. We roared about 100 yards—conservative estimate—and the same damn thing happened again. We finally gave up and just winched our way through this one bad section, sought dry ground, and gave up for the night.

We were cold and wet, with canned tuna, fruit, and old bread to eat—plus the warm beer headed for a guy already in Bardera (which we readily disposed of). Not to mention that we were completely covered with mud. We were ready to sleep—about 8:00. We had no sooner bathed (dubious use of the term) in the puddles next to the car than it started to rain. It kept it up all night, and we spent an all-time lousy night under the vehicle.

We tried again for about 5 or 6 hours the next morning, but, after getting hopelessly stuck another 4 or 5 times, we gave up and went back to Dinsoor. We got quite a few chuckles when we arrived, needless to say. We spent that night in Dinsoor. Dave Zwink had taken a room in what was the old school, until he could find a place of his own. Dinsoor was my first introduction to a real bush town—and quite revealing it was. The lack of privacy has always been a traditional complaint of PCVs. They say that it's impossible to get any time to yourself. One girl I read about couldn't even be alone to take a dump. The most curious and persistent people seem to be the kids—who do not seem to mean any harm but can become a trifle annoying after a while.

In Dinsoor, we sacked out in the afternoon when we got there, and, boy, were we an attraction. For a little ventilation, we left the door and window open, and there were at least a dozen little farts at each, with more waiting their turn behind the ones in front. Most of them know a little English, so such questions as "What's your name?" "How many years are you?" and "Where you go?" predominated. We all figured that the best approach would be good-natured tolerance, and, sure enough, most of them finally tired of our doing nothing and took off—as we hoped they would.

That night was our first bush restaurant, also an experience in and of itself. The menu at almost every restaurant in Somalia, be it in the bush or not, is usually very limited. They always have rice, probably have spaghetti, serve fantastic tea flavored with cinnamon, generally have goat meat, perhaps camel meat, and, if a starving American is lucky, they'll have beef. I imagine that the place we went must be regarded as pretty typical for the bush. The chief ingredient in all their cooking is stuff called *ghee*, which is animal fat that is encouraged to go rancid. [I think I was wrong about this. *Ghee*, called *subakh* in Somali, is "clarified butter," which is ubiquitous on the Indian subcontinent. Because there was no refrigeration it could get pretty rank.]

It's a very pervasive smell in the bush, because the people of the tribe around Dinsoor (called Rahan Weyn) use it on their bodies and to groom their enormous hairdos. Black Americans' naturals are nothing when compared to the Rahan Weyns' hair. They are enormous things and make the good-looking young men seem very awesome and fierce. The kinky African hair is just turned loose to grow, probably to shoulder-length at least, but the way they groom it makes it stand away from their shoulders.

Anyway, back to Dinsoor Chuck's Steak House: One step in the door and, man, all your senses get blasted at once. First, the overwhelming smell of *ghee* hits you, coming from the people as well as the kitchen. I don't think I'll ever get used to the smell, but I'm at least able to fake it. Next, you're aware of the noise. Although the place is not very big, there are really quite a few people in there— all sounding like they're having the time of their lives. Next, heads start to turn at the sight of a group of white people. (In the Upper Juba region, the stares are seldom hostile, generally interested and curious—although other parts of the country are supposed to be a little less friendly.) People are bellowing out their orders, rapping on the filthy, little wooden tables with a coin, trying to get the waiters' attention. Everyone seems to be having a great time. We sat down, and, after trying to choke down as much rice cooked in *ghee* as I could, I ate some liver. The one thing I always try to keep in mind is that, no matter how difficult the meal is to take, the bread will fill me up and the tea will always taste good.

That night ... was a restful one, except for the fact that I awakened to see a scorpion scurry under the mat I was sleeping on. After switching to a cot, I was awakened by a bat doing the Funky Funky Broadway [a dance in the '60s] on my face. I definitely think that 2 years here will toughen me up.

The Village of Gorisane

On the way back to Baidoa we took a side trip to the most fertile farmland in the country, an area that easily has the most potential to make Somalia a food exporter. Right now, the basic crop is sorghum, but the potential is unlimited. There is a group of about 40 small villages scattered throughout the area, connected by dirt roads that are only broad paths through weed-free fields of sorghum. With no weeds, the farmers have their biggest problem licked. Using animal power to decrease their work and make production go up, planting in rows to do the same 2 things, and thinning to increase production, they'll be in fantastically good shape. The market in Baidoa is only an hour or so away by truck, and the people are obviously hard workers and interested in improving their financial positions—or they would have stuck to the subsistence farms that so many of the people have. Before we even came to the first village, the place was looking very good to me. What followed was beyond my wildest expectations.

We were giving a ride to Baidoa to the extension agent [a Somali] from Kansahdere, which is right at the western edge of the agricultural region. We went through maybe 2 small settlements, followed by the usual very curious stares, and stopped at the third, Gorisane. The Ministry has an extension agent there [also a Somali], and it's the place with the greatest possibility for my having something productive to do. The extension agent from Kansahdere spoke to the people in Rahan Weyn, a language related to Somali, but one that even Somali speakers can't understand. He explained that I would probably be coming to work in their village and the others nearby, and what did they think about that? Well, as best I could tell, they really dug the idea. Several people voiced the opinion in either halting English or grammatically butchered but very enthusiastic Italian that they were glad to have my help, which is a situation that not a lot of the PCVs in this country are fortunate enough to fall into.

It was difficult to tell exactly what was going on, because even the Somali driver didn't understand what was being said. And the Kansahdere ag man doing all the talking was not very explicit when he related to me in Italian what had gone on. [Early in my time in the bush I communicated in Italian, which I'd learned studying in Florence during college. People in southern Somalia with some education knew Italian because that half of the country was formerly an Italian colony.]

> We had a similar experience at a second village. But Gorisane it would be.

I will for sure be going to Gorisane, probably with Tim Gaudio from LA, who just got into the country after having a security hold because of his activist background. He should be flying by Cessna to Baidoa tomorrow. He's a good guy, and I'm looking forward to living with him. Roommate should be one phase of Peace Corps that doesn't pose too big a problem.

Perhaps the only big drawback will be that there is almost no food in the town—at least no meat, except a little chicken. The people eat almost no meat or vegetables, subsisting on something called *sor*, which is a dish made of milk and sorghum. [The sorghum is mashed and boiled, resembling polenta, and is traditionally eaten with one's hands.] I imagine that the western palate could get a little tired of that sort of diet ... Not too big a hang-up though, since we can bring in some cans, eat spaghetti, raise some chickens and maybe some goats, and make sure we take our vitamin pills.

> I was initially very enthusiastic and optimistic.

[Gorisane looks] like a fantastic possibility ...[8] Although what I do have to offer in the way of tech skills is considerably limited, they should be able to handle the immediately pressing problems of Somali ag ... [The techniques we'll try to teach people are] hard for people to accept, considering they were all camel herdsmen until less than 100 years ago ... 70% of the people are still nomadic herdsmen.

... Even during the rainy season, Baidoa will be no more than a long day's walk [from Gorisane]. I'm really looking forward to getting out to my post, settling into my house, and starting to work with the farmers.

🖎 *I wrote to a friend who was in Peace Corps/Nepal.*

December 14 letter. I'll be living in what must be one of the largest of the villages ...[9] [When we visited,] each village seemed to be split into a few sections a few kms apart, with maybe a few hundred people living in each. Exactly what I was looking forward to ...

I like the size of the place, because I think it will be possible for me to become kind of a fixture. [I must not have learned yet that dozens or even hundreds of nomads came through the village every day, and, since they were always on the move, for those people I would never be a fixture.] I imagine that after everybody knows me and knows what I'm doing in their village, things will become much more natural and enable me to get a little closer to their culture. As long as I'm going to be here for a few years, I figure I might as well do that. I have found, though, that I'm not too good at going out, away from home in a big place, and trying to get along comfortably. The small village will force me to interact, and I think I can use the boost, to tell the truth. I will be living in a mud and wattle hut, with a grass roof, which doesn't faze me in the least. Hell, you can get along with anything for a couple years.

There are, of course, a few disadvantages. One is that the people don't speak Somali, but, rather, a related language called Rahan Weyn. It looks like I'll get to learn a new language. It is encouraging, though, that the higher-ups, probably including the ag extension agent, speak Italian—as do quite a few people in the cities—because of the influence of the Italian colonialists. Time to take the teachings of Signora Benini [our Italian language teacher in Florence] out of mothballs ...

Like you describe Nepal, this country has a certain charm to it, and I think that perhaps I will be able to appreciate it after being out in my village for a while ... The day-to-day life of the average man here also seems to bear similarities to that of the Nepalese. Everything closes down in the afternoon, and there is a lot of time spent in teahouses talking things over—very emotionally, which makes conversations pretty exciting sometimes. The people of the bush are proud and hard-working and possess a fascinating beauty under their coating of dirt and from behind the flies that seem to accompany them ... It's an exciting country, one that I'm looking forward to having the opportunity to get a closer look at.

> ✍ *I went back to Baidoa to get organized to live in the tiny village of Gorisane. And I reacted irritably for the first time to living in a fishbowl.*

December 15 letter. I just got back from a walk downtown [in Baidoa], and I know one thing: today was the first time that being stared at constantly really bothered me.[10] Tomorrow is another day, and I imagine my annoyance will blow over with a little time. That's one thing that we've been warned to expect: tremendous ups and downs as far as enthusiasm, general emotion, etc. are concerned. I guess, as long as I stay aware of the fact that [these ups and downs] are going to come along, I will be able to retain my level of pleasant insanity.

To get back to the subject of my assignment (for which I will be leaving as soon as I round up a few things here in Baidoa): This country does have a specific sort of quasi-charm to it, and I think that perhaps I will be able to appreciate it after being out in my village for a while. I know that my contact with Somalis in the larger cities has not, as a rule, been overwhelmingly gratifying. The day-to-day life of the average man seems to contain quite a few idle minutes, and the way they just hang around is at the same time kind of cool and, also, pretty discouraging—especially when they decide to accompany standing around with staring their asses off at the white man walking down the street minding his own business. (Right now, maybe you can tell I'm a little bit tired of it.) Like I said earlier, I'm looking forward to seeing if this can be overcome to the point where I become someone who's taken for granted to a certain extent and don't have to fight being a perpetual novelty.

Christmas in Baidoa

> ✎ *The 8s had a memorable Christmas in Baidoa, hosted by PCVs Maureen Doherty and Marianne Shank. Bill Thompson, PC/Somalia associate director, arrived at midnight on Christmas Eve with a few other people and 15 cases of beer. I wrote to my family.*

[Maureen and Marianne] cooked up a Christmas feast for all 16 of us the next night, with potatoes (which we hadn't had in the bush yet because of the season), ham, apple pie, cake, wine.[11] We couldn't even walk when we were through with the feast, but we did manage to drink some more and sing the rest of our lungs out. The girls had filled our stockings with candy and gave us each a present. Mine was an authentic sheriff's badge. We decorated a thorn bush with construction paper, strings of peppers, and strings of toilet paper balls. It was a very different Christmas. I missed being at home, but, as long as I had to be here, the party couldn't have been better.

... [The bush people here] are extremely self-sufficient. We see them walking by themselves along any bush road. They dress in once-white, now-brown toga-like outfits, and carry a knife in their belt and a stick or spear in their hand. Often they wear only one sandal at a time, we assume in order to keep the pair from wearing out as fast. They have big hairdos that they carefully groom with *ghee* ... Many of them are tall and lean and very handsome and carry a thin, wooden [comb/pick] in their hair, which is used to take care of their hair. Despite the fact that they must bathe only when it rains and almost certainly never clean their hair, many of them have the clearest skin and give an overall picture of real elegance and ferociousness.

They seem to be good people, and I appreciate the fact that they don't seem to stare as constantly or as openly as do the city people. [This proved to be a premature assessment!] Perhaps they know what it feels like—being different from people from the cities—to be targets of staring themselves when they roll into town. These people, like I say, are very self-sufficient. They herd their camels, maybe a few cattle or goats, and are a hardy lot.

Our First Eid in the Bush

December 24 letter. Ramadan, the month when good Muslims don't eat or drink from dawn to sunset, ended about 5 days before Christmas. (It's now December 27.) The difference between life during Ramadan and the rest of the year has a lot to do with the fact that, by federal regulation, restaurants and tea shops are closed during the day. A lot of Somali life is centered around these places, because, since no one can read the language (since it's unwritten), talking about anything and for hours is a very common activity. During Ramadan everyone who has been holed up resting during the heat of the day comes out on the streets at dusk and walks, talks, and sits in tea shops, having the local version of a rousing good time. The idleness still strikes me every time I go downtown [in Baidoa]. Especially during the last days of Ramadan, the pace of the night life steps up. People stay up until dawn, play drums, and march around in single file lines (dancing). There is a lot of chanting of Koranic verse over loudspeakers. It's all very highly regarded as entertainment.

When people first see the new moon, the fast is over, and, of course, people were asking each other, "Did you see the moon?" Someone pointed it out to us, and it took a real sharp pair of eyes to spot the invisible little sliver. Then Eid starts, the holiday of the year. [There are 2 Eids per lunar year. This is Eid-ul-Fitr, which celebrates the end of Ramadan. Eid-ul-Adha celebrates the culmination of the annual pilgrimage to Mecca.] It lasts 3 days, and the first day features the biggest celebration. Many bush people are in [Baidoa], with their big hairdos just as gussied up as can be, with every curl carefully worked into place with lots of *ghee*. The city people have on their finest clothes. Everyone heads for the dancing, which is held at the edge of town on the dustiest field in the country, I'm sure. We saw 2 types of dancing, both with the participants in the center of a group of spectators. Both are pretty erotic and feature repetitive chanting and lots of jumping and clapping. The people who dance, only a few of whom are women, get really worked up, get very tired, and are soon coated with red dust. We guessed that Eid is the one time during the year when people are able to stop repressing their sexual desire. Normally, this has to be as unerotic a country as can be found anywhere. Poor women are slaves to their husbands, and well-to-do women just stay shut up in the house. Now Eid is over and things are back to normal.

Preparing for Gorisane

… It only takes an hour to get to Gorisane by trade truck—the only practical means of transportation. A trade truck looks like a cattle truck without a top, and they jam in as many people and things as they can, wait around for a while, and they're off. The roads aren't too hot, and the trips are usually quite an experience. I tried a couple times to get out to Gorisane before Christmas, but my periods of waiting down at the market place where the trucks take off all seemed to come right after the last truck had taken off. We'll try to get out there tomorrow. We'll have to see … [Gorisane] has about 300 people, I'd guess, maybe a few more … The people know that I'm coming and seemed eager to have some help with their agriculture.

… We have been lucky enough to find a *boyessa* (a cook, laundress, and house cleaner combination), who will go with us out to the bush. I never thought we'd find one. Fadumo was recommended by Zenab, Mikulski's *boyessa*, and, if she's half the cook and the personality as Zenab, we'll have a real good set-up. We go tomorrow. [This is the first of three different women named Fadumo.]

January 4, 1969 letter. Since [Christmas] a process has been continuing that actually began before the holiday season.[12] Rosy optimism is gone, and the fact that we've got 2 years of pretty tough service ahead is getting a little more attention. The fascinating thing is the psychological vacillation that accompanies the realization [of the tough road ahead]. I never thought I was any moodier than the next guy. But here, one minute you're up and the next minute inexplicably you're down as hell. It happens to me, probably no more or less than with anybody else.

Reality Hits

> Tim and I went out to Gorisane to line up a place to stay and to see what was available in the village.

[Gorisane] at first glance is one thing; a longer look and it proved to be something else. The dialect is completely unintelligible, and the things available to buy are at least as limited as I thought. But all is not too bad. We're going to have to spend all our time working on the language, starting damn near from scratch. There are two people in the village who speak Italian [the chief's sons Ibrahim and Mohamed, who learned Italian during 5 years of elementary school in Baidoa], and we are taking an all-purpose Girl Friday to cook, wash clothes, keep water boiled, clean house, all the goodies that supposedly will allow us plenty of time to be good vols. She knows both Somali and Rahan Weyn, and we're hoping she will be able to help us get our heads above water. Without the language we'll get nothing done.

Right now I'm in sort of the "up stage," so things don't seem impossible. There are possibilities of getting people to use oxen power, plant in rows, then all the good things. They are convinced that pesticide is the end-all and cure-all, so maybe we can work out a little bribery: I'll get "the medicine" somehow, if they can manage to try things my way. Demonstration plots may help to prove my point. Yesterday all I could think of was the fact that the village seems to have so little money—although it's hard to know for sure—and the fact that the language will prove to be very difficult.

We'll be living in two *mundels*, circular mud and wattle buildings with dirt floors and thatched roofs made of sorghum stalks. As far as we can tell, until we build a "long drop" (a squat-style latrine consisting of a hole in the ground) we'll be taking our dumps out in the field—introducing the use of manure as fertilizer.

> *With one of my best friends from college, who was a VISTA volunteer in rural North Carolina, I was very explicit about the reality that was sinking in.*

January 11 letter. You think the first letter from the bush was something.[13] Read this, and you'll blow your mind. You wouldn't believe this place. Tim and I just had a quick review session of what's gone on during the 3 days we've been here in Gorisane … We were laughing our asses off to the extent [that I wanted to write]. Some things are very amusing, some are serious. Our present mood, which may expire any time within the next 5 minutes, is, like I say, one of great amusement—mostly at our own expense. We're not exactly living the life of Riley.

[With the help of a couple guys with donkey carts we made it out of Baidoa.] We looked like the proverbial white hunters with a couple locals hauling our huge pile of possessions for us. Americans just seem to have a hell of a lot of stuff, and we were no exception, with a trunk, a huge wooden box, 2 mattresses, 2 barrels (to eventually be used to hold water out at our town), a bunch of wood that we were going to use to build a couple sets of shelves), a bag of charcoal, a big tank of kerosene, and a big roll of bamboo mats, to be used on the floor, under our mattresses, etc. We had a whole lot of stuff, to say the least. It completely filled up 2 donkey carts.

We finally got on a trade truck [with]… all of our junk, ourselves, our girl Fadumo and Zenab (Mikulski's *boyessa* who came with us to return the next day). Fadumo has worked out fantastically well. She's a real enterprising and industrious worker. As of right now, we couldn't ask for anything more as far as she's concerned.

We had two *mundels* lined up in Gorisane, but when we arrived there were still people living in one. We moved as best we could into one of them, sweeping the spiders and other stuff off the thatched roof, the walls and the dirt floor. We sprayed the place down pretty good, spread out a couple of bamboo mats for beds and rug, and we were in business.

… By the time we were up and about the next day, the family had moved out of our second *mundel*—lock, stock and barrel. I guess the $2 per month we're paying the chief as rent was just too much for the people to match. Anyway, they set up their own place about 20 yards away. The woman of the family built the place out of parts that they obviously had lying around for just such a possible move. It's a house that the nomads live in, which can be carried around on a camel's back and consists of long flexible poles and fuzzy straw mats, all of which is molded into an igloo shape.

(Right now, you wouldn't believe it. Two men and a small boy have been standing in our house, staring in the most rapt attention imaginable during the entire last paragraph. Their gaze never wavers. It's fantastic; they never seem to tire of something strange done by a stranger. They just left. They'd never seen anything like it. Tim just came in with perhaps the best observation of our entire stay so far: "This place [meaning us] is the biggest fucking freak show in town." And it sure is. We're not just new people in town; we're the only freaks they've ever had the opportunity to stare at for any appreciable length of time.)

[The family] left the place in the bush-Somali rendition of spotless. They'd swept it out, without paying any attention to the bug- and spider-infested thatched roof (every roof is thatched) or to the cobweb-ridden walls. What they had done, however, was to give the floor a good dousing of water. The floor is the finest known—the final layer of camel shit makes the difference. You think I'm making this up, but they use shit for the final coating for both floor and walls ... While I built the shelves for our *mundel* and for the kitchen/dining room/pantry *mundel* (i.e., the newly douched out *mundel*), Tim cleaned and sprayed out our *mundel*. We moved our stuff around, and we were set.

Our house is located in a group of *mundels* that are inhabited by the village chief and his family. At first we were afraid that our valuable privacy would be threatened by our proximity to the family, but the whole arrangement has worked out beautifully. The family likes us, we like them, and they often serve as a buffer between us and the prying eyes of the riffraff. Mohamed, the chief's youngest son, about 22, has been very helpful, since he knows Italian. He is eager to exchange his knowledge of his language for ours of English. [His older brother, Ibrahim, also spoke Italian and was also very helpful.]

Mohamed is in here now, having a language lesson from Tim. He's incredibly quick and, as far as we can tell, has a genuine desire to help us out. At this point, he's one of the few people here I would trust. Not that the others are necessarily bad, I'm just waiting to see. Mohamed is teaching us Rahan Weyn and our progress for 2 days is very encouraging. It seems to be much easier than Somali. For example, there is no differentiation between present and past tense, which makes it easier to learn. Even though it is kind of difficult to understand, some things are already making sense.

[Tim sleeps on a mattress on the floor, and I have a mattress (filled with grass) on top of a bush bed made of poles set on forked sticks that are driven into the ground. It rests about a foot off the ground.] We've added many refinements to our *mundel*'s furnishings, including a large cushion to sit on, one of the bookcases (which holds everything we own), and the trunk, which doubles as a strong box (a place to store things that are not used too frequently as well as things that we don't particularly care to display to prying local eyes, e.g., typewriter, medical kits, etc). We have a small Petromax [a pressurized lantern] hanging from a rope in the center of the room and a small table that holds a genuine, made in who-knows-where, perfectly adequate portable radio, that I bought in Mog for all of $40.

[Fadumo lives in *mundel* number 2, which also] has our well-made shelves and a couple of tables. These are designated as food-preparation and eating tables. The one drawback to the eating table is that there were no chairs to buy in Baidoa … [Food available in Gorisane will be limited.] In the 3 days since we arrived we have had tea and bananas for breakfast every day. For lunch we have hard-boiled eggs, and a local delight called *arbolo*. (This is actually pretty tasty, a not-so-nutritious warmed-up dish of beans and corn. That's all. No fancy stuff like sauce or anything to liven it up.) We have had spaghetti and tomatoes for dinner twice, and—the treat of treats—chicken and rice one time. Chicken is the only type of meat that is available here, so we might get our fill of that. We also had corn on one occasion, which wasn't too bad. Just stick it on the charcoal and warm it up. There is very little of the local cuisine that we have sampled yet, such as the dish called *sor*, which is camel's milk and sorghum and which could probably take 2 very sick white boys to their unhealthy doom with the least provocation. We may eat it to be polite some time, but on few occasions, I would guess.

We eat better than the average local, who gets along without—to draw from the above list—eggs, spaghetti, tomatoes, bananas, rice and chicken. They mostly eat sorghum, corn and beans. They're no more open about their eating habits than we are, but this is what I imagine. They don't seem to eat much.

During the day, we've been eating in our *mundel*. The evening meal is after dark, so we recline on mats outside, sitting cross-legged to eat our meals of spaghetti and tomato sauce. I don't know how things are going to be when tomatoes and bananas go out of season. We're already preparing by taking our vitamins …

We draw our water from the *wahr*, which is right next to our house. It is a large hand-dug, stagnant pond dug out by a device called a *yambo*, which is a short-handled hoe. Rainwater collects for human consumption, not to mention consumption by the cattle, etc, who seem compelled to quench their thirst by completely submerging their manure-covered bodies.[14] The people don't seem to mind. There's a hell of a lot of stuff floating around in it, needless to say, but we boil it, let it settle in the pan, carefully pour it into converted wine bottles, let it settle, carefully pour it into glasses, where it settles out again—leaving only a thin layer of light brown crap on the bottom of the glass.[15] It doesn't taste too hot, but we've been thirsty enough that it hasn't made too much difference.

All told, our place really isn't too bad. Today we dug a hole for a long-drop. (This is Peace Corps jargon for a hand-dug, squat-style potty—actually quite comfy once the thighs get stronger, the knee joints loosen up, and your bombsight is perfected.) We lined it with a bottomless, topless oil drum to avoid the possibility of, without warning, taking a header into our own feces. That would be the shits. We're paying to have the place surrounded with a stick fence that will be mud-plastered, with enough space that we can take our "baths in a bucket." We're paying the outlandish sum of $1.40 [for building the fence], only $.30 of which is labor. Things come cheap out in the bush. When this little enclosure is completed, the place will be home.

… If we weren't so damned conservative, we would continue as we have been doing the last few days, like all the people here do— head for the outskirts of town when the mood hits. But we're too shy. Speaking of shit—I have been hearing a constant scratching at the outside wall of our *mundel* and figured it was just the kids farting around. But finally I decided that I'd go out and take a quick look. I couldn't believe my eyes. Without any charge whatsoever, the woman of the house is patching the holes in the external walls of the *mundel* with the finest camel shit. It is quite a present,— for the smell soon leaves and the place is improved. Fantastic!

There are a lot of interesting beasts around here. ("Here" refers to our duo-domiciled complex—since we're chicken shit to venture more than 3 steps away from home. We get tired of being stared at until our senses reel and are also unable to understand anything at all.) Examples of interesting beasts are the 3 camels, 3 cows, and 2 calves which feed tied up outside *mundel* number 2. There are a lot interesting people, kind of conversation pieces, to go with the animals. Excuse my insensitivity, but, until I can communicate with them, I'm not sure I can appreciate them fully as people.

> ✍ *My attitude about some of the people in the bush was already starting to sour.*

... There has been a slight attitudinal shift, either involving my fellow man or a decision that [a lot of] the people here don't necessarily fall into the category encompassing the rest of humanity. The majority of the people who live in town are actually only slightly interested in us, a little curious, and then they move on to something a little more entertaining. At this point at least, the rest of the people have sorted into 2 small categories. There are a few who are genuinely interested in our welfare, not necessarily our money or our medicine, and have proved to be damn nice guys. (There are a bunch of people who assume that all white men have every type of medicine to cure all their ills, including chronic malaria, TB, etc.)

The second of the small categories of people—if I may take the liberty to classify their very souls—consists of the complete and utter jerk. These are the guys you wouldn't trust as far as you could throw them, guys you don't even like to have to put up with.

There's a guy who is rumored to be a thief but who hasn't taken anything from us yet. He never says anything but the Rahan Weyn word for "my friend." Whenever he comes over, all he does is shake our hands, say "my friend" and take off. Perhaps the all-time example was a very old guy, who supposedly is the village crazy man/old mystic or something ... [The conversation started with a demand for medicine and] concluded with his wondering how, if we said we were from California (we even pointed out the location of the golden state on a world map that we've tacked up on our mud wall), he had never read about the place in any of his holy books ...

[Another] story involves a guy whose nickname is hyena. He hounded us for a day or so for medicine for his hurt foot, which he'd injured over a month ago with his *yambo*. We kept telling him that we weren't doctors and that we had no strong medicine. We were just average guys who had a little aspirin and band aids ... [Tim finally agreed to help him, but mistakenly used kerosene to clean the wound rather than alcohol.] But the patient was happy. Fifteen minutes after treatment he brought Tim an egg. He has proved to be a real friend.

> 🖎 *But, in addition to the chief's family, there were people for whom we were developing warm feelings.*

There is a cool guy who is building the fence around the long drop. His name is Malabo, which can easily be perverted into "Malibu." He knows "OK" and "hello" and never passes up a chance to use them. He'll be working and, out of nowhere, will emit an "OK" or a "hello." Tim figured that he could stand to have his vocabulary expanded slightly, so he proceeded to teach the fellow "Fuck your father" [a ubiquitous Somali insult] and "That's cool." Malabo hasn't quite mastered the pronunciation yet, but, when he does, he's going to be a real terror.

... Right now, mainly because of our language inability, we figure our impact on the common farmer will be minimal. There has been a lot of talk about our teaching school, with Mohamed leading the parade. If we can come up with chalk and a blackboard, they'll get us a building. It should be good, because it will allow us to do something for the place and, at the same time, legitimize our presence here. The first day or so there were a lot of people who wanted to know what we were doing in their fair city. They'll see. All is rosy.

> 🖎 *I wrote my family the same day.*

January 11 letter. It think that it's fairly safe to say that [Gorisane] is a pretty good example of the Somali bush ...[16] We are quite the attraction here, as we expected to be, of course. The thrill is finally wearing off for a lot of the bystanders, and we're being given a little time to work and think without a lot of help. Most of the people are only curious, soon tire of our not doing anything too amusing, and then take off. A few are just downright jerks—as I guess there are everywhere—who you would prefer not to ever have to see at all. Most of the people think that, just because we are white, we have all the answers to their problems as far as farming and problems of personal health are concerned.

The magic word is "medicine." I don't know how many people have asked us for medicine. Most of the time they don't even tell us what is wrong with them, if, in fact, there is anything wrong. They just want medicine. All we have is our medical kits, which consist of diarrhea pills, band aids, some antibiotic salve, aspirin, vitamins, and some preventive stuff that wouldn't do the people here any good anyway. They can't take no for an answer, though. I'm kind of a hard ass about giving away too much stuff [but Tim is more of a soft touch].

... Until we get pretty good [at the language], I don't think we'll exactly sweep the Rahan Weyn farmer off his feet. But luckily there seems to be a lot of interest in starting a school. We'll see. It would be great for everybody for us to teach English while we're learning their language. It would allow us to do something useful, allow us to prove our good intentions and abilities, and legitimize our presence. The people seem to have gotten used to our presence, but they have a lot of questions.

January 17 letter. The whole area [around Gorisane] is one big sorghum field for as far as the eye can see ...[17] We brought an incredible amount of stuff with us ... I think it's impossible for an American to travel in Africa with any less than a million times the stuff that the local people have. When bush people travel they take a flashlight, a stick, a knife, and a sheet-like garment, which they always have with them and serves as a blanket, a sun shade, a towel, a handkerchief, and lots of other things. That's about all they own. And somebody in the traveling party will have a teapot. [The teapot is used not only to make tea, but also to wash before praying.] Every person in the country drinks tea several times a day. Fortunately for us, it's invariably at least pretty good. Often it's the only stuff we can drink that won't make us sick.

To be honest, I can't imagine a Peace Corps vol being in a more difficult position that ours. We received 300 hours of language training in Somali and came to respect the opinion by recognized linguists that it is the hardest language in the entire world for an English-speaking person to learn. I had gotten to the point where at least I could interact on some sort of mundane level, but here nobody speaks the language. Instead, everyone speaks a semi-related dialect called Rahan Weyn. For native speakers the 2 are mutually unintelligible, so you can imagine what we've run into. If it weren't for the fact that Ibrahim, Mohamed and I speak Italian, we would be just about completely unable to communicate and totally miserable. We are presently spending quite a bit of time each day on the language with Mohamed, out forcing ourselves to interact. It can be harder than one would ever think possible ... We're working as hard at learning Rahan Weyn as our tiring psyches can stand. Progress should come sometime.

This place is real Africa. I'd like to see a place that's been touched less by the outside world ... As we duck out the door of *mundel* number two (the door is about 4 feet high) we can expect to see a camel or 2 or 3 tethered to one of the trees next to our house. The camel here is the direct index of a man's wealth, and, despite the fact that normally the camels do very little, they are all over the place. Our neighbors own nice camels. Thank God, because you know what unkempt neighbor's camels can do to property value.

For each of our *mundels* we pay a little over $2 a month ... Between us, Tim and I spend only about $.80 a day on food. Our biggest single expense is our girl, called a *boyessa*, whom we pay $14 a month.

About the food here: Not even the best restaurant in Baidoa has more than spaghetti, rice, liver, beef and goat. Other stuff is just not raised here. The people have never been exposed to much else, so they're perfectly content. There's something about past experience that affects whether one becomes discontent. The people have never seen anything different, so they're happy. Nothing wrong with that, I suppose ...

Despite the fact that the picture I've painted may seem a little negative as far as the physical luxuries are concerned, that aspect of my glorious PC existence doesn't really bother me. Anyone can live with that kind of stuff for a couple years. The people around us have gotten used to us and seem to like us as much as we like some of them. Most of the people in town know we are here, and many have been over to observe while we were building our shelves or doing something else. These people are not the problem.

The thing that has both of us wondering at frequent intervals just what the hell we are doing here is our treatment when we venture away from the safety of our neighborhood. Out in the bush there are a lot of people who seem to have no home base; there are a lot of nomads who seem to walk from some place to some place else for no apparent reason. There are many who are grazing their camels and cattle, but there are others who just seem to be existing and getting along. I guess the point is that there are always a lot of these people flowing through our town. And when we go downtown for cigarettes at the one store [more like a stall] that carries them or go down to talk to a friend of ours who runs another store or just go down to look around, we are the sight of their entire lives. And if we should stop somewhere, look out; they'll be all around us. [I used "downtown" ironically. It was an open area on the road through town perhaps 100 yards from our *mundels*. A few enterprising souls had stands where they sold what little was available in Gorisane.]

... I just threw a shoe at a kid peering in the window. I do need a day or 2 away from this place. Last night we were throwing rocks at the chickens—kid stuff, but at least we get the steam out of our systems. Right now we figure that we're not exactly going to take the farmers by storm. We're going to try and get some to cooperate the next planting season, which is about 9 weeks away. We'll see how far we get.

January 17 letter. The place ain't exactly a piece of cake, although, certainly, it has its enjoyable aspects ...[18] We're more or less set up ... We're pretty sure we've earned [a trip in to Baidoa], since we've had kind of a rugged week or two ...

[Something happened yesterday afternoon] that had Tim and me so pissed we couldn't see straight ... The people who actually live in Gorisane have gotten pretty used to us ... But, here in the bush, there is a constant flow of people going through town—bush people, who are just herding their camels or cows, or just walking from nowhere in particular to a similar place. And, man, they have never seen anything like us. If we stop to talk to someone we know or stop in one of the 3 or 4 stores, there immediately forms a group of these interested bush men. Most of them just want to look, seem to have very little against us, and only seem curious. But there are some guys that feel it is their duty to teach us the Rahan Weyn dialect—of course, speaking so fast that we're not learning anything. Or they ask us what we're doing here or what we think we're doing wearing bush sandals (a topic of discussion that is blown way out of proportion by some of the local gentry—big deal, so we wear bush sandals). And so on.

Yesterday, coming back from talking to a farmer in his field we ran into a guy I know who teaches school near here and who speaks Italian [meaning that I could communicate with him]. Well, we were exchanging pleasantries and—not one bit of exaggeration—a crowd of over 50 people formed. The teacher didn't like it any more than I did. (He apologized for the uncivilized state of the people here.) So we started to move off toward our house. At least half the people followed. As they stood at a distance and stared, Tim and I sat on a mat in front of our house and just seethed.

We were so mad. Although of doubtful benefit to forging international relations, I've found that a good string of abuse helps me feel better. The people whom I am addressing can't understand what my reaction means. [I'll bet they could figure out I was mad about something.] The whole scene is generally uncomfortable. Mohamed is damn nice about it, and, because he does hold a certain position in the community, he is usually effective at running off the onlookers. His help is truly appreciated. It is a disconcerting experience to be sitting outside our door, doing exactly nothing, and have one guy after another roll in to inspect us.

A lot of times it's very easy to take. Other times something just snaps, and you give a good goddamn whether you stay in this crappy little town another day. Attitudes change. For example, today is a fantastic day. [We're working on language for hours every day and are making progress.] The structure and most of the sounds are like Somali, and the conjugations are easier, etc. So we should be able to catch on.

January 14 journal entry. Pretty much a nothing day.[19] We spent the morning on language. We also made sure that the long drop was going to be finished today and then watched it sit. No sweat. There's lots of time. We're being seen less as freaks, although we did have some observers. The people who live around us know we're learning, and a few stick up for us. We decided that we've never had life so "easy." Food is becoming monotonous, but it's still good. This has been a strange day, with almost no ups and downs—although I did get pissed a couple times.

The people here are farmers, but they spend very little time farming.[20] When the rain starts, they plant their seed (as it were), they watch it grow, hack away with a short-handled hoe if the weed population seems to dictate, and harvest over about a 6-week time span. The rest of their time is spent sitting around shooting the breeze (although they take off from noon to 4:00 because of the incredibly draining heat) or strolling around the "downtown" area.

You can imagine in a town of about 300 just how little new stuff there is to check out on the trips downtown.

Our nice neighbor brought her young son to the "new magic white doctors" for some "medicine" for what looked like some type of systematic ceremonial incisions.[21] I couldn't talk to her very well, but she knew I thought the whole thing was a crock. Never have I been more conscious of the cultural gap than when the lady wanted medicine for her kid and then tried to convert us. Everyone is Muslim here, and when you die you're finished if you're not on the team. What B.S. I hope it's not a daily thing.

I built a very nice table from a packing crate. It was something to do. I was offered a beautiful girl today. Her husband had taken off on her, but I'm not ready for that yet.

January 24 letter. The neighborhood is fantastic.[22] There is a family that we ran out of the *mundel* in which we set up our dining room/kitchen/pantry/maid's quarters that has proved to be a fantastic couple ... The best set of friends we have. The wife is a beautiful little woman named Gurey (called Small Tits by her American guests) with dirt on her face, shit on her hands, and a little kid on her back. She is too much. When they moved out of the *mundel*, they set up a house like those the nomads live in, that looks like an igloo made of dried grass. It's the woman's job to build these places, and Small Tits did her job like a champ. Tim and I sat and watched—as men are expected to do, of course—and she taught us the names for the parts of the house and those of the portable bed made of sticks and bamboo mat. She is so too much that she's beyond description. Tim and I are going to fight at the end of our stay here to see who gets the chance to offer to buy her from her man.

Her husband, Malabo [sometimes called Malibu by his guests] is another very good friend of ours. He is also too much. We worked with him one of the first days we were here, building a long-drop toilet ... We worked alternately digging the hole (which because of its depth, should probably be termed a short-drop), and Tim and I both noticed his facility for the English language. Of course, we had to teach him and his wife "You're too much," so that they would know what we were saying about them.

... Although obviously suffering from something resembling dead-end TB, the chief [who we called Chief Green Beads] is a fantastic old man who is concerned for our welfare. We've already talked to him through his oldest son Ibrahim about running a little agricultural experimentation on his land this next growing season.

Although his wife has not yet finished the final layer of shit on the wall of sticks surrounding our long drop, Malibu is hard at work starting on a small, shaded enclosure that will adjoin *mundel* #2 and should give us a little more privacy. As it is right now, we can be in our *mundel*, trying to escape things in general, and a visitor will "just drop in." As often as not, they're semi-friends, but we'd probably be a little happier if we could establish some place as ours alone.

... Fadumo prepares food on a charcoal stove I made from a kerosene tin. She's a good cook, and we've been eating much better since the break we took in Baidoa a few days ago. A frying pan and a bag of potatoes make all the difference in the world. We had been eating hard-boiled eggs, beans, corn, a little chicken, rice and spaghetti. Now we get our version of a Spanish omelet, potatoes with our chicken, and coffee after dinner. As we finish eating dinner sitting cross-legged on our mat outside *mundel* #2, light up a cigarette and mix a cup of instant coffee—in the solitudinous delight of our own thoughts (i.e., we've finally achieved a moment of privacy after a day in the fishbowl)—that's living.

Our *mundel*, needless to say, is furnished with the styles of the 30th century as far as the people here are concerned and of about the 15th as far as we are concerned. There is a tremendous difference between our culture and theirs as far as technological advancement is concerned—not making any sort of judgment, just stating the facts ... We have my Peace Corps trunk in which I keep things that I'm pretty sure I don't want to lose—although thievery doesn't seem to be any real problem at all here, knock on wood—as well as those things that I'd just as soon not show the locals. (They have an affinity for asking for things.)

In a moment of industriousness, I made a table out of wood from a packing crate in which we hauled our stuff from Baidoa. I also made a set of shelves. The latter hold just about everything we own in the world: books, shaving kits, about 3 shirts and 2 pair of white hunter-type khaki shorts. That's it. As far as the people here are concerned, we're the wealthiest people they've ever laid eyes on. And we consider what it would be like to try to get along on a large college campus with what we have.

… There are more camels here than one knows what to do with. Although they seem to do little but carry nomad families' possessions or a load of sorghum stalks for their own feed, they are considered to be the direct measure of a man's wealth here. Alimony in the case of divorce is in the form of camels, and camels are the blood money that is paid to settle inter-tribal disputes.

… We've been learning some of the language, trying as hard as we can push ourselves. We've learned a lot of words, but it's now a matter of getting to the point where we can pronounce them so that we're understood and can pick up the words we know from the incredible flow of daily conversation that surrounds us. It's slow, but I'm optimistic. (Who knows why?) At any rate, we spend as much time daily as we can stand trying to rub elbows with people we like and trying to expose ourselves as much as possible without destroying our psychological make-up.

… We have learned that privacy is a commodity so valuable that it is seldom available. As an example, right now there are 4 or 5 beautiful, young Somali women standing outside the door watching me as my flying fingers type this letter. They've never seen anything like it, to say the least. Living with the chief, we were afraid that we would always be entertaining visitors. (Two more guys just rolled in.) As you might have guessed, we don't always have as much privacy as we'd like, but there are certain benefits from living where we live ...

The psychological fluctuations are incredible, to say the least, varying from guarded optimism to complete outrage to hysterical mirth to the lowest imaginable psychological down (i.e., "What the hell am I doing here?"). The optimism and the mirth are more or less welcome states, and the anger usually subsides quickly (usually after a form of release, such as yesterday, when I shoved some guy around, wielded a big stick, and bellowed obscenely in English to please leave my yard).

... One real psychological advantage we have here is that nobody knows any English at all, and we are able to soothe our often abused psyches by just telling someone off or telling someone just exactly what we think of him. Admittedly, I do this a lot more than Tim does. I may end up hating the place—not entirely unlikely, but, at the same time, not necessarily the case. At least I won't have an ulcer from letting the little frustrations eat at me.

A night's sleep always takes care of the downs. With each successive day the downs come more frequently and earlier in the day, but we've found that the cure is a day or 2 in Baidoa, palavering with the PCVs there, drinking beer in the city's one bar, and generally relaxing. The place never looked better than when we arrived for our 3 day break after being out here (only 30 km [18 miles] away) for about 9 days. The need to take trips into town should come less frequently as time wears on, the language gets a little easier, and more people come to recognize us as fixtures. At least we'll see. We think we're going to start a school pretty soon, but, until then, our work doesn't actually keep us here. The almost 6-week long process of harvesting the sorghum has just begun, and there's not much about our specified "job" that requires that we stay here.

January 26 letter. The roofs are thatched, with some sort of grass (non-hallucinogenic, of course) packed on top of a thick layer of sorghum and corn stalks.[23] When the roof gets a little aged (I think ours is in its second century) it makes a great home for animal life, but, of course, we pacifists love every spider, cockroach, fly, lizard, and wasp as if it were our own.

... The pronunciation of the Rahan Weyn language has to be absolutely exact or people have no idea at all what we're trying to say. To further complicate things, the people here have never heard a foreigner butcher their language. It's sort of tough and gives rise to the occasional spells of incredible depression ...

We actually look forward to seeing many of our acquaintances and get along great. But conversations with our friends are not very substantive, and there is usually nothing to say. This lack of substance characterizes most of our relationships here, but the people in the chief's family (3 or 4 women, several kids, and 2 men) are fantastic. Generally we just fart around with the language, but hopefully someday things can undergo some sort of linguistic metamorphosis. Even if we knew the language, what would we talk about during times of leisure? We were asking the kids as a matter of course what they had done during the day. But when we got the same answer every day from each kid, we decided that we'd have to think of another question.

Many people have become good friends; some have not. [In addition to the others I've mentioned] there is, Ahmed, our friend from the north, who is actually quite a turd. If they can be stereotyped, the people from northern Somalia are typified by Ahmed. He's obnoxious and doesn't know when to leave. Anyway, I guess we insulted him one night, because he said he wasn't going to come back. He's only come back once, when he just rolled in and demanded a cigarette—literally, "Give me a cigarette." (The language has no polite words. It is put together in such a way that it is impossible for the people to be polite when asking for something. There are no polite commands, no word for "please," and there is only a word translated as "thank you" as a result of foreign influence.) The guy then took off. I think we hurt the poor man ... There's another guy, who speaks Italian and should be a good farmer to work with, who came by and quite honestly confessed that he had never seen or talked to any Americans and wanted to. He's sort of full of it, but not a bad guy.

Our *boyessa*, Fadumo, has really been helping us out by chasing the crowds away. Last night, though, she was too concerned about us and not concerned enough about her fellow countrymen. We were eating dinner, sitting cross-legged on a mat with our little storm lantern, the radio turned to the 7:00 show on Radio Ethiopia, eating chicken and rice with our hands (as is the local custom—utensils just don't exist). A crowd of maybe 20 people, mostly kids, rolled in out of the darkness. Fadumo ran them off, telling them to wait until we were through eating. We asked her what the deal was, and she said that one of the kids had a cut on the back of his head. "A lot of blood or just a little?" (If you should ever have to use the phrase in Somali, it's *"Dhig badaan misseh kisto?"*) "Oh, a lot." We thought we'd better go look, and, by the light of a flashlight and our lantern, we cleaned some of the blood off and slapped a sterile bandage on the kid. *Daktari!* [Doctor.]

We've been doing a lot of that type of thing—treating people who are hacked up with their *yambos* or kids who get skewered by thorn bushes while fooling around out in the bush. That may, in fact, be the area in which we've had the biggest impact. We always make a point of telling them to leave the bandage on, that dirt and flies are bad, that medicine is not the magical cure-all, and other appropriate medical things. There has actually been a slight bit of education. One kid even came to us for a second look with his bandage still on; the others take it off, we suppose so that they will be sure to get some more medicine when they come back.

The attitude of the people concerning medicine is incredible. A little medicine from the white man's medical kit is bound to make all the difference in the world—and a little magical treatment for their crops would certainly result in all the sorghum heads immediately assuming the size of a small football. We've had so many people come and tell us that their little baby is crying, was bitten by a mosquito, and demand medicine ... [Remember that there is no word for please.] Sometimes we have to get pretty adamant about the fact we have no magic medicine. We have pills against diarrhea, pills to try to ward off malaria, aspirin, vitamin pills and stuff to dress cuts—that's it. For example, last night we gave the kid with the cut head a couple aspirin to try and make it easier for him to get some sleep. There were a whole bunch of people in attendance, and I'm not sure what the reaction will be the next time I tell someone that we have no pills.

Maybe you're wondering what else we do around here ... It's necessary to look at about a week's period of time if we're going to feel as if we've accomplished anything at all. Even then it's necessary to alter one's concept of what constitutes success. This week has been successful, though ... We've treated a bunch of kids. We worked at learning the language. We're watching our long drop reach a stage vaguely resembling completion and are organizing Malabo's labor on the shaded enclosure that will be completed sometime. Last night we rigged up a burglar alarm consisting of a nail, a metal cup, and a metal bowl. We've cemented a few relationships. We've sort of half-assedly worked at fixing up a door for one of the chief's *mundels*. We had our first one-on-one conversation with a genuine bush man. We've read a couple books apiece.

As maybe you can appreciate, achievement is measured in scaled-down, more personal, terms. What I describe would snow the top PC people in this country. I suspect that they'd think we were doing a fine job. Some of them are due any day, and I guess we'll find out for sure [what they think of how we're doing]. We're taking things pretty swiftly—and more in stride than during the first week, that's for sure.

Two days later: I'm just getting over the 3-day measles and have a fantastic case of the diarrhea (called EAWA by some—East Africa Wins Again). And we're completely out of charcoal and money. It looks like we'll have to head into Baidoa for a day or 2. We look forward to going into the big city, because of the opportunity to eat meat and drink beer. The last time we went in, we were both blitheringly bitter basket cases, but this time the hassle has been much less troublesome.

January 25 journal entry. [Our first] month in Gorisane is about up.[24] Time is passing. We're making some fantastic friends. It's starting to actually offset the impact of the staring assholes (if that's possible).

... We gave Malabo a new pair of Big Mac work gloves today and talk about excited! The last 2 nights we've had him over to our mat for coffee and a smoke. He and Fadumo (bless her heart!) talk while Tim and I talk. Communication [with Malabo] is certainly on the non-verbal level.

... This little kid, Ow, spent the whole evening here last night, and a better guest we've never had. He's the most patient and understanding person we've run into and must have a strange sort of intelligence, because he understands our pronunciation when no one else does. We showed him pictures of our families, told him all about how many cars there are in the US, and he's promised us to go there. Tim gave him a water pistol, and boy was he tickled. I think we've got a real case of hero worship on our hands.

We're still treating a lot of kids and started a medical log today, which has created some problems that we hadn't foreseen. There is a guy, a real obnoxious type, who is in the village off and on. He's some sort of government doctor/nurse/witch doctor/jerk combination. Anyway, he's no real friend of ours. He's not in Gorisane all the time, and sometimes he doesn't have any medicine. That's how we got started treating cut up little kids. Well, needless to say, he sees his position as being considerably threatened. We try to steer everyone we can to him, but people tell us that he has no medicine and is a bad doctor. They just want some of the white man's magic. He's around frequently enough to let us know that he's really on the ball. One day, he was reciting in Italian all the different types of TB; another time he covered the different types of injections. He brings a container of syringes when he drops by and talks about all the types of diseases he treats—even about cardiac injections. It will be a day without frustration in the Somali Republic before I let that guy perform an intracardial injection in my dear little heart.

I really realized today what a subconscious effect this place has on me. The evangelist came in with his kid and, in a way that seemed rude to our polite US ears, demanded a picture of him with his cute little kid. Boing! I went berserk, although slightly keeping my cool. I was in control of my words, but the reaction was certainly subconscious. I told him—in English, of course—accompanied by a waving finger, that he had no right to come into our house and demand things like that. He got the idea. Our little buddy, Ow, advised us to steer clear of him anyway.

The fits of pique are staying at a constant level of a few per day, and the downs haven't hit me this time yet. (Knock on wood.) Of course, we haven't been downtown recently either. We think that we're going today to drop in on Ahmed—who was here last night with what may prove to be our first real bush acquaintance. Big hair, the whole bit. And handsome as hell. He was interested in us, and we are in him. He's bringing a couple of headrests today for us to check out. [These "bush pillows" are intricately carved small wooden supports used when sleeping to keep the user's head and hair off the ground.] We're looking forward to the business encounter.

February 3 journal entry. Last night Tim and Malibu went to Baidoa to see the doctor.[25] Malibu's leg is really infected. I hope they get something to knock it out of him. It's kind of strange being here without Tim, but I think I actually like being alone. There's nobody to speak English to, but I think my traumatic stage is over—although I experienced a great flash of anger when the kids wouldn't leave when I asked about 17 times. I think I actually scared the piss out of them ...

Without Tim, there's only one guy who has to agree with a decision and no one whose statements have to occasionally brush the other the wrong way, no one to wonder whether he's trying hard enough or what he thinks he's doing here. There's nothing wrong with Tim. After a while anyway, anyone would provide a certain amount of abrasive stimulus.

... Malibu's back (Tim's not), having gotten a shot in each cheek and a hole sliced in his knee. It's getting better every minute. He was snowed by Tim's having spent some money on him and told everyone. He also told everyone about the rowdy group he stayed with in Baidoa—PC vols!

Downtown Baidoa—photo by John Marks

Downtown Gorisane—photo by Bob Bonnewell

Our cook Fadumo in front of her *mundel*

Tim Gaudio in front of our *mundel*

The *wahr*, our water source

Mohamed, the chief's son (center)

Gurey, Malabo's wife, building *akal*

Neighborhood kids in Gorisane

Loading camel with parts for *akal*

Woman pounding sorghum

Nomad

Three men, wearing *ma'awiis*—photo by John Marks

Phil Lovdal on trade truck

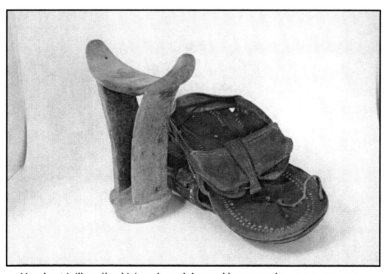

Headrest/pillow (*barkin*) and sandals used by nomads—photo by Peter McKee

Knives worn by nomads—photo by Peter McKee

Camel bell—photo by Peter McKee

Starting To Do Ag Work

> ✍ *We got off to an enthusiastic and optimistic start on our work in agriculture.*

January 14 journal entry. We'll get some seeds from the U.S. and some from people here. We're going to work the way the local people do, but with practical improvements (rows, thinning, etc.). Maybe we can get some of our friends to try things our way. We plan to build a terrarium and a chicken coop. We'll raise their type of chicken. The fewer magic white man things we use, the better off we'll be.

January 26 letter. Harvesting has started now and will go for about [4 more] weeks.[26] Planting comes in about 2 months. The first season we're going to ease into things, working with only 2 or 3 farmers to iron out our technique for organizing the agricultural revolt. But this week's headline is that the chief is excited as hell to let us run a demonstration plot on his land. We figure to put it near the road, where its phenomenal success can be seen by all who pass by. We will be running very standard stuff, but, for here, it's a very big step to take. I'm sure it was very difficult for Chief Green Beads to cut the biggest sorghum heads for seed, instead of using the smallest runts like they've always done. They figure that the good, big ones should be eaten [and we were trying to teach them to plant seeds from big, healthy heads]. We've threshed out the heads (or whatever you do to sorghum) that we're going to use for seed.

January 27 journal entry. Today was our first big PC ag day.[27] Huzzah! We had earlier hit up Ibrahim and Issak for a little plot space. [Ibrahim was the chief's older son; Issak was the chief.] As it's turned out, we may have talked Ibrahim into his whole field. (We're not sure, but he seemed to think we'd need a hell of a lot of seed.) Anyway, we went out with him, shot the breeze, learned some nature terms, and then got him to let us cut some of his largest heads for seed. A big step.

February 3 journal entry. Burns and company rolled into town from BONKA. He checked out a guy's field of overripe peanuts, and we went out to Abukar Fiko's demonstration farm.[28] [BONKA was an experimental ag station in Baidoa, jointly sponsored by the Somali government and USAID—the US Agency for International Development. Mr. Burns was the one American USAID employee. Fiko was the one farmer in the area who worked with BONKA and, as a result, was starting to use oxen to plow.] Fiko has great peanuts, houses, *wahr*, [pond/reservoir], the whole bit. I go out tomorrow for lunch with him and the ag agent for this area—whose goal is to turn the whole area into waving fields of sorghum as high as an elephant's eye, planted in rows and worked with oxen, of course. Good luck to all of us. Burns's counterpart, Olad, would be a fantastic guy to work with. It would be of benefit if Burns came out 3 or 4 times a week. But he never will. There's going to be a movie Wednesday night, put on by BONKA.

February 6 letter. We have 3, maybe 4, farmers on whose farms we're going to run demonstration plots of sorghum this next planting season.[29] (Planting will be done about March 25, before the rains, which is a real break with tradition.) We're going to introduce such advanced techniques as … getting the seeds in the ground before the rains come, planting in rows, and thinning down to proper spacing in the rows. These are all things that nobody here has ever tried. If things work out perfectly, we'll be able to get some DDT for the young plants. (They have a real problem with stalk borer.) Plans for the future involve trying to expand these practices with the first group of farmers, moving onto other farmers, and getting farmers into [BONKA] for oxen training.

We're also expecting to start teaching school pretty soon, although the dates haven't been settled on. They haven't had a school here for 5 years, and people seem fairly eager. We'll try it out and see how things go. Tim and I will teach nothing but English, and a teacher I've gotten to know in a town about 10 km [6 miles] away is planning to move from his too-small town and will teach other subjects.

If things work out—great. If they don't—we tried. If things do look good, we're talking about a self-help one- or two-room school. Obviously, we're at the village's disposal. We're trying to work with felt needs—or even with subconsciously-only quasi-felt needs.

... We've had a hell of a lot of people come to us for medical help. All we have is the standard PC medical kit, and they don't know the first thing about how to care for themselves if they get cut up. [It would be great to have a short] filmstrip extoling the virtues of soap and water and telling these ignorants that "medicine" is not the cure-all magic that every single one of them seems to think it is. It's incredible. Some guy with a huge infection on his leg, weeks old, will saunter in and—instead of saying "Hey, man. I'm hurt" or "Say, buddy, do you suppose you could take a look at my leg?"—says "Give me some medicine." Hopefully, a little education is possible. They could sure use a little, for their own good.

February 6 journal entry. Abukar Fiko and Sinay [the local ag man from the Ministry, whom I only saw 2 or 3 times the whole time I was in Gorisane] seem to have quite a bit on the ball.[30] They're going to let us know when peanuts are ready to harvest. At lunch they both seemed to be impressed by my suave manner and language brilliance. They exchanged quite a few compliments when they thought I couldn't understand. They did give me a hard time about not eating much, but they'll get over that. On the way back from Abukar's farm, I met my new "girlfriend"—15 year-old Ishi. She is too much. Very friendly, beautiful, intelligent.

Last night was a big night—movies at Fiko's. Olad and Mohamed Ali were there from BONKA showing generally irrelevant US films. There were a hundred people at least, and Sinay was giving them the straight scoop through a bullhorn. He really laid it on about us, too: "These are fine men. Go see them for help. Etc." I also got the word from Olad that, any time we want to, we can send farmers into BONKA for oxen training. Fantastic! This makes things much simpler. They walk in, train for a couple weeks, and walk back out with a pair of trained oxen. I hope they will be "training to train," so that things will be set up for more than a few years. This place has fantastic potential, even without tractors or crop dusters. But there aren't enough people with knowledge who also care enough to spread their knowledge around.

It was a wild feeling, looking around the audience. We were in rural Africa. It was quite a sight: a crowd of people whose only farm implement is a short-handled hoe, dressed in brown rags, watching movies of tractors and laughing at the overalls the farmer is wearing. The wrong guy is laughing, as far as I'm concerned, and it's on occasions like these that my core irrationality says, "Hell with you. I could give a damn if you ever get out of the Stone Age." Which brings up an interesting point: We were trying to figure out where these people belong in the scheme of anthropological development. All I know is that one of the cartoons was about 13th century Europe, and they were using the ox and plow.

Today, it's back to the role of super-vol. We're going to get Ali to collect seed, taking pictures for the filmstrip [about ag techniques, more on this idea later] all the while.

February 7 journal entry. Ali wasn't there, but I had several conversations on the road back.[31] One guy insisted on asking the price of everything I own. After giving ridiculous prices for everything, I finally got him to admit that it was really *eb* [rude] to ask someone how much everything costs.

… Abukar's peanuts are supposedly ready to be picked tomorrow, with Sinay coming out to help. I have to talk to Ali Wer and Ibrahim about selection and land prep and to get a few more names. (Ibrahim is still a genuine friend. I hope my negative reaction to other people doesn't foul my relationship with him.) Then it will be time for a few days' break.

February 7 letter. Work, as defined by the Peace Corps I guess, is picking up a little as we get acquainted with farmers, become friends with them, and lay a few of our revolutionary ideas on them.[32] We're going to be working with 3 or 4 of them, all of whom seem interested in letting a friend help them out. Why waste our time with them if there's no interest? ... In my perpetual state of quasi-organization, I envision urging the farmers to take advantage of BONKA ... during the next dry season to learn how to work with oxen. Then, if all works well (*insha allah*, as the people say here—if Allah wills), we'll expand to include more farmers and larger operations.

February 7 letter. The school is no closer to the opening than it was when I wrote my last letter.[33] We have, however, run into a teacher from a nearby town who wants to move up here ... At any rate, he'll be a hell of a guy to have in town, being one of the most understanding and all-around nice Somalis I've met here.

　... Because of the fact that a lazy American is running the show [at BONKA], it doesn't do nearly as much as it might to promote new ag practices out here. Things may be about to improve, however, and we're hoping to send a few of our Beverly Hillbillies into BONKA during the next dry season for oxen training. If things get planted in rows, oxen would definitely help these guys out.

　[The demonstration plot that BONKA has set up at Abukar Fiko's] is, for some reason, ignored by everybody in the area despite the fact that the results are fantastic. It's truly an amazing specimen—trained oxen, peanuts planted in rows, a little American sorghum—really something. It's enough to make a well-meaning PCV wonder why the concept of doing something right in the field of agriculture for a change hasn't spread even a short distance in one direction or another.

More Challenges of Day-to-Day Life

　✎　*I wrote to my college friend who was in Peace Corps/Nepal.*

February 6 letter. At least on the surface, Nepal and this place sound like they have a few things in common.[34] You expressed the opinion that Somalia just might resemble somewhat the conditions found at that place known as the end of the world. Well, you're not too far off—speaking from all of about a month at our post. It would seem that previously we were only approaching the end of the world, while now we're dwelling on the actual parapet. It's bad, but I'm just trying to be sensationalistic about the environment. Sometimes it's great, sometimes it's the shits.

... [Tim and I are] not overly similar in a lot of respects, but there is very little overt friction between us. Our approach to the PC is quite markedly different, but he doesn't call me an overly energetic, hyper-organized, goal-oriented [jerk], and I don't call him a lazy, pseudo-intellectual utopian. We get along all right.

... I made an oven, and Fadumo [our cook] is a whiz with bread ... [Baidoa is 18 miles] away, but 3 hours by trade truck—truly a revolutionary way to travel over undulating local versions of super highway. We're able to bring back a day or two's worth of beef and fruit. The first few days after a trip to the big city are filled with beef, papayas, grapefruit, peppers, potatoes. Then things settle down to normal, when we eat scrambled eggs and tomatoes, bread, tea, rice, spaghetti with no meat sauce, and an occasional chicken.

... We eat a hell of a lot better than the rest of the people here, whose diet consists entirely of sorghum, camel milk (the combination of which, as you seemed to have noted, is called *sor*, eaten once or twice a day, every day of their lives), beans and corn. That's it. Tomatoes are grown locally, but nobody but us buys them. Nobody ever eats meat, although there are goats, cows, camels and chickens all over the place—living in our front yard as a matter of fact. People seem very contented with their diet (and the rest of their existence, for that matter), I would guess as a result of never having been exposed to anything else.

From our point of view, we brought the absolute bare minimum as far as furniture, clothing, everything, is concerned. But we still have so much more than anyone here that it is a little depressing. If it ever became known that we pay our cook 100 shillings a month (about $14), we'd be considered in the same breath as Allah …

Because we do have more stuff than anyone else, we are getting hit up for things with amazing regularity. This language makes it impossible for anyone to ask politely for anything, in the sense that we're used to … "Give me a cigarette;" "Give me that pair of shoes." It's definitely a cross-cultural experience, because here, supposedly, the well-off are supposed to take care of the down and outers, and the language seems rude to our ears. [I learned later that Zakat or alms-giving is one of the five pillars of Islam. Helping the poor is an obligation if one can afford to do so. I don't think we were taught this in our training.] It is getting easier to handle. We just say no, or lie to them, or, in the case of someone we know asking for a cig, give him a cigarette …

Tim and I … had to get at least a slippery grip on the language. We were really pleased to find that there are a lot of similarities between the two languages [Somali and Rahan Weyn], with differences in pronunciation and different nouns being the biggest differences between the two. I've been pleased with my progress and am now able to pass the time of day, engage in the all-important process of greeting people, and ask diddly little questions. It's coming, slowly but surely. I've got to admit that my progress has been the result of pretty hard work, though. (I just sprained my wrist patting myself on the back.)

… Tim and I boil our water; I think we'd probably be dead now if we didn't. But I've still got a good little settlement of amoeba, bacteria, or something developing in my alimentary tract. As a matter of fact, this is about the first time that I've physically felt like writing to you … We never feel real bad, but we seldom feel up to complete par (the standard for which, I'm sure, will be dropping as time passes).

… [We've been setting up our long-drop toilet.] The Muslim culture is big on one's not seeing the private regions of another (female breasts excluded out here, of course), especially while taking a dump or a leak. As a result, even though people piss in the streets of even the biggest cities and take a crap only 5 steps off the road in a field of sorghum, people won't watch them. It's nice. [I do remember that it was different with the kids. They would follow us at a discrete distance and inspect our deposits once we'd finished. Because of the difference in our diets, they must have been spectacular.]

... In a move to create a little more private atmosphere, we erected a fence of thorn bushes [where we can sit on the ground and have our meals]. Actually, it was the idea of Fadumo and Malibu, working in a combined effort. It has helped, because, although it is easy to see through, people get the idea that maybe the place isn't a public gathering area. Our neighbors are fine, and we like having them come over any time; and they're good about not visiting when it's chow time ...

... You asked how I pass the time. For me, like for you, the working day is actually not too long. We usually spend some time each day learning the language. I usually carry a pen and a piece of paper around with me to take down things as they come up. And I usually work on them some time during the day.

We've built quite a few things to improve the place, including shelves and a couple small tables. We built a hell of an effective "refrigerator," we call it, although it's nothing but an evaporator cooler. We lined a large wooden crate with charcoal, put a lining of burlap inside that, and covered the top with another layer of burlap. We try and keep the top layer wet, and, using the charcoal as insulation, we keep things pretty cool. We figure it'll give us an extra day's worth of meat and papaya on our trips to Baidoa. And if we ever get any beer out here—to be drunk privately, of course, since there are strong feelings among true Muslims about drinking liquor. Sorry, guys: we're not Muslim and have absolutely not one small idea of ever becoming one.

We're starting an insect collection. Tim made a net yesterday to help us round up the fantastic variety of weird insects that are found on our very door step. We listen to the radio quite a bit, although it's usually just background. I, too, have been reading quite a bit—more, in fact, than I've ever had time for in my life. Most of the selections are [Peace Corps] book locker specials, which, although often falling short of classic, have proven to be pretty adequate. [These include Ring Lardner, 9 by Salinger, The Cave, by Warren, The Heart is a Lonely Hunter by Carson McCuller, and Barth's Floating Opera.]... Anyway, enough meaningless titles. My point is, I guess, that I, too, have been reading.

We're also constantly trying to improve on our living conditions—hope against hope—before the rains come. We have a solemn promise from Chief Green Beads that, within a few days, work will start on a new roof of sorghum stalks for our *mundels*. We should also get a new layer of cow shit on our floor and our inside walls, the latter frosted with a layer of whitewash. [Other places I say it was camel manure. Now, years later, I don't remember which it was. I suspect it was cow.] Really right uptown. It works very well, since the smell departs within a few days, leaving a dust-free, durable surface.

February 6 journal entry. Tuesday morning I played doctor just about constantly until time to go out to Abukar Fiko's for greasy chicken, rice and tomatoes.[35] It was all right ...

Yesterday I did absolutely nothing except watch Tim make an insect net—and stay out of sorts for about 6 hours. It was the first time I've been like that for a while. I also had Hussein, an old friend who we just found out was a leather worker, make a sheath for my knife. It came out very well. After he's done harvesting today, he's going to come get Tim to show him leather for a belt.

February 7 letter. Things have smoothed out considerably for us here ...[36] That's not to say that life doesn't still have its rough spots—usually recognizable by intense feelings of being [out of sorts] or an incredible eruption of rage. But things have improved, generally speaking, of course ... The chief's family has proved to contain its share of truly fantastic people. I've got the hots for a couple of the various young wives—the one big problem being that they smell pretty bad. We spend enough time just fooling around, laughing our asses off, to offset the "times of trial," as it were.

The language is getting closer to something vaguely recognizable. I've worked pretty hard at it—at times awfully hard, in fact. Those first few days were pretty rough. And results are starting to show. We have just about conquered the amenities. These are very important to the people here in their completely verbal culture. Small talk will be next, along with farm talk. The language has actually reached a plateau, and it's going to be necessary to kick myself in the ass to keep improving. There are a lot of things that I don't know, that I've figured out how to grunt-and-groan, sign-language my way through. That's no way to do it. The reaction that I get when I successfully use the language can be pretty frustrating. Either the person goes into hysterics, repeating in amazement the phrase I've used, or else he wonders why in the hell I don't know more. There are only a few truly understandable people around here. One of the biggest problems is that the people have never heard a foreigner use their language, and the slight differences in pronunciation are a real problem. I have recently spent a lot of time trying to educate both my tongue and other ears for better communication.

We had a real proud moment about a week ago. Tim and I went into Baidoa, having run out of money and charcoal this time (rather than patience as happened the first time). While there, Jim Mikulski, the vol who has been established in Baidoa for almost 2 years, and Bill Thompson, the associate country director in charge of our program (and one hell of a good guy), rolled into town after a 3-week tour of the posts where guys from our group are living. After a night of getting absolutely drunk on rotten red wine (there is no such thing, is there?*) and playing cards, it was off to our vil-

---

* A word about drinking: It surprises me now to see all the references in my letters to drinking and wanting to get drunk. My college experience, and particularly our training camp in Fort Yates, included drinking a lot of

lage for the quicky tour. The big shots were snowed, I think, with how many people we know, the work we've done arranging our place to look like the finest suburban home, what I know of the language, what we know about the farming situation, the arrangements we've made for the coming planting season, etc ... We wandered around our small town, of course attracting crowds rivaling the 7th game of the World Series.

Our *boyessa* Fadumo is the absolute joy of joys; without her we would be nothing. I happened to mention to her that it would be nice if she could bring enough meat and papaya from Baidoa to feed the whole group. There were 8 of us in all. She gave me sort of a weird look but said yes. So, we settled down to the meal of our young lives. It was fantastic. We spread out mats, like we do every night, and ate sitting on the ground, like every night. We are a little short in the utensil department, having only 3 spoons and 3 forks, but we got along tremendously eating with our hands, which is, after all, the way Somalis eat. Fadumo was the picture of organization, presenting rice, beef, lettuce and tomato salad, papaya—all prepared sumptuously. Everyone had been grumbling about having to stay out in the bush for dinner. I guess we showed them. It was an example of how, in this environment, a minor achievement can be viewed as an astounding conquest. In this shit hole, little successes mean a lot.

> ✍ *I put it a little differently in a journal entry the same day. I was starting to get a little ragged psychologically.*

February 7 journal entry. I recall reading about the "limp wash rag syndrome."[37] Never have I felt more beaten up by my social surroundings. My spirit is too beat up to have much anger.

Mohamed [the chief's younger son] got back day before

---

beer. We were young guys in the '60s, and, for most of us, it was what we were used to. As the difficulty of our assignment became clearer, it became a way to escape and regroup.

yesterday from Mog, and we'd forgotten how hectic it is with him around. Not one moment of peace, although—through pretty blatant hints—we think he's figured out that we like some time to ourselves. He never works and Tim's laziness sets us up as targets.

Yesterday I made a door for Habibo's *mundels*. (She's one of the wives in the chief's family. I love that wonderful creature. The women are all so fantastic. They can't possibly realize that they're the only people with whom we have relationships on our own terms. They're great and they don't ever push things like the men do.) Making the door was quite a big job, needless to say, but then listening to the cackling in our *mundel*, as everyone who was crowded in there jumped through hoops for each other, drove me insane. To top it off, I busted the ax handle! I was so pissed off!! It's been uphill ever since, with not even the Saturday sounds being much help. [This must have been a program on the radio.]

Malibu is back, having spent our rent on an ugly pair of plastic shoes and a fantastic new dress for Gurey. She looks great. We have to get things back on a work relationship with Malibu. He's been spoiled. Tim's paying for his trip into Baidoa, a meal, shot, etc, has changed our relationship. Now he's taking advantage of us. He never asks for a cigarette any more, just reaches for it.

The drums are going tonight, but I have no inclination strong enough to overcome my condition of ethnic shock fostered by the cross-cultural exchanges of the past few days. Earlier in the day, maybe we could take it. But at night we just want to escape. We had forgotten how relatively little hassle there was when our "friends" were gone.

Things are relatively easy when the antagonists come and go, but, when the same group hangs on, it wears me down. I made it a week with absolutely no problem. Two days later, I'm a 30 year-old, tired pile of crap. [Thirty must have seemed so old. I was not yet 23.] All the structures of rationality that I thought my behavior was hung on have proved to be made of nothing sturdier than spaghetti. My responses are not predictable, as my mind seems not to be in charge. It's almost like there's an externally-created psychological nihilism, in which everything is just thrown into a jar like numbered balls in a game of bingo; and responses are drawn at random, with no consideration of the previous or the following response to a similar situation.

✎ *Ten days later I wrote:*

February 17 journal entry. I got back from Baidoa yesterday.[38] Of course, the *mundel* is not done. We were only gone 8 days! The old lady did get the inside and outside walls done perfectly—as well as most of the floor. As a result of its not being ready, I'm living out of my suitcase, sleeping on a mat, "waiting for the van to come." [I think the quote is a line from a Beatle's song.] The place looks great; we have the *nuriyo* [maybe the "whitewash" that was the final coat for interior walls] and the place should be in great shape soon. This morning I cleaned the *ulbangh* of the wasp nest. [Apparently, I had developed my vocabulary for elements of the *mundel's* construction. But that knowledge didn't last 45 years. *Ulbangh* may well have been the word for "roof."] The place is really going to be something—a veritable show place.

I have no idea when Malibu is going to finish the porch or the *maskola* [drop toilet]. He didn't seem to have worked very hard putting things right while I was gone. The walls have some shit on them, and part of the roof is covered—*bis* [that's all]… The phrase that best epitomizes local workmanship is slow and unsteady.[39] Things may or may not get done, and they may or may not be well done. One just has to wait and see. I've found that the advice, "If you want something done, do it yourself," is very applicable.

Baidoa wasn't too much fun.[40] Most things in this country seem to be not much fun. Banzoni's was out of beer, and Fadumo was very lazy as far as getting stuff organized for the trip back. She likes the big city better than the suburbs, that's for sure …

I had a real bad time coming back on the truck. I was in a crabby mood. I dipped to my all-time low when a guy, who I thought was part of the shipping company but who was actually a free agent, demanded 25 shillings [about $3.50] after carrying our stuff from downtown. If I knew he was going to pull that, I would have carried the stuff myself. I ended up lobbing the coins into the dirt at his feet. Pretty rank on my part. We bellowed at each other, and Fadumo finally picked the coins up and gave him his money. That afternoon things settled down.

The next day was a good day. It's strange how this place is now actually home. Very little hassle about medicine, etc. Pretty nice overall. I built a window for our *mundel*, with very little trouble, surprisingly enough. The chief's wife immediately mudded up the outside. We have her solemn promise that the rest will be done today. Issak also assured us that we're getting a grass roof. He and Malibu seem to be in competition. They're both throwing away 30 shillings (2 month's rent in advance, as far as we can tell) trying to show off for each other. Once we put a coat of *nuriyo* on the *mundels*, we'll be the local pacesetters …

I had my first good trip downtown. I hung around the *tomals* [blacksmiths] a while, learned a word or two, learned about poison arrows and their effects, and generally had a pretty good time.

Still Trying To Do Ag Work

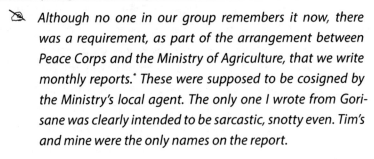 *Although no one in our group remembers it now, there was a requirement, as part of the arrangement between Peace Corps and the Ministry of Agriculture, that we write monthly reports.* These were supposed to be cosigned by the Ministry's local agent. The only one I wrote from Gorisane was clearly intended to be sarcastic, snotty even. Tim's and mine were the only names on the report.*

---

* This requirement was described in a memo dated December 7, 1968, to PC/Somalia Director Felix Knauth from Dr. Abdul-Rahman Elmi, Director General of the Ministry.

Periodic Report of Peace Corps Volunteers in Agriculture
Covering the Period through January 31, 1969
James A. Douglas and J. Timothy Gaudio –
Assigned to the Shevello Region

Owing basically to the difficulty inherent in endeavoring to firmly ensconce oneself in a culture foreign to one's own, the two of us have experienced only minimal success concerning the ultimate goal of revolutionizing and mobilizing the agrarians of the Shevello Region. The amount of time that we have found necessary to devote to acquainting ourselves with the many cultural nuances involved in attempting to establish ourselves in our community has been considerable. A second problem, most paramount, has been that of achieving a grasp of the regional patois sufficient to allow us to proceed with our efforts to affect, even minimally, the agricultural techniques presently in practice. In short, the amount of time that we have found necessary to devote to becoming settled in a physical sense, as well as the number of hours that we have chosen to devote to the task of starting up the trail—which it is hoped will eventually lead to a mastery of the local parlance—have precluded any full-time involvement in the field of agriculture—to this point in time, at any rate.

But now to direct ourselves to the matter of the achievements that we have experienced in the field of agriculture, which, after all, is what this report is purporting to deal with: We have succeeded in establishing excellent business relationships with two agriculturalists of the region, Ibrahim Issak Gorisane and Ali "Wer." The proposal for the upcoming period of cultivation is for these two men (plus additional interested parties, if located) to inseminate with selected seed in stands carefully delineated in a longitudinal sense—under our mutual auspices, of course. As the revelations of modern agricultural technology dictate, this is to be done prior to the period of imminent tropical deluge. Upon appearance of substantial germination, selection within the individual areas of delineation will be made, leaving the remainder spaced as per professional instruction. We are hopeful that the production of the above-described areas of demonstration will manifest a marked improvement in technique over that exhibited by methods presently being utilized.

✎ *How arrogant! The following letter to Bill Thompson, the associate director of PC/Somalia, must have been the cover letter for the report.*

February 8 letter. That should hold the bureaucrats for a while …[41]

And I have what I think is a fantastic idea for my monumental work—my masterpiece. I've decided to go into the movie producing business. The stimulus for this little brainstorm was the evening at the cinema that we attended [at the demonstration farm]. The films could have been a little more directly applicable, but the idea was a damn good one—going from one little village to another out here with a little educational entertainment. My idea is to make a filmstrip, using slides that show the correct practice in our demonstrations—showing Ali Wer cutting ideal heads for seed, showing Ibrahim Issak planting in rows and thinning. Hopefully, we'd have an accompanying narration in Rahan Weyn that everyone would understand. I'm pretty sure that we'd have to take a local around with us to do the explaining—our Rahan Weyn is never going to get that good. We'd probably be able to get a car for a couple months, and just hit this area, a different town every day.

Seriously, I think the idea of slide shows, utilizing a projector as described in the Village Tech Handbook (made of a flashlight and a few lenses), might have some kind of understandably minimal impact. (I'm sure that Kodak in Milan could rig up a filmstrip or two.) At least it's something to dream about. There's no education out here, in any form. The farmers have no idea how to carry out correct farming, even for the conditions found here. It would certainly be easy to attract the crowds (witness your recent brief visit), and I'm sure that we can find someone easily enough who is fluent in Rahan Weyn, with whom we could also converse. After a few showings you could probably send the ag PCVs home, Somali agriculture having been completely revolutionized and all.

February 17 journal entry. I had a great talk with Ibrahim [the chief's older son].[42] He's a hell of a good guy. He knows who wants to change and who's not interested in trying something new. We talked ag while we supervised the filling of the enormous family *got* [probably an underground storage hole for sorghum]. We talked with Ali Wer, and he's not up to trying new things. He wants oxen, medicine, and everything else now, or he's not going to do anything at all. After a good conversation with Ali and Ibrahim, Ali and I agreed to disagree … That afternoon I talked to Ibrahim again and helped him and Ali Wer cover up Ali's *got*.

Ibrahim and I are supposed to talk to a few progressive farmers, Alio Hhumo and Sherif Jiis.[43] I have talked briefly with Alio. I figure I will take a few photos of his "seed selection techniques" [for the filmstrip] and we'll be all set. He and Ibrahim are buddies—which I'm sure must be one of the criteria for selection to the ag improvement program—so things will be great … Those 3—and maybe Abukar Fiko—will give us plenty to do … Today has to be the day for seed selection, since most of the [harvested] sorghum is under the ground by now.

The mark of a progressive farmer out here, that is, one who's interested in something above subsistence living, is fields of peanuts, and we've latched onto one of these.[44] [Sherif Jiis] must be the local millionaire, since he just spent 350 shillings ($50!, a truly incredible amount out here) to have the Russian-run farm implement rental outfit [ONAD] come out and plow up 2 or 3 acres of land. He was planning to grow peanuts on it, and, since he's game and the big field is right on the road where all the people can see the magnificent success of the white man's advice, we're going to give him the benefit of our fantastic ag backgrounds. Additional incentives are that peanut crops almost never fail—and the margin of profit is 2000% or some place in that neighborhood.

February 19 journal entry. Alio Hhumo and I selected his seeds and took pictures.[45] I talked to Sherif Jiis. We'll plant peanuts on the tractor-plowed ground. He's a real mover. We will get seeds from Ibrahim's brother-in-law. I have 4 farmers, and we have plots picked out for Ibrahim and Sherif Jiis. I'm very pleased.

We've set up 5 demonstration plots, 4 of sorghum, 1 of peanuts.[46] We've looked for people who want to change, who will do exactly what we tell them, hopefully will be able to see the reasons behind what we do, and—if things are successful—learn from the success. The sorghum plots are going to be 40 meters square, planted in rows, thinned, and perhaps sprayed with DDT if we can get it. Almost all the farmers here grow sorghum almost exclusively, so we've chosen to work with it for starters. Then, hopefully, we'll diversify to crops such as peanuts, maybe cotton, beans, and other vegetables if a miracle occurs. The people are used to growing only corn, beans and sorghum. They are also used to eating only corn, beans and sorghum. No wonder we're stronger than they are.

February 25 entry. Last week we got seeds from Alio Hhumo and eager permission from Sherif Jiis to work the plowed land just outside town.[47] It's quite a set-up. Peanuts are supposed to grow like hell during the *gu* [rainy season]. According to locals, sorghum has trouble every time it turns around. We'll see.

I also got seeds from Ibrahim's brother-in-law, and Malibu talked his way into the program. I don't care—if he'll improve. He has to get working at a little better clip, though, or the rains will catch us at the half-finished stage, where we are now.

Daily Life Unchanged

February 18 letter. I just re-read a copy of my first letter [to you] from Somalia [written in mid-December].[48] I'm keeping carbons of all my letters, so that I can read them over in a couple years and see how my attitudes have changed—or warped as the case may be. Anyway, that first letter was total BS. It could have been written by a high school sophomore, as unrealistic as it was. Talk about ridiculous optimism.

... I've been very pleased with my progress in the language ... I'm to the point where I can deal with the amenities, which are very important to the culture here, and have built a pretty good vocabulary of words for the parts of a bushman's outfit (long stick, fringed robe, big hairdo, very sturdy sandals, etc), ag terms (there are a million different ways to describe a head of sorghum, for example), names of birds, thorn trees, etc. Not too useful for urban use, but very handy out here. It always makes for a good snow job on some bushman to be able to name all the things he points at as he checks out how much of his language we know.

... We have gotten used to a hell of a lot in the 5 weeks since we first arrived here. A great example: I told you that the people use cow shit as the final veneer on walls and floors. When we first moved into our *mundels*, the one that Fadumo now lives in was inhabited. The family moved out and left the place as nice as they could imagine. They even wet down the floor [made of manure], the purpose being to make it even harder and dust-free when it dries. Tim and I were appalled. We didn't know what to do. After all, we'd never seen it done before.

Today—just 5 enlightening, adjusting weeks later—I sat and watched the sweet little old lady as she put the final bit of frosting on the floor of our *mundel*. I guess the point is that one adjusts, given a little time. We're getting used to a hell of a lot, e.g., shit on the floors, runaway camels running through our yard as we're eating dinner, people coming over to stare. Every day fewer people do the latter; every day more people say hello by name as we walk out in the fields or walk downtown. The aspects of our existence that seemed so sensational to us when we first got here don't seem too bad now. We have learned to take a hell of a lot of things in stride.

[Having said that,] the effect of the immediate moment is really interesting … Sometimes I can withstand anything. Other times, the smallest things just send me into a rage. I've pulled enough crazy stuff here that I don't get much trouble from people any more. After all, you don't give some crazy white guy too much trouble if you've seen him threaten somebody with a stick or seen him suggest that you take off—using a Somali dagger as a pointer. To say the least, the rational is not always in control. The lasting ill effects on my own psyche and on my relationships with the people don't seem to be bad because of my occasional outbursts. The bad ones stay away, and the good ones come back a little better trained.

It seems terrible to act as if the people are animals, as if they have to be trained. Is that bad? Are they animals? Are we being grossly culturally insensitive or are they? What can we expect of them? Their culture, especially out here in the bush, is so completely different from ours that the only way people will respect the few rights we wish to hang on to will be for us to "train" them. Their culture is very verbally oriented; they can talk for hours about nothing. They just go on and on, talking trivia. The people don't read because the language is unwritten. These people don't even know where the U.S. is. (I just talked to a bushman who had never heard of America.)

How can they understand that we can read, for example, or talk about some of the things we do? Things are just too different for us to completely adopt the ways of their culture or for them to be able to understand some of the things we do. Things like our reading books, my typewriter, our lack of enthusiasm for what they consider the greatest things in life. An example of the latter is their games and dancing at political rallies. One guy chants through a bullhorn, one guy beats on a drum, and the people walk around single-file. Big deal. Seen it once, you've seen it every time. And yet, when it's all you've ever known as far as raising hell and having a good time are concerned, it's a hell of a big deal. No wonder neither culture understands the other too well.

There is a girl PCV who spent 2 years in a bush town in the north who maintains that she has enjoyed her time here because she has ceased to think of herself as an American. She feels she is a Somali. Her language ability is fantastic, but it's still got to be BS. Because of the color of our skin we can never be anonymous. (Sounds like another contemporary problem, right?).

Even if you could get into the culture completely, who would want to? I have gained an appreciation, in just the short time I've been here, of the marvelous complexity of life in the western countries. Sure, there are things wrong, but these problems are just the result of the complexity that gives us so many other things. It's a good lesson to live here for a while, to see what the simple life is. It's different, something that, for a person of my cultural upbringing, must be supplemented by fragments of the culture back home. Complete fluency [in Somali] would not make reading any less desirable. After what we've all been used to, there's not enough in this culture to take up all our time.

Well, I've told you about everything but our official Peace Corps work. Owing to our different personalities, I end up doing most of the stuff that would be classified as PC stuff. Tim isn't very work-oriented. That's OK; we complement each other pretty well. He does one type of thing; I do the other. And I, for my part, am pretty satisfied with the way things are going ... At least we have our little ideas and it does seem like we may be able to affect a few lives, a few men's farming techniques. That and staying out of the [Viet Nam] war would seem to be my reasons for being here. God knows it can't be because of the soft life or because of all the exotic activities that fill our every waking moment.

✎ *I wrote a long and informative letter to the sister of a college friend.*

February 23 letter. [Right now I'm] lounging around in my skirt.[49] Called a *foorungh*, it's worn by the great majority of men here [that is, of the men who reside in Gorisane; most nomads wore a robe. Also, *foorungh* was probably a Rahan Weyn word. It is not the Somali word, which is *ma'awiis*.] It looks exactly like a skirt, extending down to about mid-shin or ankle level. It's as comfortable as one can ever imagine. Right now our *boyessa* is washing practically everything else in my not so extensive wardrobe.

Apparently, the rains and incredible discomfort are just about a month away, so the 2 of us have started the process of battening down the hatches ... The rains here are supposed to have a debilitating effect on the social life of the village, which right now consists almost entirely of walking around, talking to friends, checking things out in general. The mud is supposed to be about mid-thigh in depth ... We're planning to hole up with a lot of good books, a healthy supply of spaghetti and vitamin pills, and see what happens. Even the little things may be tough. We have been told that the rains hit this area about every 4 or 5 days. The rain comes down very hard for hours at a time and then stops to build up until the next deluge. As they say, the farmers like it.

... I was just interrupted by the first shower of the season. There's not supposed to be any rain until the first of March, and we're getting some today. Not too much, but a good shower. I had to bolt outside to help our *boyessa* take the clothes down off the line, and, now, of course, they're strung all over our *mundel* ... This shower would seem to be a good indication of how the ground will turn during the rains. Despite the fact that the amount of rain has not been too great, the surface of the ground is just like library paste. It should be a lot of fun when it's up to the bottom of one's white-hunter type khaki shorts.

Tomorrow is supposed to mark the beginning of the re-roofing project, or so it is said. We were first told that it would be done "tomorrow" about 2 weeks ago. Maybe the unbelievable will happen. Then we'll whitewash the inside walls and be ready for the rains.

Yesterday we had a visit by the Peace Corps doctor—a guy named Don Parsons ... He's just checking around, asking very good questions concerning our present state of contentment. (Mine of which is very high, especially on paper, considering language prog-ress, ag progress, etc—in the parlance, a real super-vol.) We walked around town, and Don asked us very good, probing questions.[50] For example, is there still reason for two of us to be here? Are we going to stay 2 years? I told him the truth, and he spent some pri-vate time with Tim. Tim's and my approaches to this place are dif-ferent enough that we always have to be making agreements. I'm not an arguer, so we end up doing things his way. It never bothers me intensely, but little things do add up to slight irritation.

Since Don doesn't often get the chance to get away from Mog-adishu, he eats up the chance to see different aspects of bush life.[51] [Something] the people do here that we're getting used to doing ourselves is just going downtown (all of about 100 yards away) to look around. Earlier, like I'm sure I told you, the trips downtown were pretty rugged. But now that we know a little of the language and know a few people, we can walk down to check out this guy's little blacksmith shop, that's guy's shop, see if so-and-so is selling bananas today, see if his brother is selling sorghum, have a cup of tea. It's not exactly what one imagines he'll be doing for a good time when he's a senior in college, but here it's all they've got. By enjoying what local people enjoy, or at least doing what they do, I think I'll get a little better insight into the way they work.

I've been pleased with what I've learned about the people and their way of life. Knowing Italian has been very helpful, since I can have some interesting conversations with the chief's sons about their attitudes toward politics, toward other sub-tribes, about social customs and practices. Sometimes I could just give a good god damn; other times I've got a million questions, all of which have interesting answers. I was never too excited about the city Somalis, because of a million little reasons that add up to a gen-eral lack of affection. The people in the bush—or at least the ones who eventually accept us as a new set of neighbors rather than freaks who can't possibly mind having their every move carefully followed and questioned—are really something. Their lives aren't very complicated, but they've figured out survival very well, and, for their way of life, that's doing pretty well. They utilize everything they have to keep themselves and their livestock taken care of as best they know how.

I'd been told before coming out here that the people didn't know their environment, but I've found the opposite. Knowing that for spider bites one uses a wasp nest as a poultice; that the sap from a certain tree is not only very irritating to skin and eyes but also makes good glue; that Venus always comes up in the same place—they're not completely out of touch with their surroundings.

I've seen 3 types of people out here. There are people who live most of the time in permanent houses, like the people with whom we live. They leave only to take their stock out to feed in the bush after the sorghum stalks have all been eaten. The second type is the real wild and woolly bush man who, with nothing but his stick, flashlight and knife, wanders from place to place, seemingly doing nothing but wander—with no animals, no family. The third type is very interesting, a group with which I'm getting a little better acquainted as time goes on. They're the people who have a few camels, maybe a few goats, a few cows, but no permanent farm. They graze their stock wherever they can, carrying their homes (made of sticks and mats) and all their belongings on the backs of their camels. Real subsistence, but one look at the Somali bush makes it pretty obvious that they have to be pretty hardy folk.

I just finished dinner of camel meat and rice. Not too bad. We were eating mostly spaghetti for dinner, but recently the market has been getting some meat. The other day we had goat, today camel. It isn't exactly rare sirloin, but it is definitely meat.

In reading back over this, it looks like a goddamned term paper. Sorry. It's the first time I've written a lot of this stuff down, and I just lost my head.

In about a week, we're going into the capital city for a conference of the guys in our group. We're going to declare all of our good intentions once again and discuss successes and problems. I think that perhaps the biggest reason for holding it is to give us the chance to go into Mog, spend a few days at the beach, stay drunk for a few days, entertain promiscuous women, etc., before the miserable months that accompany the rains. I'm game.

Having run the anthro lecture into the ground, I was getting ready to close this, but our buddy Hassen just entered our shack and informed me that he'd never seen me work the "machine." [I think Hassen was Ibrahim's son.] So I have to type a few lines to show him just how talented and wonderful those acquainted with western technology are. He's a hell of a nice kid, and it wouldn't do to leave him disappointed … I had to show him how the paper is removed [from the typewriter] after one is through with it.

There are so many things that we take so completely for granted that people here can no more understand than that men recently went around the moon. Things like American matches just amaze them; the only matches they see are the ones that come in the little wooden boxes. They can't imagine owning more than one shirt, a *foorungh* and a pair of shorts. They can't imagine why anyone who wasn't just struggling to survive in the bush would wear their sandals. And on and on.

We amaze them with damn near everything we do. Right now, 2 guys are looking at the stamps on this envelope—their own country's stamps, and they can't believe their eyes. If nothing else, we're exposing them to something different, and most of them certainly cannot be harmed by learning that the United States ("Where?" many of them would say, having never even heard of the place) is farther away than French Somaliland, that English and American are the same language, and that the Italian westerns do not present a totally accurate picture of life as it's lived in the US today. It's really Africa, not the kind that makes the movies, but the kind that makes the documentaries. And it's home, through thick and thin, until November, 1970.

February 24 letter. Another thing that is troublesome is that people are always asking us how much things cost.[52] How much did your shirt cost? How much do you pay your girl? How much did the lantern cost? Etc. We are only being treated like they treat each other. In training we were told that the people here don't care a thing about money, and this statement typifies the accuracy of the information we received [in training, in general]. It's a crock. The people are very money conscious, and since we've got it all—being paid about $140 [must have been 1000 shillings] a month, as much as the chief has saved in a lifetime, for a fact—we get a lot of attention and questions ...

The new grass roof [on top of sorghum stalks, as I recall now] was supposed to be put on today. We're leaving in 2 days and everyone knew that we wanted the damn thing put on before we left for [the conference in Mog] before the rains come. We'd first been told that the job would be done "tomorrow" about 2 weeks ago. Now we find out it takes 4 days to do. They said before that it took 2. Very definitely a small failure, but, with nothing to do today to clean the thought out of my head, there was little to do but sit like a little baby and let it eat on me.

February 25 journal entry. The end of last week, Tim and I spent more time downtown than before.[53] It's getting to be a lot easier. I've been watching the *tomals* [blacksmiths], learning the words. At present, I'm not overly enthusiastic. In rationalizing, it might be because I have the language coming out of my ears. A few of the days have really been full of new stuff.

I took a quicky trip into Baidoa on Saturday ... The driver of my trade truck turned out to be Little Jerry's brother, taking a one-shot trip around the Upper Juba for his dad's corporation. [Little Jerry was the singer with the rock band at the Bar Lido, on the beach in Mog. More about the Lido later.] We had a few beers at Banzoni's. He turned out to be a hell of a good guy. The trip was fast, but I'm getting sort of tired of having Somalis ask why I'm not married, how I possibly get along without a wife to wait on me, do I want to buy a girl, do I like to fuck, etc.

National Elections in Gorisane

February 23 letter. Last night there was what is called a "party."[54] The national elections are coming up in just about a month, and, since they occur only once every 5 years and are very important in maintaining the system of graft and corruption that completely dominates the national political system, they're a big deal. You ought to see it if you're disillusioned with the hypocrisy and dishonesty in American politics. It's truly incredible here. Of course, the party presently in power has all the government vehicles at its disposal for campaigning. The opposition parties get along as best they can. (There are about 100 of them in the country, a dozen in Baidoa, and they contest maybe half a dozen seats in Parliament.) Hardly a real egalitarian system.

Categorized as a whole, the politicians are solely interested in making their money, living in Mogadishu, and generally selling out their constituents. There are few with anything resembling what we would consider a social conscience. Within each parliamentary district, the party bosses figure out the line-up within their party, of course dictated by the size of the pay-offs by the individual candidates. Then the campaigning begins. But rather than the individual campaigning, the entire party campaigns. Also, people vote for the party rather than the man with, I would guess, the majority of votes being bought—24 cents or so easily being enough to assure the vote of many of the people in a place like our village. The number of parliament seats awarded to each party within a district is determined by the percentage of the vote the party receives, and the individual parliamentarians are determined by their standing within the party. Obviously democratic in principle, but something is lost in practice. It's so corrupt and selfish that it's all a farce.

Anyway … Last night the majority party came to town, as the parties are wont do to. With the election so close, they're coming more often. There's another big to-do tonight, as a matter of fact. Campaigning takes a very interesting form, with no speeches, no nothing. Instead, there are a couple of drums (played by anyone who feels so inclined) and a guy sort of chanting through a bull-horn, bellowing everything from the Koran to spontaneous pro-party crap. The reason the people look forward to these events as much as they do is that it's their chance to "dance." The men line up in one single-file line, the women in another, and then they walk back and forth. It's sort of the bunny hop without the hop. And that's their biggest form of enjoyment. I'm sure that they will miss it when the elections are over.

Last night the 3 white guys [Tim, the doctor Don Parsons and I] went downtown just to check it out. People were glad to see us, we were shown to a bench that someone had set up, and we settled back to enjoy the festivities. Needless to say, we saw a lot of walking back and forth. It was a little different from the previous times, though. We've gotten to the point where we know quite a few people in town, and I enjoyed watching our friends "having fun." They've never known anything else, so they definitely groove on this stuff. And I'm getting used to the place and its people to the extent that I enjoy watching their good times. After all, there's nothing else for them to do.

Eid in Gorisane

✍ *I was really looking forward to experiencing Eid in Gorisane.*

February 23 letter. Coming up in 3 days is what is referred to as Eid-Aareff.[55] [This must be the name in Rahan Weyn for Eid-ul-Adha.] As best I've been able to ascertain, this marks the beginning of the brief period of time when Muslim pilgrims can enter the holy city of Mecca. [Actually, it celebrates the end of the annual pilgrimage to Mecca.] The historical significance has something to do with the Prophet Mohamed's visit to the same city, but the details of that visit have eluded my intellectual search. There is another Eid [Eid-ul-Fitr], which this year was at Christmas time and that I saw celebrated in Baidoa. We expect the celebration in the bush to be something right out of Lowell Thomas documentaries.

There are tame things like gambling for 1.4-cent pieces, and shooting a pellet gun at a target for the same amount. Tame stuff. But ... authentic Africana comes in during what is called *saar*, a type of dance. From what we saw in Baidoa last Eid, there are a couple types of dances besides *saar*, some of which involve just men and some involving a few women as well. There is a lot of stamping, chanting, wailing, jumping and crotch-flexing. The people get incredibly worked up psychologically—who knows how; the use of alcohol is forbidden, and the only ones in this country who know about grass are PCVs. These dances go on, quite monotonously as far as we're concerned, for hours, and the participants get pretty worn out.

On the other hand, *saar* is something that I've only heard about. I imagine that there is the same chanting, wailing, jumping and stomping. The one big difference is that each guy, instead of keeping his knife in his sheath as in the other dances, clutches it firmly in his sweaty, dust-covered hand. The guys are supposed to get really worked up, and, when they reach a certain point, they start working over their own arms and legs with the knife. It sounds just a little primitive, doesn't it? Especially when the number of scars is the direct index of your stud factor. One of our neighbors [Malabo] is nothing but scar from shoulder to wrist and all over his thighs. The number of individual slashes he's inflicted must be in the hundreds, and they're not little cuts, but healthy slices. Like I said, it seems a little primitive.

Another aspect of Eid that I'm looking forward to almost as much as the knife games is the eating that goes on. The people here eat exclusively sorghum and milk, and corn and beans, practically all year. Eid is their chance to chow down on some meat. Each family slaughters the type of animal it can afford: the richest slaughter a camel; the next financial grouping, a cow; next, a goat, and the poorest families, a chicken. Tim and I are slaughtering a goat and having all our friends over. Three or 4 volunteers are coming from Baidoa, having never seen Eid festivities out in the bush. And the 20 or so people in the chief's family will be there. We're going to have a great time eating greasy goat, rice and tomatoes. In the Somali bush, that's living.

> ✎ *But Eid does not go as planned and my mood sours.*

February 25 journal entry. Tim left for Kismayo [to visit other volunteers], rather than staying around for Eid tomorrow and the big goat feed we're having.[56] I wonder if he ever considers anything like a sense of duty. Sure, it's easier to just take things easy, but I can't see where that's the point of our being here. He never went with me to select seeds, doesn't even know 3 of the 5 farmers "we" are working with. I'm not going to tell him what to do, but I don't have to agree with his approach.

March 16 journal entry. It's been a long time.[57] What has happened in 3 weeks? The first day of Eid really started things going downhill, as far as I could tell. I went downtown with Mohamed and was mildly provoked to the point that I hit a guy in the face—I tried to miss him, but he moved into it. I got into a playful stick fight (utilizing unorthodox *gaal* style), which ended with my rapping the guy's ribs a bit. Both guys had started the conversations with "Hey, buddy, I'll bet you don't know how to ..." Now, maybe they know.

Eid was a bad time, because there were a hell of a lot of bushies in town who had never had the chance to look at my white body. ["Bushy" was our term for Rahan Weyn people who both lived in the bush and had large hairdos.] I had also been out here a while and was getting tired of all the BS. Still, I should remember I'm a civilized human being ... I went back downtown the afternoon of Eid for a little of the warm-up "games." Of course, I was the show. Fuck! All I wanted to do was go down there with Mohamed and check things out. No way. The only game going on was the inter-sub-tribal slap contests that featured some of the greatest monotonic, extended rank jobs by one of the participants. He was excellent.

Jim Mikulski, Phil Smith, Maureen and Marianne showed up that evening with Zenab and food for dinner. The place had worn me down to a frazzle, but the 2 girls wanted to check things out down town. Well, they got no farther than the banana stands when the rush and the shouting started. They were rushed by an excited crowd of hundreds and coolly returned to the *mundels*, followed, of course, by about 200 bushies. It took an army guy to try and turn them back. It was just another incident to make things less enjoyable. That night we were surprisingly left alone, since everyone was down town digging what was going on. We played hearts and split a bottle of wine they had brought.

The next day there were bushies all over the place, and I treated a couple who came by. There was one little kid I can remember vividly. She had fallen into the fire, burning a hole in her back. It had started to heal remarkably well, but she was so skinny and dirty that I was just about sick. I washed her back, treated the burn and told her she could go. As she got up and adjusted her filthy robe, I remarked to Smitty that the little guy just didn't have a chance. So skinny, so dirty. All the time I had thought it was a little boy. But he had seen that it was a girl when she adjusted her robe. Jesus! I was really sick then.

I had bought a nice goat. To feed all my friends at Eid, a little PR to all my new friends, right? Ha! The white people ate in my *mundel*, the men ate in Ibrahim's *mundel*, the women ate outside, and the kids ate who knows where. It was far from what I'd expected, but at least people had something to eat—although no one actually likes meat. (Not as good as a few handfuls of *sor* [boiled, mashed sorghum, like polenta, eaten with milk].) I learned. No more big spreads from this kid. Why bother? I'm an outsider. I think that fact just has to be accepted and worked around.

✍ *With 45 years of hindsight, this seems like a remarkable overreaction to the fact that people with very little in common culturally chose to eat separately. People ate with their own, as I now know happens in many cultures. I was starting to lose patience with just how different the Somali bush was from everything I was accustomed to at home.*

The big dances hadn't started by the time we finished eating the goat. So we took off for Baidoa ... Dinner the next night at Burns [the guy at BONKA] was casual, but I decided to do it up right. Long pants and shoes felt strange. It was the first time for long pants since Thanksgiving, and the first time for shoes since getting into the country. [We always wore flip flops or bush sandals.] Quite the young dude.

Advice About Whether to Join the Peace Corps

🖎   *I wrote a letter to a friend still in college who was thinking about going into the Peace Corps.**

February 24, 1969. Maybe some of the potential draft dodgers in the class of '69 would be interested in a small evaluation of my brief term of service.[58] First, this country is not too typical. We get absolutely no government support (Somali, that is), which is quite the exception. In Kenya, for example, the government actually pays the PCVs' salaries. Here, in most cases, we don't even get a government agent to work with. We're just out here hacking along as best as our initiative will allow. The system of politics and government appointments is so screwed up with graft and corruption that there are very few politicians or appointees who give a good god damn about anything. Everyone who works for the government is a product of a great deal of blatant brown-nosing and ass-kissing. I have a "colleague" who is a good example. He is the ag extension

---

*   A somewhat different letter about the Peace Corps to a different friend still in college is in Appendix A.

agent assigned to this area. He very seldom comes out here, except to supervise a huge, tremendously successful demonstration farm that is run by one of his buddies. No one else manages to concern him. And he's pretty typical. They all talk nice to your face and then never do anything.

It's quite frustrating, because some of the people do care about improving their farms and their way of life. But, even if the advice is available, the materials are not. For example, DDT is not sold in Baidoa, one of the biggest cities in the country and the capital of the ag region in which most of my group is working. The only place it's available is at an experimental farm, and there you can only get it if you're a farmer with a little clout, for example, if you have a worthless ag extension agent running a huge demonstration farm on your land or a red hot PCV giving you advice. Without someone on their side, the little farmers don't have a chance to improve.

There are other reasons why this country is not really typical Peace Corps. Like I think I mentioned, Americans are not overly loved here, for fairly insignificant political reasons. [Over time I learned about the reasons for this, which were, in fact, fairly significant, including the fact the U.S. had sided with Ethiopia in a war with Somalia.] Some areas of the country are horrible this way. I'm sure that my part of the country is one of the best as far as this is concerned. I think most volunteers spread out over the world would be helping people who have at least a vague idea what the Peace Corps is trying to do (at least what it is) and would probably (or certainly) know where the US is or at least have heard the name. The people here don't have any idea what's going on, other than the fact that we're white and living in their village, working with the farmers.

Perhaps—perhaps, hell, certainly—the biggest disadvantage to this country is the language. It's incredibly difficult, supposedly the most difficult in the world [for an English-speaker to learn]. Only about $1/3$ of the volunteers in Somalia come out of their 2 years with even a working knowledge of the language, and only a very small percentage of those become semi-fluent. Understandably, the result is a lot of bitter returned PCVs.

I don't think that I will end up bitter, maybe I will. But I don't think I will remember the country or its people on the whole with a tremendous amount of affection. Individuals are a completely different story. I kind of like my village—that's as far as I'll go right now. As the language becomes less of a problem, I think I'll like it even more. But the individuals in many cases are just about all that's keeping me here—that plus the possibilities for "job success" and the vague feeling of having committed myself in some way. That's reason enough.

… The physical discomforts, housing, diet, camels shitting outside our door, are almost never a source of discontent. As a matter of fact, there's a sort of masochistic pride based on the belief that a guy has to be quite the stud to handle conditions like these.

To those who would ask me for advice [about the Peace Corps], I would say that it's all right—rather than the pits. This is speaking for myself, serving in what has to be considered one of the "worst" Peace Corps countries in the world under what have to be as primitive conditions as a PCV would ever have to live with. I think that another country might be easier to handle, perhaps making for a more completely enjoyable experience. A country with a language that's easy to learn would make things a lot more comfortable. When the big US government tosses in the trump card that is conscription, [the decision to go in the Peace Corps] looks even better.

Into Mog for a Conference

    The purpose of the conference was to discuss problems we were having in the bush, particularly having to do with our work, and to get some new ideas. Although I now remember nothing about the details, I described it as "a success." But perhaps more important was the fact that I got really sick, which seems like another pivotal experience that continued to sour me on being in Somalia. This trip to Mog now seems like a key experience in losing my enthusiasm as a Peace Corps Volunteer.

March 16 journal entry. On March 1 we went into Mog.[59] Talk about psyched up! About Wadlee Weyn, I started to sniffle. After arriving at Thompson's, getting drunk, making my first trip to the Lido for all of an hour, Mikulski and I both collapsed into bed for several days with some form of the flu. The next 5 or 6 days in Mog were no fun: flu with all its miseries, bad sores which wouldn't heal—every little thing becoming infected, including a couple on my face—a hemorrhoid, a false alarm on an itchy asshole, a couple shots, etc. Talk about pissed off. It was a hell of a way to enjoy Mog. And it was then that my disgruntlement at the general situation began to grow. But then, as I regained my strength, I gave drinking and the beach their due consideration. And then came the Lido and my Fadumo [not to be confused with either our *boyessa* or the Fadumo who will appear later in the story].

> ✍ *But first a few words about sex: To a certain extent, particularly when we first arrived in Mog, our only friends were prostitutes.* We called them "hookers." We learned dialogues in training about how to take a taxi to the Bar Lido— and, for all I remember, those exercises included negotiating prices after we arrived.*
>
> *Somalis practiced the most extreme form of female genital mutilation (so-called "female circumcision"). Reportedly, 98 percent of women in Somalia are still subject to the practice. Traditionally, this involved a cliterectomy and "sewing" the labia together with thorns from the bush. Under this barbaric practice, it's easy for a man to confirm he's marrying a virgin. Traditionally, girls marry at 13 or 14 years*

---

*   Later in our stay, I expanded this group to include basketball players.

old. Unfortunately, if the husband tires of his wife, he can end the marriage by saying, "I divorce thee," three times. Because the woman is then "damaged goods," no self-respecting man would want to marry her after divorce. At least in 1969, a divorced woman's options were to stay with her family in the bush and become an old maid or come to the big city and try to make a living as best she could, perhaps at the world's oldest profession.

The hookers were damaged goods and we were on the outside of Somali culture. A pretty convenient match, all things considered. If a male Peace Corps Volunteer wanted female company, the Lido was frequently where he started.

The Lido [is] perhaps the only institution in this entire country that is worth a damn.[60] As an introductory note, the social situation here is really something. There are few girl volunteers, and the Somali females lead a very sheltered existence—one that certainly does not include spending any leisure time drinking, dancing and generally hanging around with any white infidels. So what is left, you ask? Hookers: fantastic, beautiful local women who have been divorced or would rather make a little scratch by working on their back than some other way. The Lido is a club [on the beach] in Mog that is actually a pretty decent place, where the hookers go to get picked up and people like the Peace Corps go to drink, dance to a pretty decent band, and maybe end up going home with some young honey. I'd never been out there before. The first time we were in Mog, I didn't have the urge. (I was also sick.) But the second time was a charm ... One of the saving graces of this hole is that about a third of the women are absolutely beautiful, and the hookers are among the cream of the crop.

March 16 journal entry. If I never see Fadumo again, I'll remember my 23rd birthday for a while.[61] A huge group of us went to the Lido after steak at the Beach Club. [This was the Anglo-American Beach

Club, one of our refuges. I now wonder why I spent so much of my leisure time there. I guess mixing with Somalis in Mog proved to be unrewarding.] I watched her dance, danced with her a couple times, then drank some more … We were leaving when fate moved me to sit down with this new young friend of mine. In about half an hour we were engaged in beautiful, sweaty love. What a great girl—in every way imaginable. Not all wogs are bad. They can't be. Wonderful, wonderful girl. Perfect! I had wondered, from sort of an academic point of view, whether any subconscious racism would manifest itself and whether the fact that I was paying for it would spoil things. No. I can't wait to get back to Mog. I'll live with her!

Back to the Bush

Coming back to Baidoa was traumatic. Who knows why? Everyone was belly-aching about the place, everyone compounding everyone else's complaints. After the relative anonymity of Mog, the stares and attention of the people gathered in Baidoa for the elections was depressing. Harvey [a PC teacher in Baidoa] had made arrangements for us to stay at the hotel, which pissed all of us off, especially Thompson. Nice hospitality … So there we were, stuck in the fishbowl. Having 20 PCVs in town didn't help my situation any. I like seeing everyone, but not 20 at a time. Banzoni was out of beer, etc. A horrible time was had by me, anyway, and I don't think many enjoyed it very much. The guys from the south really had their eyes opened. [Three people in our group of 15 were farther south in Somalia, on the coast south of Mog. Two others lived in Mog.] From what someone had said, they thought we were a bunch of belly-aching pussies—pissing and moaning without any reason. Admittedly, we shouldn't talk about it so much, but having everyone together breeds gross discontent.

After racing around Baidoa, it was finally off to home sweet home. God, what a horror show. A lot of people are beginning to congregate now for politics in the larger villages. The pickup full of *gaalki* [plural of *gaal*, white infidel] blew some minds ... We were greeted in Gorisane by about 75 people I'd never seen before. We sat around among millions of people. Jimison and Merry ate up completely all the wild types. Maybe I'm a different person, or maybe it's just that, for me, it's a 24-hour a day job and it gets a little tiresome. Thompson and I exchanged cute remarks, and then they took off, with Duane knocking people off the back of the truck as they tried to climb on.

And there I was, left with only my thoughts. The roof wasn't done (although it was completed that afternoon), and all I could think of was Fadumo's beautiful body and affectionate manner. There was nothing to do but sit on my ass and get stared at by a million new people.

I arrived back here day before yesterday, and, I guess because of being absent for 2 weeks, it took [a couple days] to regain my sanity. (Not a perfect term but an adequate one.) I'd forgotten a lot about the place and had to recover my techniques for dealing with it. The people had me completely naked, clawing me to death psychologically. I'd forgotten how I'd figured out how to handle it.

The first night here was the most horrible time I can remember ever having in my life. I was tired as hell and went to sleep about 9:00, miserable and thinking too much. I got to sleep but woke up some time about midnight. I couldn't get back to sleep and was really scared at the thoughts that were going through my mind. It was like being high in that my thoughts were going so fast that I could not keep up with them or follow any one of them through ...

One minute I'd be thinking of Fadumo, the next minute about getting stared at by hundreds of people, the next minute about plowing with camels—but never thinking slowly enough about anything. It bothered me tremendously, because everything seemed so insignificant. If the thoughts weren't important enough to allow me to think about them, Jesus, what was I doing? I didn't want to think about anything; nothing made me feel right. This must have gone on for an hour at least—the worst psychological experience of my life. Thinking about my night with Fadumo, about visiting [college friend in VISTA in North Carolina], about the fun in California last summer—nothing helped. My life seemed so ridiculous. The height of boredom: when there aren't even any thoughts that will entertain me.

I was also listening to the bullfrogs, the cows, the chickens, a bunch of voices near the *wahr*, hallucinating. Returning to Gorisane had left me without any rational defenses. I thought I was losing control. I felt that, if I could have turned on the light and had a cig and a glass of water, I would have been better off. But that was impossible, so these thoughts took their place among the string of disjointed fragments sprinting through my consciousness. I don't need to do that again. I hope I've learned from the experience, because there are potentially bad times yet to come.

What saved my sanity was 2 very busy days. Yesterday I spent all day cleaning the roof inside and white-washing the inside walls part-way up. I'm back in the routine. Thank God! It was full-day job, a hell of a lot of work, and I was as dirty as I've ever been in my life when dark came. And I'm starting Royal Canadian Air Force exercises.

Last night was better, but still not normal. Thinking too much about this place without one's defenses can screw you over.

Today I set up the strings [for planting in rows] and row markers and made a rain gauge. It was a hard day physically, an easy one mentally. Just the kind I like. I wish they could all be like today. I taught Fadumo (wrong Fadumo, unfortunately) to make banana bread. Something is not right, but it's still pretty good. I've also been working on a list of recommended things for the 9's [the next PC group] to bring, which I'll send to Thompson.

A wedding celebration started yesterday afternoon, but, not being in the mood, I'm not partaking. My paranoia about being the sole center of attention is no doubt affecting my mood. Yesterday the women marched through town dressed in beautiful clothes. Marching like a corps of cadets (crossing quasi-intricately, etc), some carried spears and knives. There must be some symbolism in that. The celebrating is not supposed to end until tomorrow. Maybe I'll feel like checking it out tomorrow.

Barsho [one of the kids] showed me the most creative thing I've seen in this country. He'd made a miniature microphone out of clay. I was really excited. I'd never seen such creativity here.

... Never have I been so conscious of how culturally dependent things like personal philosophy are. One's environment has to act and react somewhat similarly to what one has been reared with if one is to apply the personal philosophy that has been the product of life within that certain culture. For example: "I am unemotional. I will be in complete control of my reactions." That works fine at home, no matter how unusual the situation, if enough thought or experience has served as preparation. And now, here I am, trying to see and learn a pattern of cultural behavior—specifically as the people react to me, one of those strange *gaals*. The pattern would seem to be fairly predictable as far as the locals are concerned. Now, what's left is for me to prepare some reactions for them. Maybe if I approach it from this point of view, it will be easier.

I know how people are going to act and react toward me, which, after all, is all that I need to be concerned with as far as maintaining my psychological well-being is concerned. Now, all I have to do is control how I react toward them. Simple, huh? 1) All Somalis are wogs and should be treated accordingly. 2) I must do what I want to. Please myself. Keep my psychic well-being from time to time. 3) Stay in control of myself and the situation, e.g., walk away if there's no good reason for hanging around. [I now wonder why it took me so long to come up with number 3.] Better to be lonely than nuts at the end of 2 years. I'll have to see. I think that writing this out may have started to establish a pattern. Tim's return, of course, will mess things up. He's buying a horse!

March 17 journal entry. A very good day. An un-PC day, but one which always found me in control of myself ...[62] This morning

I finished the classical advice for the 9's.[*] Kind of simple, but it should be useful. Not being a brown-nose, just trying to be helpful and, at the same time, trying to keep myself busy. This afternoon I finished painting the walls. I worked hard and now it's all done. Clean the place up tomorrow, move stuff in, and then go to work on farms. Ibrahim [the chief's older son] is back from Baidoa and asking when we're going to work.

... Today, while I was painting, I got pretty dirty, and, of course, everyone got a good chuckle. I was pleased with my reaction. Keep walking, keep working and a no-sweat, silent "Hell with all of you." There are 3 cops living in Mohamed's *mundel* now who will be staying through the elections. I had a conversation with one of them. "No assassin, Somalia." That's not all they've got nothing of.

March 18 journal entry. Another good day.[63] My technique seems to be working well. It was tested downtown and worked OK. I had to check out Sherif Jiis' field south of town. It needs some rain before we plant. We finished the *mundel*, and I moved stuff in, including one of the big tables. Things are much nicer. Tim probably won't care for it. Today, Ibrahim and I will start to work on his field. We hope to get it all *yambo*ed [worked with a *yambo*, the hoe used by every farmer]. We have a lot to do before April 1.

Even the little babies know I'm different, breaking into tears whenever I even look at them. And, the young people in the US consider themselves to be outcasts from the surrounding society.

Status Quo in Gorisane

☞ *I continued to be frustrated by life in Gorisane.*

March 18 letter. [We finally got our *mundel* renovated.][64] You ought to see the place sparkle now. We had offers of 3 camels and a wife

---

[*]   This was a letter for the 9s with suggestions about what to bring to Somalia. It is in Appendix B.

for it, but I ain't selling. Place is too nice. Let those rains come. Seriously though, the hermitage [I meant "the life of a hermit"] is about to begin, since the rains are due to begin in about 2 weeks.

… As they say, the worm has turned. Four months ago an inspired youngster landed in Somalia. Within a month or 2 my initial rosy optimism turned into a solidly realistic, but nonetheless optimistic, approach. Now—does this place suck. Jesus. I can't put it strongly enough. Everything about this entire country—with the extremely notable exception of numerous individuals—is so small-time it's a big joke.

… There is no real unhappiness on my part. [Oh, no?] And I don't think that I'm particularly bitter. [Oh, no?] I think the closest I could come to defining my attitude right now would be the phrase "loathing and disgust"… The physical conditions—call them hardships if you like—aren't the cause for complaint. The fact that the particular dialect is still more or less unintelligible isn't actually digging at me too much. It's the people as a whole that are the problem.

… [The] *gaal*—that's me, the white infidel—is never ever going to fit into the culture here. I could speak the language perfectly and it would still be a matter of being looked down on as some sort of freak. The background that our exciting, vibrant, always moving culture has provided me makes the lives of these people seem incredibly drab. There is absolutely nothing to do. If I didn't wander around creating little projects for myself, I'd be completely out of my head. Right now, for example, harvest is finished and there's nothing to do but sit around and wait to plant. But the people sit around and talk a lot, blithering on about nothing. It's amazing. They have the same kind of conversations a half dozen times a day. No substance at all.

… [I describe an incident when we were surrounded by a crowd of people.] We're something extremely unusual, but that doesn't mean that I have to like it when it has happened every single day I've been here and will no doubt happen every single day until the end of 2 years. The people have absolutely no concept of how to treat an outsider. Other Somalis from other areas can come here and get no trouble at all from these people. But let the *gaal* show up ... It's a real pain in the ass, and the fact that it recurs time and again certainly affects my present mood ... This place can have an amazing effect on one's sanity.

... If you don't hear from me for a while (say 3 months or so) it'll be because the rains have closed the roads to mail trucks and everything else. The work is just about to start, with 5 demonstration plots, some seemingly cooperative and enthusiastic farmers lined up, some plans for the future, etc. In view of the negative opinions I cast out earlier, I guess I would have to say that it's the good individuals I know and the possibilities of getting something small accomplished in ag that keep me here. Perhaps the opposition party will win the election and we'll all be thrown out of the country. That's probably what would happen, and I don't particularly fear the possibility. It might be all right to try another country for a while.

🖎 *I put it a little differently to my family.*

March 18 letter. Things in general are all right, and my health has been good other than a dandy bout with the flu and occasional to-be-expected diarrhea.[65] Speaking of diarrhea, excuse me—I'll be back in a minute. While the variety of food hasn't picked up to any appreciable extent, there's enough to eat and vitamin pills make a dandy dessert. I've lost quite a bit of weight. Everyone in our group of 15 has. One guy, who was a little chubby to begin with, has lost 30 pounds. I'm down to my high school baseball playing weight, 145. But I don't think acute malnutrition is any real threat.

... The rains are due in 2 weeks, and about 6 inches of rain are expected in the month of April. Gorisane is supposedly isolated from Baidoa for only a month, so things shouldn't be too bad. We'll haul in enough spaghetti and rice to last us, and wait it out. We've already beefed up our library.

… The honeymoon is over as far as this little PCV is concerned … Even if one wanted to become part of the culture here—which I'm beginning to see is not going to be one of my goals—he would never be allowed to. They're them and I'm me. And the twain meet only on certain playing fields … Especially out here—in what must certainly be one of the most uncivilized (for want of a better word) posts for a Peace Corps volunteer anywhere—the differences are really accentuated … The people here are living at a level probably comparable to that of 2500–3000 years ago, and the majority of them and I have a little trouble getting through to each other …

And, dearest mother of mine—I may not dig the place to any incredible extent, but I ain't sick and I ain't overly unhappy.

March 20 journal entry. I just got through one of the worst experiences of my life …[66] [After returning from Ibrahim's field], I strolled back to my *mundel* and collapsed. The siege had begun. It must have been heat exhaustion, although I'd only been in the sun for a little more than an hour. I figured it was a lack of salt. I was dying for about 4 hours, sleeping restlessly. I wasn't sweating, but I was hot all over; then I felt cold. The most miserable was yet to come. [At some point I mistakenly drank water from the *wahr* that had not been boiled. A big mistake.] About 4 PM I started to shit. It started off slowly, but by 11 PM I was taking one every 5 or 10 minutes. It was nothing but water, with some blood. I figured about 60 times in a 24-hour period. I finally gave up and began to shit into a pan in my house, perched backward on the chair to zero in. Paragoric and polymagma did no good whatsoever. [These were powerful anti-diarrhea medications in the PC medical kit. I remember that one of them had arsenic in it.] For a long time, of course, I could not sleep, but now things seem to be slowing down. I sure hope so. It was terrible.

I will try poached eggs for breakfast and then maybe try to plow. I probably shouldn't, but now we're way behind schedule. I also want to go into Baidoa to say goodbye to Mikulski before he leaves. We'll really miss him around here.

More Status Quo in Gorisane

April 4 journal entry. [I just got back from a trip to Baidoa.][67] Before going into Baidoa I had thought very strongly about the possibility of moving in there, still working out here, or maybe finding some other work. It seemed like I would be happier. The idea began to grow when I saw Fritz's new house. What a set-up compared with Gorisane. There would never be any getting around the fact that Somalis are fucked, but at least I would have a little time to myself and a little peace. In Baidoa there are places to go, and people staring can be laughed off with a *"Nabat mia, Abdi?"* [*Nabat mia,* literally "Is there peace?" was a very common greeting.] I'd made my plans assuming that Tim was still hot to get away from Gorisane and that Thompson would go for the idea. Neither was the case. Although Tim and I are getting along OK now, this place is still not for me. It is not a 2-man town, and it's not for me. The big question is whether I can find work near Baidoa. Right now I don't know what I'm going to do.

… Leaving Baidoa [to return to Gorisane] was quite an experience. Tim and Fadumo were going to leave the day before me, because I wanted to talk to Shermani and Thompson. Tim had free space booked on Abukar's truck for himself and all our stuff. After about a 24-hour delay while the chief farmer looked around for his plow, the word was that we and our stuff were to be at Banzoni's immediately. We had a beer and kept watch for Abukar's truck, but it never showed up. But Abukar did, on another truck, which sat outside about 10 minutes before Abukar came to tell us to load up. I guess we were supposed to know that his truck had gone to Mog. We were messed around either by Tim's language ability or, more likely, by our buddy Abukar. This place wears me out.

We got out to Gorisane to absolutely nothing. No camel [to

use for plowing]. No nothing. We spent the first day cleaning the place up. It looks very nice with the colored cloth up and the 2 tape recorders. A little cramped, but not bad. I talked one morning to Ibrahim about our farming techniques. He sounds interested, but, with all the fooling around he's doing, he can't be that excited. Tim's horse showed up, only 2 or 3 days behind schedule. It had gone 200 km [120 miles] without food or water, and they'd tied his mouth so severely that he had a great big sore. As a result, he was ready for a little rest. Of course, everyone in the entire village knows more about horses than Tim. "Feed him this." "Water him." "Why don't you ride him?" We went through a couple alternatives concerning housing for the beast during the rains and finally decided to let him show how tough he is [by staying outside].

I just about killed a kid when he cracked up when the horse stepped on my foot. Also, I was shocked when I saw Ibrahim blowing up a cow's asshole. The cow must have had some kind of an obstruction, but it didn't seem like a very sanitary thing to do.

I've done very little else. I'm getting an incredible number of vocabulary words from *Time Magazine*. How's that for a surprise?

I remembered today that many of the women here eat dirt.[68] Just pick up a few small clods and chow down. There just may be a deficiency somewhere.

Also, I remembered the time a few days ago when a woman brought her infant for "medicine." I was puzzled by the small scabs on the child's head, and, after a few questions, learned that a few days earlier the baby had been "sick in the head," and they had burned her head—presumably to drive away the evil spirits. I gave her a hard time about that.

Yesterday the lady with the incredibly swollen wrist paid us another visit, after we told her 3 weeks ago to go to the mission clinic in Baidoa.[69] We had Fadumo tell her to go there. She refused, I think because of something about being handled by *gaal* ladies. If she won't help herself, let her arm fall off. It may; her wrist was much worse.

April 8 journal entry. Hassen hurt his head on a tree and was being carried to our *mundel* for treatment, crying at the top of his lungs, "I don't want that *gaal* to touch me."[70] We've only been here 3 months.

A kid came in: "Jama. Give me a cigarette." "No." "What's wrong?" "Nothing." I gave him a long butt a little while later. "But, Jama, this is too small." "Get out of here." Aden asked me why I didn't have black skin and a flat nose.

7:00 AM. Tea is late. Fadumo is at the market. It's getting bright. It should be hotter than the hinges of hell today. Tough on man and beast, as they say.

It's now 9:00 AM. Scratch one well-intentioned experiment! [The details about problems plowing with a camel are in a later letter.]

I still think that I'll go into Baidoa as soon as things settle down here. I'd like to break Tim in as to what has been arranged here before I take off.

April 10 letter. I appreciate letters that talk about people at home and their situations, plus a lot of obscene and humorous bullshit.[71] It's been interesting, though, that every time I get a letter that I really enjoy the writer has to apologize for being so superficial and for leading "such narrow, square lives." For me, the serious and the ideal have just gotten lost in the shuffle. In other words, except for books and an occasional *Time* or *Newsweek*, there is very little stimulation. I look at this as a 2-year coffee break for my intellect …

A little girl just came to our door. It seems that yesterday she ate a worm, or so her father said. I told them, "I have no medicine for your stomach, but wait a day or two and she will shit it out. All will be OK. Just don't burn her stomach with hot coals to cure her. (That's a favorite remedy with the people here for what ails them.) Just wait a few days." Despite the fact that we understand quite a bit of what people say, they cannot understand us at all. They've never had to listen to a foreigner struggle with their language. Understandable, but it is just another thing that makes this place a farce as far as our being here is concerned. When we talk to people, like I was with this guy just now, they say "I understand," nod their heads, roll their eyes, and make a gasping noise that means, "I understand." But they have no idea what we've said. Just another example of how unfulfilling communication with these people is. The guy will probably go back to his home in the bush, lay his little girl down, and proceed to make little holes in her 7-year old belly with a hot coal.

Politics and Elections

March 17 journal entry. Fadumo and Mohamed have had some interesting conversations about the upcoming elections.[72] "*Dub* is the best." [*Dub*, literally meaning "Fire," was the main opposition party, allied with the Soviets and the Soviet-sponsored army.] "No. SYL is the best. They will win because all the people in charge of the elections are SYL." [Somali Youth League, the incumbent party, was allied with the U.S. and the U.S.-sponsored National Police.] Voting will be held in Issak's [the chief's] *mundel*. That should provide a few laughs. Mohamed doesn't want the opposition to come and vote because they'll cause too much trouble. Why any bushy would favor SYL is beyond me, since the government has never done anything for them and they say so. They had a lot of trouble with 2 *Dub* Land Rovers in the bush, and they were escorted through town with police escort. If *Dub* wins, maybe we'll get thrown out of the country.

March 18 letter. The big national elections are coming up.[73] Held once every 5 years, they're quite the farce. Everyone gets all fired up about them, and they're a constant topic of conversation. The people are so politically aware and so interested in the functioning of their democracy, right? Shit. The graft and corruption even surpass the tactics of Capone's Chicago or Tammany Hall. The people's discussions consist of shouting matches encompassing such important subjects as "My party's better than yours." "No, it's not." It's not very substantive, mostly noise.

The people out here, or at least the majority of the ones I know and have heard about, are in favor of the party presently in power, but there are 2 prime contenders that also have a little support. In addition, there are about 100 others that don't have a chance, but are only in the game so that they can be bought out at the last minute by one of the bigger parties. Of course, the government in power has allocated an amount of money equal to 5 times the annual budget of the Ministry of Agriculture to see to it that their party wins. It's hardly democracy at its finest. As a result, national government Land Rovers are seen all over carrying political banners, etc. Nobody can ever, ever, ever knock American politics again.

The people are expected to cause quite a bit of trouble over the elections, and some of it has already occurred. One of the other guys in ag, located in another small town near Baidoa, got to listen to a 3-hour [shootout] right outside his *mundel*. Ten killed. Another guy in our group was riding in a USAID Land Rover when they were stopped at a barricade of thorn bushes thrown across the road by a bunch of guys who wanted to kill the leader of the opposition party in Baidoa. This goes on all the time. And believe it or not, the people think that their form of governmental selection is virtually flawless compared with any other in the world.

March 18 letter. The national elections ... are coming up in 8 days.[74] It's been quite something to observe ... Apparently, in the last election a town about the size of Gorisane turned in something like 17,000 votes. There are so many nomads who come from out of nowhere to vote (having been paid a shilling or 2 by someone or another) that it is impossible to check up on things. A couple of corrupt cops, or no cops for that matter, and there's no telling what sort of stuff can be pulled.

April 2 journal entry. I got back from Baidoa the day before yesterday.[75] I went in for a 2-day trip, to drink up a case of beer I had left with

Mikulski, say goodbye to him, buy a bunch of stuff, and get back out here to go to work. Well! The night I got to Baidoa, there was a political assassination. ("No assassin, Somalia.") [I ended up staying 8 days.] The head of the elections was rubbed out, evidently out of fear that his SYL sympathies would have an effect on the election. The details were unclear. One story was that he was accosted by a group of 3 or 4 bushies on a dark street. Another was that he got shot after answering a knock at his compound door. Anyway, the killers did a good and thorough job, and they never did get caught.

April 4 journal entry. For the next 8 or 9 days, there were no trucks allowed more than a km out of Baidoa.[76] At one point there were 400 people in jail, but the number had gotten down to 60 by the time we left town. [At the beginning of my time in Baidoa,] I had a tremendously successful day and a half shopping and drinking, and the day to leave dawned. The travel restrictions were only being applied to certain trucks, and I went down to check out the truck situation. People were getting on a truck, and the kid told me to bring my stuff down. OK. I brought all my booty down to the market. "Sorry. The government won't let the trucks go."

So I settled down for a week or so in Baidoa. There was a curfew at 8 PM, and everyone was off the street except for hobnail-booted police and army in their fatigues—all armed to the teeth. Perhaps the only time a rule has ever been obeyed in this country. All stores, restaurants, and Banzoni's were closed. Most of the street lights were off at 8 PM. No movies. [There was an outdoor theater with movies in Italian.] It made for very little fun.

We did have the opportunity to hear a lot of scuttlebutt about the election from Dulbane, Daad, and Giumale. [None of us remember now who these guys were. They may well have been teachers.] We heard stories of people voting more than once. Dulbane got in about 5 votes; Giumale, 3. Democracy in action! The police power kept the trouble down, and voting day was pretty tame from what we could see. The results were delayed for a few days, probably out of fear of violent reprisal. The earliest rumors were that only 6,000 people voted, and the worry was that reapportionment would result from such limited participation on the part of the constituents. Well, when the results [for the Baidoa area] were announced over Radio Mog: SYL, 27,000; *Dubka*, 2100; SANU, 1200. Six seats went to Lega. [This must be the Somali Youth League.]

Considering *Dubka* and SANU had considerable backing, people were pissed off. It was blatant cheating. Everyone was saying that blood *badaan* [a lot of blood] was going to flow afterwards, but there was none. All talk. I don't see how this country will get anywhere with the present governmental set up. And it doesn't look like the democratic process can be used to shift power from one group to another. A military take-over looks like a winner to me. Oh, also: Shekh Banane of Ghil Ghel, called the king of the Rahan Weyn, was put in jail for having a guy cut in half. A fellow shekh at that. Good for the police.

We got strange treatment in Baidoa as far as we were concerned. It seemed that election time was not the time for being friendly with the *gaals*. Perhaps there was some official anti-intruder propaganda being spread around, or maybe there were just a lot of things on people's minds. Anyway, except for Daad and Dulbane, the few friends we do have in Baidoa wouldn't even stop to talk. And the girls were really something. Not even short Fadumo would talk with us. [These were women who worked in the restaurants and Banzoni's and were usually very friendly to us.] Who knows? Luckily, 3 or 4 days after the elections, things seemed to have returned to normal.

People warned us to carefully observe the curfew and to be careful in general. Dulbane said, "You know you might be killed." That was certainly BS, but that's gratitude for you. [I now realize that, in view of our estrangement from Somali society and the somewhat arbitrary nature of political violence during the elections, we probably were not as safe as we thought we were at the time.]

Still Trying to Work in Agriculture

✍ *I was still optimistic about what I could accomplish in agriculture.*

March 18 letter. We just had a conference in Mog where we discussed problems, asked questions, and got some new ideas.[77] The conference was a success, although things were a little ragged.[78] The 2 days in Mog and the morning at BONKA [in Baidoa] with Chuck Allen were very helpful. I have my 2 years pretty well figured out: working toward plowing with camels, plant in rows, then weed with a *yambo*, sorghum/peanut rotation with beans and corn (and vegetables) as desired. At least for now there's no possibility for seed prep, insect control or use of manure. As far as I can see, the key to progress in ag here boils down to "instruction and follow-up and availability of plows." In my case the latter will be crucial. Thompson's working on it, and Zwink is going to hunt around Nairobi for plows to import. Row markers, seeders, levelers aren't nearly so crucial. The farms aren't big enough to warrant a lot of money on equipment. Two or 3 mo-board plows in this village, a little instruction and follow-up, and the people should be quite a bit better off.

The work in ag seems to be shaping up nicely.[79] We're working (or more accurately, I'm working; my roommate doesn't overexert himself) with 5 farmers, running demonstration plots on their farms. There will be 4 plots (40 X 40 meters) of sorghum, and one large one, maybe a hectare [about 2.5 acres] of peanuts. Tomorrow I'm going to start working one of the plots, with the farmer's help, so that we'll be able to plant before the rains ...

This season we'll be working with just a hoe and will work for acceptance of the ideas of planting in rows before the rains, thinning, and keeping the weeds down. Following the advice of the guys at the experimental farms near Mog and Baidoa, the only crops that I'll be working with will be sorghum and peanuts, working for crop rotation between the two ...

If all goes well, we'll get to camel-power for plowing the planting season after this next one. (There aren't enough bulls around here to make that a paying proposition.) Things could work out well if, somehow, the villagers are able to buy a plow. Right now there are none available for purchase in the entire country.

March 20 journal entry. Wednesday morning I got up and went out to Ibrahim's field to start to work.[80] We staked out the 40 meters square and talked about the possibility of getting a plow next season, to use with a camel. He said fine. I said "Let's work." We started to hoe, with every bushy in Somalia watching and laughing, of course. After a minute or 2, Ibrahim said, "Maybe tomorrow we can use a machine and a camel. There's a machine in the silos." [After weeks of understanding that there were no plows in the area—it was a plow!] Thanks for telling me, Ibrahim. We got it out, used a locally-adapted harness, and it looks like it will work. We had even more skeptics around than usual, which is saying something. I think I overheard Alio Hhumo say that it can't be done, that we need to have bulls. They don't have any bulls.

April 4 journal entry. Because I was interested in the possibilities of extension work with the ministry, while I was in Baidoa I went in to see Shermani.[81] [He must have been the local Ministry head.] God, what an incredible windbag ... I'd gone in with 2 simple questions concerning extension; in about 2 hours in his office I got one of them answered. The rest of the time, Zak and I listened to him blather on about the great SYL victory, the democratic elections, and his conception of extension—which involves cooperation with a minimum of 20 participants. What BS. He started talking about his conscientiousness and I just about gagged. His heart is kind of in the right place, but, man, can he talk ... It would be very interesting to work with the gentleman.

The elections put us way behind schedule, as have the past habits of the people concerning when they plant. (It seems the local soothsayer thinks it's going to be a little late this year.) Ibrahim's camel is off in the bush and has been coming back "tomorrow" since we got back here. [He is] getting money for working with the election. Nobody else will let us use their camel, or so he says, since the work is too hard for the poor beasts.

Sherif Jiis is due back soon. [He's the one who had his field plowed by ONAD.] We have to wait for another rain to plant his peanuts, though, since the ground is too rough now. We'll have to see about the other farmers. BONKA planted 2 $\frac{1}{2}$ weeks ago. They may not have gotten enough rain. We're also going to work with Abukar Fiko, although he needs minimal assistance. [He was the one farmer working with BONKA, the experimental station in Baidoa.] He's such a bullshitter that that's all I feel like giving him. He's Tim's buddy, since he helped Tim in Lugh when he was getting his horse. He's also the biggest farmer in the area.

Yesterday Tim and I went out to Abukar Fiko's, supposedly to see the oxen in action. [We got there about 9:30, just as they were finishing.] Apparently, the oxen are still very skittish, but they're supposed to settle down soon. He wants to plow 5 hectares in 5 days for his peanuts. I'll believe it when we see it. That's all he's plowing. He's planting 2 hectares of cotton, the rest in corn (18 hectares in all), without a plow—just plant. I think all that we can do with him is to get him to plant his peanuts thicker and to plant his sorghum in rows and thin. There's not much else to do.

When we were sitting around drinking tea, he [Abukar] really pissed me off. "Issak is old and gets money from the government. Ibrahim is not good; he has no animals, and has a small farm. Get the American government to give me a tractor. They cost so much. I got so many shillings for peanuts. I've spent so much on my 2 trucks. Bulls are bad, tractors are good. My family has 2 farms. My brother has a garage and 50 taxis in Mog. Etc ..." Somalis are always bragging or complaining or asking us to give them something.

April 5 journal entry. Ibrahim is back from Baidoa, but the camel is in Bur Acaba ...[82] The rumor is that the other farmers think that using animal power is "too much trouble." That'll be the topic for our group discussion tomorrow.

April 7 journal entry. Ibrahim went off to the market, where he spent several hours, doing what only God can imagine. [83] This was before we could talk to the other farmers regarding their plans. He got back about 11:00, and I decided to run an experiment: let him bring up the subject of our going to work. About 15 minutes of conversation, still no mention. And the work day was over! I brought up the subject in the afternoon, and he said "Yeah, tomorrow." I think I'm going to let him take a small part of the initiative. No sense riding him if he doesn't want to be ridden.

April 8 journal entry. Another big day.[84] It's early now, and, in about 15 minutes, we're supposed to start working Ibrahim's plot. Sherif Jiis is still sick in Baidoa and his son is not here either. His peanuts will have to wait. The field needs some more rain before we plant anyway. The others are going to wait and see how things go this morning with Ibrahim. They're not very interested in taking a chance.

There has not been a drop of rain, although yesterday and today there were grayish clouds on the horizon in the early morning. Early in the day it seems cooler, but yesterday it got hotter than hell very early. We came in from outside about 10:00.

Ibrahim mentioned a village near Baidoa on the Wedgit Road called ____, where people plow with a camel, then broadcast the seed. That would be worth looking into. If it would rain soon, and if Sherif Jiis gets back from Baidoa, I could help Ibrahim and S.J. and maybe still try something at the other village.

Ibrahim told me another way to determine when to plant (other than the holy man's vision). It's time when, near dawn, the two stars forming an edge of the Big Dipper dip below the horizon. I should check that out.

April 10 journal entry. We're getting weak from hunger.[85] This morning I went out to Fiko's to help him plant to find out "3 or 4 days from now." We're going into Baidoa to regain our strength. Every minute I spend here just reinforces the idea that every additional minute is pointless.

April 10 letter. We had been advised that, although the locals have no understanding of it, scientific research has shown that the rains come every year close enough to April 1 to warrant the necessity of getting seeds in the ground before then.[86] [After getting stuck in Baidoa after the assassination,] we got out here on the last day of March, afraid that we'd be caught unawares by the imminent deluge. Not hardly. Today's the 10th and there's not a cloud in the sky. We haven't had rain enough to wet down the dust of a good fart. Everyone says that it's coming, it's coming. It's very good thing that we didn't succeed with our plans. There would have been a few pissed-off farmers if we had to go back and replant.

> ✎ *We were going to have camel problems.*

Early the next morning we agricultural commandos were at our posts. No one else in town would let us use their camel, except [Ibrahim]—who is a hell of a guy as far as I'm concerned. The others were afraid that something they'd never heard of being done [that is, plowing with a camel] would damage their poor ugly babies. The camels are stronger than an ox, literally, and yet they do very little work. Their sole value is in being the yardstick of a man's wealth. Anyway, we had all our eggs in the basket also containing this damned camel—who worked out, you must have guessed, to be the laziest son of a bitch ever to be hitched to the dreams that are a Peace Corps plow.

We utilized a clever set-up involving a harness for the camel adapted from 1) a rope/grass mat/pole set-up used by the local pastoralists to haul sorghum stalks, 2) a long rope, and 3) a sturdy 3-blade plow-cultivator that was in one of the USAID-built silos (that we "discovered" after we'd been here 3 months). Things were working well. The 4 corners were laid out without a hitch. Off we went—turning up maybe 8 inches to a foot of soil. We made it about $^3/_4$ of the way down one side of the quadrant when the camel got uppity. The work didn't seem to be too hard on him; it was just new and he apparently has a stubborn streak in him anyway. We pulled on him, beat his ass raw with a stick, let him rest, called him names in 3 or 4 languages, and, finally, after one trip around our 40-meter square plot, had to give up the ghost. The family has another camel, but, since there is not enough food for it here, it's in a village 80 km [50 miles] away and won't be back until things turn green.

That took care of our plans. And all because of one lazy camel … As a result of the camel's laziness, we lost the patronage of 3 semi-enthusiastic farmers who now must think that we really have nothing on the ball. In addition to being white and non-Muslim, eating eggs and spaghetti instead of camel's milk and ground sorghum, those fools tried to plow with a goddamn camel! Can you believe that?

As a result of the hump-backed insolence, our plans in agriculture have shrunk a bit. We'll have [Ibrahim's] 40 X 40 meter plot of sorghum, planted in rows and thinned, but without any soil preparation. We're just going to wait until the first day or so of rain loosens things up enough to plant. [We will also work with Sherif Jiis, who is the man who] paid a hell of a lot of money for these parts to have the Russian tractor rental outfit come in and disk up about 2 or 3 acres of land. We're planting peanuts for him, which is the big money crop. The margin of profit is incredible. (Our advice for people is to grow sorghum to eat and peanuts to sell.) The first few days of rain will have to break down the clods for us on this plot, and we'll be out there with our sticks and our string, laying out peanuts in 30-inch rows, 6 inches within the rows.

[Abukar Fiko] is the local version of J. Paul Getty, being the owner of a couple big trade trucks, several teams of oxen, etc. The whole deal. His family has quite a bit of cash, and, as a result, he's received the favors of both the regional office of the Ministry of Agriculture and [BONKA] … when it comes to instruction, supervision, insecticide, sprayers, etc. He does a hell of a lot of things right, but we figure that we can correct plant population by increasing the amount of peanuts in a given area and getting him to thin his sorghum. He plows, like I say, with oxen, which, for here, is tremendously advanced. (He's the only guy I've heard of in the entire area who uses animal power.) He plants earlier than most, so we don't have a whole lot we can teach him. He's even talking about buying a tractor when he gets enough money together.

... That'll be the extent of our revolution this season. Damn camel ruined everything. If he would've produced, the other farmers would have been hot to try the idea (maybe).

Our other farmers could just give a damn what goes on and, besides, their camels are too valuable to do something as unheard of as pulling a plow around a field.[87] Hell with them. There seems to be no alternative to waiting for a day of rain and just sticking the seeds in the ground in rows. It all boils down to introducing proper plant population. What a come-down from [the idea of] using animal power. Maybe next season, we can try the other camel. Mikulski's successful experience certainly seems to bear out my conviction that, with a well-behaved camel, things would be a snap. The work is simply not that hard. Maybe a little training when the animal is young would help.

Near the End of My Rope in Gorisane

April 5 journal entry. I treated a few people, that's it ...[88] There should be a few plusses somewhere. Here, there is no such thing as something "good," that is, something that is unique to here. Never could it be said that "That thing, unique to Gorisane, is good. I look at that as something positive." Here, there are only negatives. Things that are "Hey, that's all right" are like that only when compared with the minuses. They would be no better than neutral anywhere else. Here they just stand out by comparison. That's no way for me to live.

- To have volunteers in ag in the bush is a farce. It's pointless. They just sit on their asses all day, thinking about how little there is to do. The environment precludes any projects concerning community development or self-help. (With teaching at least there is something to do.) Boredom is boring but it's not too bad, as long as you can be bored on your own terms.

- Some people might enjoy the life. All my encouragement and best wishes go to anyone who likes it. Not me.

- I would prefer, and would be more comfortable psychologically, somewhere that it's possible to escape, even if boredom is the only thing to escape to.

- One good test is whether it would have some sort of disheartening effect if I were leaving tomorrow. I would leave gladly. There must not be much attraction.

- My scorecard is the only one that counts. Seeing "how much I can take" is not worth any points.

- It's not a matter of "not being able to take it." It's a matter of "why?" when there's no point in any of it.

- I don't think the place has whipped me, whatever that means. I don't think I've lost at any contest of life. I think I've just discovered that I don't like being a part of the social and cultural existence out here. I don't dig life in the Somali bush—as it is lived by the people either between themselves or as it involves me.

- I've seen a negative change as far as my personality is concerned. Considering the lack of work opportunities here and the little that will be accomplished, I might as well not leave here screwed up psychologically.

- This whole experience is a 24-hour a day ball game. Spectator-ship is unlimited and admission is free. Come one, come all.

- This place is not for me.

April 10 letter. Every Somali in the country is an absolutely know-nothing, but they have the fascinating penchant for telling the *gaals* everything that there is to know.[89] It's as if in every conversation they see us as 2-year olds who have to be clued in on all the wonderful facts of the world and all that is entailed in handling its intricacies. Things like ... How come you guys aren't married? You can't have kids if you're not married, you know? Do you have a penis? Do you shit? Do you know how to fuck? Do you know your horse is skinny? Why don't you ride it? My family has 2 farms. I own 2 trucks. America is wonderful. Somalia is much nicer than the US, isn't it? No assassins, Somalia. Do you know that you just said 'Good Morning' in the Somali language? Did you know that your horse is eating sorghum? When are you going to ride your horse? Why do you work with those other farmers? They are lazy, they have no bulls for plowing, they have no money and their farms are small ... And on and on. It must sound like I'm being sort of picky, but practically every word that is exchanged with a Somali involves his treating us like dumb children—when it's pain-fully obviously that the shoe is actually on the other foot—asking a stupid question or asking us for something.

I'm kind of glad that we don't have any materials. Otherwise, when we gave them something or sold something to someone, we'd get hit up by everyone in town. Maybe I've driven the point into the ground, but the whole thing—the whole concept of "Give me something for nothing"—just dominates almost every relationship or contact we have. They even have a word for getting something for nothing: *baksheesh*. [Definition: "a tip, gift or gratuity" (or alms or a bribe); in Somalia, asking for something for nothing] They're either telling us something so elementary that they think we can't possibly know. Or they're bragging about their nothing country, or asking for something—or, more correctly, telling us that we're going to do something for them or give them something.

... Another example of our feelings for most of the people here is that right now we're trying to think of one person, child or adult, to take care of feeding and watering Tim's horse while we take a break of a day or 2 Baidoa. We can't come up with one person who we figure would do it right without starving the horse to death or trying to screw us over. And it's not sour grapes on our parts—it's the way the people are here.

... Right now, if it's up to me, this village will have seen the last of my infidel white ass right after the seeds are in the ground—as far as permanent residency is concerned. I would like to live in Baidoa, where the hassle is much easier to take. (No one comes to your door, peers in, and bellows *"Baksheesh"* at the top of their lungs.) I would continue to more or less work out here, but, when there was nothing going on in ag, I could be holed up in Baidoa. There seems to be very little to be gained from extensive contacts with the locals—other than a chronic case of being pissed off at every human being I see. What a thing for a PCV to say, huh? ... I'm going to be a sour asshole for years, if this place has its say. But I'll fight it. A place as screwed up as this doesn't have the right to strike me down.

The Bush—Kansahdere

🖎 *Within the next 10 days, I left Gorisane and relocated to Kansahdere.*

I Move to Kansahdere

April 20 journal entry. Things have changed a lot![90] I'm now living in Kansahdere with [John Marks, a good friend] after a fairly complicated evolution of circumstances. Tim and I got into Baidoa, almost literally starving to death and encountered Thompson and Ali Jama as they returned from Bardera. I had promised myself that [Thompson] was going to listen to me and my reasons for having decided that Gorisane sucks. I got good and drunk (as did everyone else) and got really wound up. It took a hell of a long time, but my bellowing and previously thought-out arguments—in the form of out and out ranting and raving—had the desired effect. The conclusion was a genuine concession by Bill that the experiment involving placing volunteers in tiny little bush towns was failing—at least as far as my experience was concerned. What to do about my discontent was left until the next day, when Bill and John suggested that I come out to KD to work with John. I was eager to get out of Gorisane, but also to stay in the Upper Juba if possible. Bill ruled out Baidoa—so here I am … There were very few alternatives to Kansahdere.[91] The other towns of any size whatsoever (say 750–1000 or more), where there was any ag at all, already had someone there.

About the last month I was [in Gorisane] the place started to eat me up completely ... It was time for me to get out, especially when my mind started to quiver out near the limits of self-control. [The place] just did not offer compensation enough for all the pains in the neck that I had to put up with living there ...[92] Added together, they were greater than the sum of their parts and were not balanced by any positive aspects. Being there was pointless, and, although there was a degree of excitement and adventure for a while, that faded once things settled down to incredible tedium. There was really no form of gratification (and it wouldn't have taken much to satisfy); and there were a million small hassles that made for a pretty unpleasant existence. Tim is still in Gorisane, not out of any love for the place, but because of the difficulty in getting himself and his recently-purchased horse to a new post before the rains come ...

There was literally zero enthusiasm for any sort of agricultural innovation, and the extremely primitive conditions in which everyone lived were really depressing me.[93] Due to all the little hassles, some psychological problems were starting to appear. That is, I was just about to lose my mind with all of those completely heedless savages around every single second of every single day ... It was truly a 24 hour/day ball game and the white boys were the stars of the show.

The totally lethargic existence, involving nothing but sitting around and talking about nothing, was impossible to work with.[94] After things settled down a bit, I felt I was getting nothing out of living in that village and, because of the very minimal stage of development the people have reached, they weren't getting anything out of my being there either. We were just the white guys in town, people who should be taught the correct way of life. There was no establishing any credibility. We, and everything we did or said, were absolutely incredible.

April 20 journal entry. I came out [to Kansahdere] with Don and Dan to check the place out and enjoyed what I saw.[95] There are a lot of the same hassles here, but the problems aren't as acute. It's more of a city, and a few people have some idea what the hell the score is. [I remember that its population was about 1,000 people.] Things are also a lot more spread out and, although we have no compound, we have a big lot with some buffer space between our *mundel* and our tormentors. On the check-out visit, the morning we spent here was enjoyable. We visited the son of a deputy [member of parliament], spoke a bit with a few other reasonably understanding individuals, and checked out downtown. There is more to downtown here than in Gorisane, but no more reason to go down there. Exposure is bullshit; it just gets you pissed off. This place is big enough that everyone doesn't have to wonder where the *gaals* are today and then drop by to see. Nothing in this country is heaven, but the Kalahari Desert would look good after Gorisane.

... The next day I went out to Gorisane to get all my stuff. Fadumo hadn't been heard from for about 5 days, and Tim was going out to Gorisane without her. (Last I heard he'd fired her.)

Mohamed and Ibrahim were very sorry to see me go, and I was sorry to leave them. [They were the] 2 guys with whom I had developed a friendship founded on some sort of mutual respect and just general good feeling.[96] They were the only 2 in the village who spoke Italian, and I was able to explain my reasons for leaving to them using Italian. (Handling the subtleties of the local language is totally out of the question and always will be.) Mohamed knew why I was leaving and was very understanding.[97] Ibrahim was a little incredulous and was concerned with what would become of our work. I've prepped Tim—he knows what to do. Like I say, I was sorry to say goodbye to those 2, but all the ogling bushies made it very easy.

I said a sincere goodbye to Tim. (His change in attitude has been interesting—life ain't too groovy all the time anymore.) While driving out of town I was surprised at how sorry I was to leave

Mohamed and Ibrahim. It didn't last too long (about a minute), and we dashed back to Baidoa to celebrate my leaving Gorisane. The next day, with all my things in the truck (including 4 ½ bags of cement and wood for a bed and set of shelves), Dwayne, Dan, Zak and I headed for Lugh at breakneck speed …

The next morning we looked at Dan's plots, mostly very small and irrigated. [Lugh is on the river.] He kept telling us that there was very little work in Lugh. I don't know who he is kidding. There are not a lot of farmers and none of them are full time, but he has the possibility of affecting them all.

On April 16, we had a miserable drive from Berdale to Kansahdere, which featured getting lost in the sorghum fields near Ghil Ghel. We got to my new home about 9:00 PM. I slept in dirt pajamas [I think that means in my clothes without bathing], and the next morning John and I sat around with Dwayne and Zak. After a *sor* lunch, they were off for Baidoa.

April 23 letter. Now I'm in Kansahdere, and it's the difference between night and day.[98] Many of the minor headaches no longer exist. Our cook [Olat] knows his stuff, and there is a lot more food available here.[99] They butcher every day (as opposed to almost never in Gorisane), and we get lots of meat. In Gorisane, we were eating bananas, eggs, rice, and spaghetti without sauce and figured we were getting maybe 800–1000 calories a day and hoping to stay alive on vitamins.[100] I was down to about 135 when I moved here and wasn't feeling too healthy in general. Here, I don't have diarrhea ⅓ to ½ the time. These may seem like petty points, but, looking back on things, they had a lot to do with my discontentment in Gorisane. When these small negative points were added to the reactions we'd had from farmers when discussing different ag practices ("Oh, working with animal power is just too much trouble.") and all the other negative aspects, any more time in Gorisane would have been completely pointless.

Just the change in diet has done a hell of a lot to boost my spirits and allows me to accept the fact that I have about a year and a half left in this hole.[101] KD is still Somalia, and there is still a preponderance of jerks, but things like food, privacy (relatively speaking), etc. are a lot nicer here, which makes life easier in general ...[102] Here there aren't 6 people watching me brush my teeth (to all of whom I have to provide a jovial one-sentence explanation about what I'm doing) or 11 people watching with wonder while I shave or 25 watching and commenting while Tim feeds his horse.

April 21 letter. Kansahdere is located about 4 hours from Baidoa (when the roads are good), at the other end of the huge sorghum region that begins at Gorisane ...[103] The agriculture situation here is very similar to that in Gorisane, with the exception that here there is some money. And we've concluded that only those who have had a taste of the green are eager to change their techniques so as to rake in a little more.

Here, there are many of the same problems I experienced in Gorisane, but most of them don't seem to be so acute. When we're outside, bushies still stop and stare and ask questions, but there aren't as many of them. This is the city, and there are some people who are willing to listen to some of the things we have to say, rather than wondering why we don't change to their way of life. Here, people eat meat and spaghetti because they know it is good for them, rather than sticking to sorghum, corn and milk. I can't play this place up too big—experience has proven to be too good a teacher for me to do that. I'm just going to wait and see how things work out.

Settling Into KD

April 25 journal entry. Olat and Jamila [Olat's wife] are getting used to me a little more.[104] Between the 2 of them, they will be getting 200 shillings a month from the 2 of us, which is a lot. But they do a very good job, aiming to please above all else—even if their

John, Olat, and group in Kansahdere

approach is usually a very Somali one consisting of telling us to do something or telling us what is good for us. Jamila is pretty neurotic and does not understand the speech of the *san goleh*. [I was born with a cleft palate. As a result my speech is somewhat nasal, not extreme but apparently noticeable. Not one person in my entire life called this to my attention or teased me about it until I arrived in Somalia, where many people did both. *San goleh* is a nickname for someone with nasal speech.] Honestly, Jamila doesn't understand one word I say. She has a lot of annoying habits, but I'm getting to the point that I can very easily ignore her. Because Olat is also here, her impact is blunted to a considerable extent. Sometimes they're bothersome, but they mean well. And Olat is loyal as hell to John and to me by association. I imagine that he's very interested in keeping on our good side. [Because Olat spoke English quite well, much of our communication with him was in English. Conversation with Jamila was in Somali.]

And then there's Hassen Hhumo, that jerk. He was commissioned to build our *dersi* [the fenced-in shelter adjoining our *mundel*]

137

and billed us 55 shillings for materials. We were even working with him. But then we found out he was taking us to the cleaners. (Another Malibu, our buddy in Gorisane.) We made it very clear that he was screwing us and that we weren't too excited about the whole deal. He ended up finishing by himself, with nothing but grief from us. We ended up having to pay him even more—62 shillings for the porch and the fence around the vegetables. [About $9.] We're through with him.

But the *dersi* is finished and things have sort of settled down. There's no local music coming out of our radio, and there's no group of a dozen cackling locals settled down to chat outside our home. Our place is better.

Thursday we had tea at Shekh Sapri's. We talked hunting with him and listened to him complain about not having any money. He showed us his arrows and the banner that proclaims that he is Caliph of Shekh Abdulkadir, told us again how little money he has, and asked us for the hundredth time if we had any seeds. He said he would look for some and pray for the rain to come ... Like Hassen Issak when he got seeds from us and took them to a holy man for a blessing. Or Olat, when he tried to see if a sufi reading the Koran over him would cure him of worms.

We got our *mundel* arranged, built a door for the *muskosha* [long-drop toilet] and just put in another window. Now we're waiting for the woman to come in and slap some shit on the rough edges. We've also built [a window for Olat's *mundel*], which we will put in soon. He's still sick, having left Baidoa before the doctors could issue a verdict. We'll probably head into Baidoa very soon, to take him to the hospital, to try and pick up some beer, and to try to meet that lovely girl at the Bar Hargeisa.

We're both so goddamned horny we spend most of our waking moments thinking about the times of loving tenderness that await us in Mog. We also have a colony of beauties down the street, which may be a possibility. Medina has no husband and would seem to be interested. (One indication of her willingness may be the day she grabbed her crotch and asked "Is this what you want?") It's now a matter of getting time and place and proper moves worked out. She sure seems ready, and if she weren't such an Amazon (with a hefty aroma to boot) she could be very good. Time will tell.

Thursday night they had a *dikhri* outside our window. The local holies sang the God song and hyperventilated for who knows how long ... [Because there was no apparent reason for doing it near our house, I wonder now whether this was some effort to convert us.]

Yesterday started out as a hell of a good day. About 2:00 or 3:00 John and I had settled down outside with a few beers. We were having an enjoyable time when the locals started giving us trouble. First it was Hussein, the little fart, whom we finally drove off by ignoring him. Then Buro and Aimoy [Jamila's son, age 8 or 9] showed up to piss us off and make the beer in our stomachs turn sour. Buro had been here in the morning with a tremendously obnoxious little fart from Dinsoor. ("I'm a friend of Daud [Dave Zwink, PCV in Dinsoor]," etc.) He was the quintessential Somali. What an obnoxious little jerk. He knew a little English, and we told him he'd better not come back or we would kill him. ("Oh, no. I will come back.") He's liable to be dealt with quite sternly if he does show up.

After Buro finally left, the little kids started acting like shits. After calmly suggesting that they had better leave, I nailed one at about 20 yards with a big rock. Right in the back. I hope they've learned their lesson. Please people—don't get us pissed off. What started out as a beautiful afternoon was spoiled ... We decided that each time hate shows itself, it is the product of all the earlier bad experiences piled up on each other. They all come back.

April 26 journal entry. Today we put in Olat's windows and had both his and ours shitted up.[105] One of the women who did the work was an incredible whiner. They charged us 2.50 shillings—certainly mostly gall tax—and the shrew hounded us for a *kumi* [a tenth of a shilling, less than a couple cents] for tobacco all the while. [I'm not sure what explains our stinginess. Perhaps it was the fear that, if we gave a little money to someone, word would spread and we'd be inundated with people asking for *baksheesh*.]

Yesterday afternoon we got a good rain, but the rains still may not have started.[106] There are differing opinions as to whether there will be rain. Some say yes, some say no. Anyway, for about an hour it really came down.

During a normal season, there is 6 inches of rain in April.[107] This year I'm sure there hasn't been more than $1/2$ an inch. There are daily showers, only drizzles, but unless yesterday's good $1/4$ inch of rain changes people's minds, the consensus is beware of a real bad season. The stories are that people and animals are already dying in central and northern Somalia. The next rainy season starts in October. It could be a long time. We, for one, are holding off doing any more planting until the people tell us the rains have arrived.

April 28 journal entry. We finished our beer and most of one of the bottles of wine.[108] John gave Jamila some wine, and I guess it was pretty amusing. She didn't lose her mind like she had anticipated. The night before we'd put down a lot of beer and were lying around in a stupor when a guy walked in. He just couldn't believe we were drinking the forbidden potion and tried a little taste in his palm. It all of a sudden dawned on him what he might just have done, and he couldn't rinse his mouth out fast enough. He kept on saying "That wasn't *khambro* [alcohol], was it?"

Yesterday was an average day, but one not without a little excitement. Brazen Medina came over. She asked if I would marry her. I told her that I would a little later, and then she asked for *baksheesh*. That was my opportunity: "If I give you *baksheesh* what will you give me?" "My kunt." I mean, what could I say? We made an appointment for last night. I was naked and oiled [just a saying], but she no-showed. Oh, well. She's going to get a hard time from me the next time we exchange words.

Yesterday at sunset (it was fantastic) this teacher from Offaro came by: I said, *"Nabad mia?"* [Literally, "Is there peace?" A very common greeting.] "Oh. Do you know the Somali language?" "No. I was kidding. I actually spoke in English." "I can't understand you. Your nose is ..." Then the guy says, "Give me tables and chairs." Screw you, buddy.

I'm getting so tired of having people making fun of the buzz in my voice. There are a lot of people here who don't understand a word I say. Jamila, for example, is becoming slightly more impressed with my language ability, although I'm getting worse rather than better because there's no motivation. In the US I don't think I ever had anyone make fun of my speaking voice, or even mention it for that matter. Here, everyone has to say something. Maybe it's just more noticeable in speaking Somali, or maybe they're just jerks. Thompson gets the same insults about his stammering. I think the fact that I have to take shit from them pisses me off, but I'm also pissed because it's something I can't do anything about.

April 29 letter. It could be pretty rugged for everyone here if there's no rain.[109] Kansahdere is lucky because they have a very good well that shouldn't run dry. But other places aren't so fortunate. We figure that most of the plots that we've planted are doomed for lack of water.

> ✏ *I wrote to a friend from high school who was waiting to hear on his application to the Peace Corps.*

The actual work in rural development is definitely not a full-time job ...[110] Other projects [different from the work in ag]—or whatever some hot-shot PC/Washington type would suggest to fill the time and make us super-vols at the same time—have no chance for success, due to the centuries of tradition that we would have to overcome and the inherent know-it-all attitude that seems to be a part of just about every Somali personality. So, we spend time on projects around our *mundel*, recently putting in another window, planting some flowers and vegetables, having an adjoining shaded enclosure built where we can have some privacy to sit outside and read, write, or whatever. We spend time ogling the incredibly beautiful women as they go down to the well to get water ... We spend time reading books or month-old copies of Time ...

We're getting ready to go into Baidoa for a few days. There's nothing to do here and the rains haven't sealed us off yet ...

I just realized that you and Barbara are going to get married in less than 2 months. Wow! Time is passing. I hope by now that you've both heard something from the Peace Corps. The organization can be pretty good at keeping you hanging. I've been disappointed with the organization and its bureaucratic hierarchy in general, but my experience isn't necessarily typical. Besides, with "the Uncle" (as you so cleverly put it) waiting for you [this must have been the draft], the alternatives are limited. Living somewhere in a mud and wattle house with a thatched roof would be quite a honeymoon. I've thought about what it would be like to go into the Peace Corps right after getting married. At the end of 2 years the couple would either be clawing each other to death or have established one of the ideal marriages of our time. There are 2 couples who just finished their 2 years here who have had things work out very well [at least to that point].

Keep in close touch. It'll be interesting to see how your experiences in the PC compare with mine. I hope yours will be better. After having been in Africa for 6 months, I think I would have been happier in Latin America, where the language would have been much easier to handle, and there would be a few more similarities in the way of life. I don't know, though—I've only seen one country.

May 19 letter. The rains, or at least a scaled-down version, finally did hit, and we'd gotten used to the idea that mail was going to get neither in nor out of Kansahdere.[111] But the roads have dried since the last rain 5 days ago (a nice one, about 2 1/2 inches worth), and a Land Rover is supposed to be taking off that can take us with it.

But right now, the skies are cloudy and rain may unleash itself on us any minute—so we'll just have to wait and see how things come out.

The rains here are grim and gloomy affairs. It's gray as hell, good and cold, and the sky just opens up. It comes down in incredible quantities and leaves the red ground muddy for days. We just have to give up any idea of keeping ourselves or our clothes clean until the ground dries up. Living through the rain in a rather imperfect version of a thatched mud hut has its drawbacks, as the rain manages to find its way through the walls to such items as books and shoes, which it promptly tries to turn to mold. The ventilation is not too good, and the floor is still damp from the last rain. Not real cool, but not as bad as it may seem on paper.

    I ranted to one of my best friends from college, who was a VISTA volunteer in the Mission District of San Francisco.

I don't think anyone at home can ever imagine what [the Somali bush] is like or what [living here] can to do an individual and his approach to things …[112] I'm sure that a lot of the complaints are almost subconscious—things like language difficulty, housing, food, a million other minor inconveniences. I accept these as just being part of the nebulous concept of the Peace Corps experience. But there is something about the country and its people that somehow kicks things way into the negative side. I've tried to figure out from a detached point of view what there is about the place, but the complexity of the whole fucking experience and the fact that there is a tremendous amount of personal emotional involvement makes it a pretty tough one to figure.

It seems like I'm trying to explain why this place is impossible to explain—which doesn't seem to make a lot of sense … To be honest with you [everything going on in the U.S. in 1969] seems so far away to me. Here I find myself worrying about things like "I wonder how many times I'll have to take a crap today." "I wonder how close I'll come to hauling off and slugging somebody today." "I wonder if we'll get anything to eat today besides tea, eggs, and spaghetti without sauce." "I wonder if that jerk Ali is going to show up so we can work on his farm today or whether he'll have some convenient excuse to avoid having to get a little sweat up." "I wonder if the rains will ever start or whether there will be drought like 7 years ago, when thousands of people and animals died."

... I'm hopeful that my original attitudes toward those around me will be recoverable when I'm through with this place. Time will tell. But for now, this is a very different place, and, in reacting to it, I've become a different person ...

I have definitely reached one conclusion: understanding and compassion are not necessarily interrelated. I feel I have a fairly good understanding of how this culture operates, at least as far as my role as an outsider is concerned. I understand why everyone has to treat me like a dumb 3-year old kid who has to have everything explained to him. I understand why the people out here in the bush don't understand the words that a white mouth forms when trying (actually quite admirably) to communicate in their impossible language. I understand why people feel they can ask us for anything we own—or anything else in the world for that matter. I understand why the most common word for white person—a word that we'll probably hear as often in 2 years as we will our own names—carries with it the connotation of being inferior, unclean and damned to hell. I understand why a crowd of gaping idiots has to gather every time we pause to do something in public, for example, a yard from our own front door. I understand all this—and a hundred other similar everyday experiences. Understanding and compassion are synonymous the first million times this stuff happens. After that one begins to tire of the unique quality of the experience and decides that the less he sets himself up for situations like those I describe, the happier he's going to be. They cease to become learning experiences and only result in a perpetual state of being pissed off ...

My reaction has seemed so strange when I think about it myself that I don't see how anyone who hasn't lived through the experience second-by-second could ever be expected to understand the turn that my approach to dealing with people around me has taken. For all we have in common, these people might as well come from a galaxy light years away. [And we must have certainly seemed the same way to them.] ... After being around them for quite a while, it's easy to intensely dislike most of them. I don't think I could have made that statement about anyone a year ago—and now it describes my relationship with a nation of 3–5 million people.

✍ *I wrote to a high school friend who was going into the Peace Corps in Sierra Leone.*

I've been keeping carbon copies of letters I write for my own record.[113] It's very interesting to go back and see how my attitudes have changed with time. I just read over the last letter I sent you—a long time ago. A whole hell of a lot of water has passed under the bridge, resulting in quite a few changes in approach.

... I'm convinced now that this is just not a typical PC country. Other PCVs in other countries come back saying they had an enjoyable time and that they gained something from extensive contact with another culture. Volunteers here leave, and I'm sure to be one of them, so pissed off and disgusted with the national personality that he doesn't care if he ever lays eyes on a Somali again for as long as life goes on.

Anything goes in dealing with a *gaal*. People never ask politely for a white man to do something for them. Instead they command or just state that you will, in fact, do this. Examples: "Give me a tractor." "Give me a pair of shoes (shirt, money, etc)." "You will give me desks and chairs for my one room school." "You will take me into Baidoa." Etc. If they treated each other in the same way, then our reaction would be unwarranted. But they don't.

The Longest March

May 19 letter. Right after the last letter I wrote you, John and I decided that we would take a quicky trip into Baidoa, to see if there was any beer in town, pick up some supplies.[114] There was nothing keeping us here. The rains were a month late, nobody was planting and 3 or 4 days away from our post certainly wouldn't hurt anybody, least of all us. But what was in store!

We got a ride part of the way, to Dinsoor, where we planned to spend a night with [Dave Zwink] before going on to Baidoa. The ride was very typical, with the Land Rover filled to the gunwales with absolute jerks who felt it their responsibility to check out how much we knew of their language. ("Let's hear you count. Do you know 1, 2, 3?" "Where did you come from?" "Where are you going?" "Do you know ...?" Man, it gets tiresome.) But we politely ignored them, vowing under our breaths to take a bona fide poke at some random jerk before the end of our 2 years ...

As we rolled into Dinsoor, we saw a Land Rover leave, asked a guy in our vehicle where it was going, and he told us what he thought we wanted to hear.[115] ["To Baidoa."] John and I hustled over, to see the tracks turned onto the road out of town. Desperation. Screwing up the courage to get into a conversation with wogs, we strode up to a group in front of one of the official buildings. More ridiculous BS. In answer to our questions, we again got what people thought we wanted to hear—lies! "Yes. The Land Rover goes to Baidoa." "No. It just went to get gas." Nothing [we could rely on].

We returned to the building where we waited, since they had told us that the Land Rover would be back. Of course, we had the usual scintillating conversation, which, when added to the BS we'd already gotten from these guys, made for a couple of sullen volunteers. ("Are you in the military? Daud [Zwink] is in the military." "Are you going to marry a Somali girl? Daud is going to marry one so he can fuck all the time." "Why do Americans work so much?" "How can you be so young when you look so old? Look how young this guy looks and he's 35." "You don't speak very good Italian." You get the idea.

Finally Zwink and Big Abdi showed up—in the Land Rover that

we'd been assured was soon to go to Baidoa, but which had plans no more complicated than taking Zwink and Big Abdi out to farms every morning. It looked like we'd be spending the night at Zwink's.

He'd fired his *boyessa*, she was reportedly in jail, and he'll probably starve to death if he doesn't make some sort of change. He doesn't seem to eat very much and really likes his own spaghetti sauce. But we were leaving the next morning and appreciated the quantity of food and the hospitality.

The next morning we were checking the market when Nooro (one of Jamila's sons [a teenager]) showed up. "Good old Nooro. If we show you where we're staying will you make sure we get on the truck that is about to leave?" "Sure." Well, while he sat and listened to Abdi's *af ingresiga* (English language) version of tribal disputes (2 more were killed in Dinsoor the night before), the truck left. Nooro checked once, "No sweat, not leaving yet." The second time he checked, he didn't come back. When we checked after noting his failure to return, the truck had gone. Words can never describe our psychological state while walking back to Zwink's. So pissed at Nooro, at the asshole town that is Dinsoor, at the transportation in this country, at this country—that we couldn't even see straight. That's when it's all you can do to keep from popping some little fart who, in his sweetest little voice, says *"Gaala. Abaha wass!"* ["Infidel, fuck your father."]

Because of the tribal trouble, Zwink didn't have his Land Rover after all, so we all sat on our asses. I read *Tear for Somalia*, written by a guy who spent the '40s here as a military post leader and then as a DC [District Commissioner]. Some of the facts of life are presented, but more about the physical existence than about the cultural personality that we feel so completely. But the conclusion is more of an "I am an adventurer and a romantic and I love the desert and respect its independent inhabitants."

Yusuf, Abdi's son, told us that he would tell us when a truck was ready, and, to our great joy, came back about 4 PM with the word "go." We went down to check the truck out and got a resounding

"Go get your stuff. We're leaving right now." So, we trooped back to Zwink's, grabbed all of our stuff, and under breaking backs hauled it back to town, where they were more or less loading. We scrambled aboard, ignoring the people giving us crap, found soft spots and were ready to go.

Then the rainy season hit. After a month of waiting, here it came. The rain just poured down, but quite a few locals were thankful for its arrival and were like robins in a bird bath (ha ha—poetic use of our language). They covered up the top of the truck and there we sat, waiting to see how much rain was going to come down, to determine whether we would have to wait until the next day.

More stimulating conversation, needless to say. The griping part is, of course, that people always have to discuss us at length behind our backs. ("Do they know Somali?" "Yes." "No." "What are they doing here?" "I don't know." "They're teachers." "They're in agriculture." "How old are they?" "Yesterday I heard that one say ..." And on and on.) Finally, picking out one guy, I said that he talked too much and we'd appreciate it if they left us alone. Great gales of laughter. "He knows Somali." Then, "Oh, do you know Somali?" "No." "Yes you do." "Tell me what you know in Somali?" "But I don't know your language." (Aside: "Does his friend know Somali?" "Yes." "No.") "Yes you do." "Fine. Leave us alone." "Do you know Rahan Weyn?" "OK. Yes." "Where are you going?" "Baidoa." "Where are you coming from?" "Kansahdere." More laughter. "By God, these *gaals* do know Rahan Weyn." "Are you going to marry a Somali girl?" "No. I have a wife in America." "Do you know how to fuck?" Nod. "Do you want to fuck this girl?" (pointing out a real beauty). "No, I want a clitoris [remember that, unfortunately, Somalia practices the most extreme form of female genital mutilation]." Great gales of laughter. Finally, they leave us alone. When I was asked whether I wanted a Somali girl, one of the kids felt called upon to repeat the question in English (our being stupid *gaals*, of course we need all the help we can get). I said in English, "Do you want a broken neck?" He didn't understand, and

I sought to explicate. "Do you want to be killed." "Oh, no." "Then you will be quiet." "All right."

The rain stopped and we carted all of our stuff back to Zwink's. We were so pissed we couldn't even breathe. We would leave at 7:00 the next morning. That night it rained like hell, all 3 of us sleeping like mummies in Zwink's incredibly crowded mundel. The way he lives is incredible. They're the most depressing conditions imaginable. He really gets a masochistic delight out of roughing it, so he seems happy.

The next morning, we checked at 7:30 to find nobody near the truck. At 8:30 they told us to get our asses down there with our stuff, which we did. Then we ducked in a tea shop, where we were joined by some crazy guy who had a wild speech impediment that made him impossible to understand. We were in a good mood, though, and would interject "*runtees* [he's right]," "*sass wye* [that's the way it is]," "*alhamdulillah* [thanks to Allah]," or "*aahey* [similar to OK]" at appropriate breaks in the conversation. It was perhaps the only even vaguely enjoyable moment in Dinsoor, as a friendly group of people sort of gathered and we got no trouble.

Then we went back to the truck to wait—which we did, needless to say. Things were all fouled up. Nobody knew whether we were going to go or not and, of course, we would have been the last ones to hear the truth from anyone. We just sat and waited 3 hours at least, under the shade of a *dana* tree in the square of downtown Dinsoor, being stared at, talked about, and generally just sitting. We did get a good flow of nice looking women going to the market and watched an incredible chase scene featuring an aroused male donkey and his fleeing, kicking target. The big chuckle came when he fell down negotiating a corner and went limp. At the end of 20 or 30 minutes he was bloody and beaten and never did get his rocks off.

Of course, the school kids around had to casually use all the English they knew—in the course of conversation with each other, no less. Just to let us know that they really knew what was happening. We also had to sit and listen to the same little fart, whose life had been threatened on the truck the day before, sit and relate the entire encounter to a bunch of bushies. A point was finally reached when it seemed necessary to suggest that it wasn't very nice to talk about people behind their backs. After making the point a little more sternly, the second time the topic of conversation finally changed.

Finally, the truck was leaving. I sat down next to a beautiful young thing, who promptly shattered all affectionate illusions by wondering why the *gaals* had paid the normal price of 10 shillings to Baidoa instead of getting screwed for an extra 5 apiece. We were off.

We sailed along without too much trouble, but, in the back of our minds we were thinking about how much rain had fallen the night before and the fact that our truck was filled with bags of sorghum and had to be pushed to be started.[116] We were sailing along smoothly enough, the clouds parting to show a little innocent sky, when the driver got cold feet as he started to drive through a big puddle. He panicked, stopped, started to back up, and killed the truck. You incompetent bastard! "What are you doing?" thought the indignant *gaals*. But there were about 25 people on the truck. Maybe, we thought, something can be done about pushing the decrepit truck out of the mud. But, as our luck would have it, about 15 of the passengers were within walking distance of their village and decided to part company—without any protest from anyone even faintly resembling "Hey, why don't you guys help us push this thing before you take off?"

We tried such clever techniques as jacking up one of the rear wheels, spinning it and popping the clutch, but with no success. So there we were, maybe 50 km [30 miles] from Dinsoor and 100 [60 miles] from Baidoa, without food or water. Hmm … wonder what we'll do now. The Somalis were very accepting as far as their fates were concerned. After all, Allah must have willed it or it never would have happened. The *gaals*, on the other hand, were not particularly excited about the concept of divine guidance and were so pissed at being screwed again by local incompetence that we couldn't see straight. On top of that, we had no idea how were going to stay alive while we tried to get wherever we ended up trying to get to.

But luck was on our side. A Land Rover came along, and we paid the jacked-up-rainy-season-you're-in-trouble-and-don't-forget-to-add-in-the-*gaal*-tax price and scrambled aboard. Everything worked out as well as possible, because the road turned much worse before we finally got to Baidoa. We had to get out and push, the rain started, and, by the time we got to Baidoa it was dark and the 2 travelers were covered with mud.

But there was beer and for a day or two things were dandy. The problems came when we thought about getting out of town. It rained every day we were in Baidoa, and there we were no trucks going anywhere. We decided that the best tactic would be to get a ride on a truck going to Lugh, get off at Berdale, and walk the 45 km [a little less than 30 miles] or so to Kansahdere. OK. As it turned out, we waited 10 or 12 days for a truck. We had a ride all lined up in a government Land Rover, but, after about 4 days of continually checking with people and getting affirmative responses, at the very last minute the head big shot told us that the truck was full because there were a lot of party people who needed rides to Lugh and, of course, *gaal*, you know who comes first ...

The whole time we were in Baidoa, Omar Chicago was looking for a way for us to get to Berdale ...[117] Finally, he came with the news that a truck was leaving immediately. Dan, John and I gathered our stuff, leaving behind items like the tape recorder (broken anyway on the trip from Dinsoor).

[It was] a small trade truck, [a Russian-built power wagon] headed for Lugh.[118] It was the first truck of any size to leave town in more than a week, and there was a hell of a lot of hassle between a group wanting to go to Dinsoor and the group already loaded in the truck and ready to go to Lugh. The truck's owner, of course, was stuck right in the middle, trying to figure out which option would make him the most money and the fewest enemies. The truck was incredibly full, with the *gaals* taking very precarious perches on the roof of the cab—holding on for dear life. The real adventure had begun.

[A mile or two outside of Baidoa] the road turned really bad.[119] There had been 2 whole days without rain, but the night before there had been a healthy shower, just enough to turn the black mud into real shit. We plowed ahead. Most of the passengers must have been wondering, as we were, just what the hell we were doing trying to get through with the road that bad.

But never fear, help is here, cruising up in his caterpillar tractor. The guy proceeded to pull us—at a snail's pace admittedly—to the elevated road, about 10 km [6 miles] short of Ow Dinle. We couldn't possibly have made it without his help, but with his help we did, in fact, get to Ow Dinle—only 4 hours after leaving Baidoa. A rate of 7 or 8 km/hr [5 miles an hour]. It must have made quite a sight for the nomads who popped out of the bush to see the procession go by—a huge caterpillar pulling a trade truck filled with people.[120] Oh, Somalia.

[A brief digression:] The experiences we had travelling really provide a little additional insight into the way Somalis think.[121] For example, while we were sitting on the cab of the truck waiting for the argument to conclude between the prospective travelers to Dinsoor and the man with the money, the people who had succeeded in getting on the first truck in 2 weeks [headed for Lugh] scarcely batted an eye. They just sat and waited for God to settle the matter. But those who were involved in the argument were really worked up—pushing and wielding sticks. How to explain the difference? [Another example was] that no one got upset when we were starting into the bad section of road. ("We'll make it if Allah says.") Too hang-loose for us, but one is never called on to explain failure at any rate.

[From Ow Dinle] we made Berdale in another half hour, where John and I found a spot for the night in the teacher's room of the one-room school.[122] We first tried a room that smelled like a stable in what had once passed for a police station, but the inevitable crowd that gathered included a guy who sought to provide the finest in accommodation for the white tourists. Hence, the school. Before heading for the tea shop and a specially-made dinner of *basto* [pasta] (normally the tea shop is just that, with nothing else on the menu besides bread), we were treated to the welcome sight of about 30 bushies rolling up to play the "Hi, dumb *gaals.* Do you know etc?" game. This time it was wrestling, Somali-style. We immediately tired of being the objects of attention and just got up and left.

[We] got to sleep about 8:00 PM, to rise at 5:30 the next morning for the walk.[123] Oh, what a horror show was in store. I had a pack on my back, and John was carrying a KLM bag and his sleeping bag. We had 2 wine bottles of water, a couple tins of tuna, a couple of cheese, and one of pineapple. So … about 6:00 AM the 2 crazy travelers, veritably giggling with excitement at the very idea of the adventure on which they were embarking, headed down the camel path that was the road to Kansahdere …

Oh, boy, were we in for it. The first stretch was through bush and went by without any sweat. We saw few people, our spirits were high, and we were young and emboldened at our spiritedness in striking out a la Norman Nomad—who supposedly, when hyped up after chewing *khat* can walk 100 miles in a good day, which is believable when you see them step out. [Chewing the leaves and stems of *khat* provides a stimulating effect; historically it's been widely used in the Horn of Africa.] We'd also been told that it was only about 45 km [a little under 30 miles], which had also been my guess, made on the basis of an earlier trip, by truck, over the seldom-used road. I was in tennis shoes, John in sandals, and we stepped right along. We stopped in the middle of a sorghum field for breakfast of cheese, tuna and water. We took a few deep breaths, over-estimated how far we'd come, and struck out once more, walking at a good Somali-nomad pace.

Shortly thereafter the downhill slide commenced. Blisters began to pop out on various parts of our feet. But the ground was soft and damp, so we took our shoes off, going really ethnic, since that's the way the authentic local traveler does it. We soon hit the only muddy part of the road, which would have posed a problem [if we'd been in a vehicle]. We were lucky all things considered, for we had no rain and the road was pretty dry. When things are muddy, walking is supposed to be hard.

After an hour-plus of bare-footed tramping, our tootsies begged us to give up on that idea, and the two troopers went to the only alternative left to them: flip-flops, thongs, whatever you call them, called *da'as* in Somali and usually worn as shoes by just about everyone, including us. Right about then, maybe 4 hours after departure, the thrill started to vanish. The light-hearted conversation became harder to come by, and it became a matter of forgetting how much every part of our bodies ached from walking and just carrying our things. And forgetting how hot the sun was getting. We just kept putting one sore foot in front of the other. We'd figured that we could walk 6 km/hr [4 miles an hour] and that should have put us about halfway there. We figured the end was in sight. It wasn't.

By 11:00 or 12:00 the two crazy *gaals*—just barely conscious—stumbled into the shade for lunch. But first we passed out for a little mid-day nap. After a couple hours' rest out of the noon-day sun and some more tuna, cheese and water, the two idiots struck out again. We guessed there was maybe an hour and a half to go. We certainly hoped so, because we were getting a little peaked, our feet were getting sore, the sun was hotter than hell, and our water was getting low. We were screwed, in other words, and couldn't wait to get to goddamn Kansahdere. We stopped a nomad: "Hey, Abdi. How many hours to KD?" "Four." "Hell, he doesn't know. Let's polish off the water." "OK." We'd decided long before that we couldn't believe anything any of these guys told us.[124] It's still not bad policy, but this time it got us in trouble.

While we were walking, it seemed no wonder that the nomads

are incredible simpletons.[125] [I cringe as I type this.] They do absolutely nothing but walk, pray, eat and [have sex with their wives]. It would be tough to get them into the mainstream of world events.

It was about 4:00 PM, and we knew KD was just around the corner.[126] Not quite. Out of water, we kept on walking. We were really worn down—every step, out of necessity, something to be done completely without feeling. "Just put one foot in front of the other. That's a good boy." The hallucinations began to get good, as visions of cold beer, the girls in Mogadishu, cold Coke, cold lemonade and good food danced through our minds, at least distracting them from our aching feet. We met a couple guys who told us that we would make it by the time the sun set. It was about 4:30 or 5:00, and their estimate was closer, although they still didn't have even the foggiest idea what they were talking about as far as we were concerned. After a mouthful of water from one of the guy's gourds, we followed them until we came to a small water hole, supposedly near to our objective. These guys kept telling us "Walk a little farther and you will see the town." Liars. All they did was get our hopes up. Some people said we were near, others said that we were far. Who do you believe?

We filled a bottle with the brownest water in the world, dropped in a couple iodine tablets and laid back to wait for them to work. We were dying of thirst, but we weren't ready for a three-day case of the drizzling shits just yet. Unfortunately, the water hole was very popular at dusk, and the sight of the two defenseless white guys fostered an almost unbearable number of the usual questions— questions we had encountered from every single person we met that entire day. "Where are you going?" "Kansahdere." "Where are you coming from?" "Berdale." "No?!" "Yes." "Where's your truck?" "No truck." "What's the matter?" "We have no truck." "You walked from Berdale?" "That's right." Great gales of laughter and *"Illahi"* (one of the forms of "Allah," meaning roughly translated, "I'll be darned.") It was just inconceivable that we would be out on foot in the bush. After all, white men have trucks, just like they have a limitless supply of money, cigarettes, clothes, medicine, etc. We got exactly the same series of questions and exclamations from everyone we met, and, although their interest was very understandable, it became a little tiresome.

With a little left in our bottle of new water, we took off, figuring to be less than an hour at most from our goal. Two guys we met as dark came on told us an hour or an hour and a half. As dusk turned to night, we staggered to a halt, flopped down at the side of the road and both went to sleep. When we woke up it was dark. We split the last can of tuna and drank the last inch of water. By this time we were both numb as hell, but determined to see what we could do about actually getting to our destination.

But walking along with my tiny little .7 candlepower flashlight was no picnic, and we both had the idea of sleeping in the bush that night. We would complete the ill-fated safari the next morning. Maybe 20 minutes later, 2 very tired boy scouts stumbled off the road, found spots between thorn bushes, rolled out damp sleeping bags, and sort of got a night's sleep. We were so tired and sore that we couldn't actually call what we got sleep, but we did, at any rate, put in the time working at it. We were thirsty as hell to boot. During the night about 3 groups of nomads walked by, with camel bells clacking, laughing and wondering if those were people over there—and if those were the *gaals* who were walking from Berdale.[127] Word was out.

The next morning we were up and off who knows how early.[128] We walked maybe an hour, maybe more—actually feeling much better than we had when we crashed for the night—stopping only to rinse our poor dry little mouths out with the urine-water mixture in puddles along the road. And, low and behold, we rounded the corner and there we were. Finally. We found out that the trip had been closer to 60 km [a little less than 40 miles] than to the original estimate of 45 [a little less than 30 miles]. What a horror movie. But, after about 3 days of resting our abused feet, we were as good as new. And of course, the town couldn't leave us alone, but had to come around while we were trying to recuperate and ask exactly the same questions that the people on the road had asked. Oh well, part of the glamorous life of a PCV. [The punchline was that we found out a child had recently been hauled away by a hyena in the same area where we spent the night. We were just lucky, I guess.]

We'd been lucky—no rain and little mud.[129] All things considered, the only things we needed to make the trip come off without a hitch were good shoes and socks and more water. Otherwise, it was not too bad. (We can do anything. Now we think the people believe us.)

During the early jocular phase of the trip, John and I tried to compare our hike in the allegorical sense to our 2 years in Somalia. It was truly amazing: once we left Baidoa, [we didn't talk much about possibly terminating from the Peace Corps]. That place must be poisonous. Besides, upon application of cognitive dissonance theory, the 2 of us could not have been busting our asses like we were to get back to a place that we couldn't stand. Right?

My theory was that the light-hearted beginning of our hike, the happy and determined optimism, the eventual realization, and the struggle as the end approached (with the travelers heedless of absolutely everything but the end of the experience) could all be seen as having definite parallels [with our 2 years in Somalia]. But John's analysis was better. The trip will be the nadir of our Somali experience—a catharsis that will make the next year and a half a casual cruise to the finish line. It seemed very fitting that we made the hike exactly 6 months to the day after we arrived in country. I hope his interpretation of the experience is the correct one. That would sure be nice.

Our Efforts to Teach Ag Techniques

April 21 letter. The big pushes in ag will be the same here as in Gorisane.[130] We're trying to get people to plant in rows, thin, and eventually

157

step up to oxen power if their finances permit. We're dealing solely in peanuts and sorghum, like we were doing in Gorisane … John has done a very good job of making his presence known, and, as a result, we should be working with a lot of farmers—as many as we can get in before the rains get here. They're on their way, as we've had a little rain every day for about the last 5 or 6 days, and the roads in and out of town are reportedly getting pretty slick.

Today we planted a demonstration plot about half an hour from town, 30 X 15 yards of sorghum. We worked hard and it didn't take long. We're going from day to day. Sometimes the farmers don't show up, sometimes we can grab a substitute if they don't. Every day is anything can happen day. We're doing a good job remaining flexible and getting in as much demonstration work as we can. Here, people are coming to us, something that makes the job fairly enjoyable and something that would never have happened in Gorisane. We've got the approach down pretty well. We provide the brains and part of the work; the farmers help with their work, keep their eyes open, and provide the seed.

April 25 journal entry. We planted some peanuts on Alio Buro's place maybe 4 or 5 days ago.[131] Thirteen rows, 20–25 yards long. No sweat. John and I have also planted Nooro's farm. He's a dumb little twerp, but it was a chance to put some seeds in the ground. No spectators showed up, which was good in some respects, bad in others. We got no bullshit but had little chance to spread the word. We planted 5 rows of American white sorghum, 3 $1/2$ of American red, and 10 or 12 of his seeds. The plot is maybe 30 yards long. It was a good workout. John had 3 plots in before I got [to KD], so we have 5 in the ground now. We'll see how they work out. There are a lot more possible farmers, but without rain the plots aren't going to pan out very well …

Olat is convinced that the rain will never come this season. Abdulkadir told us that little beasts have eaten the peanuts John planted. Let them sit around long enough without any rain to germinate them, and the time will come for the clever Somali beasts to get them. We're not doing any more planting until the rains come. No sense wasting seed or energy—or getting hopes up.

May 12 journal entry. Soon we will check all the farms. The word is that Warsama's and Abdulkadir's [seeds] are up. Buro says that the insects ate his. We don't know about Abdi Noor's, and good old Nooro is nowhere to be seen. Soon we'll take a look and see for ourselves.

May 15 journal entry. We dropped by Abdulakadir's, had a cup of tea in his absence, and jumped through hoops for the women folk ... Then we found Abdulla Carter, checked out his farm—growing very well. The peanuts are [tremendous] (in one stand at least), although the sorghum must have been eaten or washed out. Not real good. Later we checked Warsama Jama's farm. Fantastic peanuts and he was out weeding. He could be a mover.

May 16 journal entry. [We had our own plot.] I was hoeing ala American, just knocking the weeds down, and Olat had to give us a lengthy demonstration on just how one is supposed to hoe: digging up dirt for six inches and working your ass off, just to kill a few weeds. I resisted his training and just about drove 2 other guys crazy. We'll see. If the weeds stay dead, my way is perfect as far as I'm concerned.

Some beans are up and growing, but a lot are not. We don't understand. The watermelon and cantaloupe are the best, and we thinned them. Zak had gotten the melons from a friend in the states. Zwink brought the beans from Nairobi. He also brought tomatoes, lettuce and carrots, which never sprouted. My radishes from Warsaw, NC are growing well, and today we planted Warsaw carrots, tomatoes and lettuce to see how they do. [I got the seeds in Warsaw when I visited a college friend in VISTA before I left for Somalia.]

May 19 journal entry. Before dinner last night Hassen Issak came by with Olat. We had given him some seed maybe 3 days earlier to take to the *shekh* [to be blessed] and had expected him to return early in the morning to go out to his fields. We had the new idea of planting in rows in clumps, with a *yambo*, without sticks and string, simply eyeballing the line. For small-timers, it could really improve things. But in the course of conversation it was revealed that Hassen had sent a couple guys out to plant for him. Oh well, maybe next season.

There's no motivation for change or improvement here. All we get are words saying, "Yeah, groovy, plant in rows, plow with oxen. Yeah. Groovy." Nobody will follow through. After all, everything is up to Allah. His will guides life, and, if you believe it hard enough, you'll never do anything to improve your own lot.

May 19 letter. Being away [on our trip to Baidoa] when the rains finally did come screwed us as far as getting more demonstrations in the ground.[132] But, like so many things about this culture, it's just written off as *naseeb* (luck). The plots we'd put in before are working out (a couple of them very well), and we have guarded hopes of doing something with oxen training after the rains stop. We'll have to see. (That's another one of the guiding maxims of PC life in this country of unpredictability and peopled with unenthusiasm. "We'll have to see," and "*Naseeb*," those are the two we live by.) There is also the evidently very real chance of not getting enough rain to bring any sort of luck. We'll just see how things work out, see what god wills. If we don't get enough rain or something else goes wrong, that would just be our luck, wouldn't it? (You get the idea.)

✍ *I wrote to my college friend in Peace Corps/Nepal.*

As you have discovered, the work is anything but a full-time job.[133] But here there is the additional problem of almost complete lack of enthusiasm for changes on the part of the farmer. Most of them will tell us, "Sure, we want to learn to plant in rows, to plow with oxen, all those things." But when it gets right down to it, they just couldn't give a damn …

We get tired of having to kick them in the ass all the time, but it's understandable that the people are content with the status quo. After all, it's Allah who determines whether you have a good crop or not. Why bust your ass to try and better your lot yourself? It's kind of paradoxical, though, because the most successful non-Europeans in the country are the Arabs, who are also by far the most devout Muslims. Everyone says that they're eager to try out our new methods, but, when it comes time to sweat a little bit and work to produce a little cash, the ranks of the dedicated shrink to just about nothing.

There are other things wrong with the job aspect of being here. Because of the alternating 3-month seasons of rain and incredible dryness, all the planting is done just twice a year. In our area the only crops people plant are sorghum, peanuts, and beans. So, farm work involves planting, thinning, harvesting, and maybe plowing— if the guy has bulls. (As of now there are no animals in Kansahdere trained for farm work.) All of this is jammed into very small, not very intense, periods when it's time to work. The rest of the time, there's nothing. We're on our own.

May 28 journal entry. This afternoon John and I learned a big lesson. Aimoy took us out to Madd Shurie's, where we had planted sorghum in rows. We should have gone out there before, but we'd heard he was sick. Today he was out working—and had even thinned most of our rows for us, doing it the Somali way. He left clumps of 3 every yard or so, not exactly what we had in mind. But—he'd failed to weed most of the American sorghum, probably because it looked so weak. (In talking with him we almost forgot that American and local sorghum are not the same.) So we thinned what little was left (most of the American), trying to explain what we were doing to the 4 or 5 bushies around us. Aimoy understands, but the rest of them just walked off after seeing that their efforts to convert us to the correct way of doing things were not going to work. Even Madd Shurie didn't stick around.

There were a lot of weak spots in our work. We should have had the old man there when we planted, instead of his dumb kid. We wonder if the kid even told his old man what we'd done. We could've checked on the plot before we did. Thinning would do less damage to the roots if it were done after a rain. But this year no luck, as they say. It would probably be better to work with guys who feel we have something to teach them. It's tough to teach incredulous people how to plant in rows.

It was very gratifying, though, to come home and find Jamila thinning the sorghum in the yard. She'd been there a few days earlier when we were talking to Olat. She may be the smartest person in the whole town. If we work with friends next season, the backyard business could really be big. I'm interested in trying techniques with those who have no possibility of using oxen: plant in rows, in clumps, with a *yambo*, without lines, and thin very early.

June 1 letter. Like I say, our demonstration plots so far are looking good, and one of the fields of peanuts has caused quite a stir in town [because it was growing so well].[134] That's what we're after, a little hubbub as it were. Just about the only thing these people understand is the buck, and this one guy is going to rake in a lot of cash from his peanut crop. That is, if somehow they do mature— that is, "if God says" in local jargon.

> *On June 1, John and I filed a "periodic report" to the Ministry of Agriculture. (I don't remember who actually drafted it.) A copy is in Appendix C. We radiated optimism, and the tone was much less sarcastic than the report I wrote from Gorisane.*

Daily Life in KD Continues

May 9 journal entry. The day's big crisis was when the guy weeding our neighbor's sorghum felt called upon to decimate our freshly sprouted morning glories.

May 12 journal entry. We were very good today, dealing with an incredibly boring procession of visitors without anger. We weren't always attentive, and John told Nooro that we didn't understand what he wanted, hanging around all the time. But we were pretty nice. We never even got mad. We're watching our flowers grow, talking about Mog, the girls, our house. [We were planning to build a house; more on this later.]

May 14 journal entry. Later Hassen Issak came by ... to invite us to the big SYL bash the next day. [SYL was Somali Youth League, the political party in power.] Drink a little of their tea and get hit for a lot of our money. But, of course, our government won't allow that. We mustn't get involved in politics overseas.

May 15 journal entry. We got up at 5:00 to hear Nixon announce his plan for Viet Nam. No surprises, but he's got Lodge, Abrams, and Rogers racing all over the world. Maybe something will happen. If they'd get rid of the war and get the lottery system for the draft (as [Secretary of Defense] Laird and Nixon are preparing to suggest to Congress), and forget about the ABM system, then uplifting the poor and eliminating hunger and poverty can receive a lot more attention—not to mention money.

During breakfast we witnessed a very interesting discussion between the 2 adult members of the family. Jamila was more than a little upset, wondering where her laundry money had gone. Several things puzzled us: 1) why she expects the money when she doesn't do the clothes; 2) what Olat had done with her money; and 3) why she'd forgotten the 50 shillings he'd spent on her new clothes. It really made the point more clearly of the differences between marital situations here and in the US. There, a couple operates as a couple; here it's each for himself. [I now realize that this perspective about couples in the US was based on my observations of my parents rather than on any universal truth.]

In the afternoon we went to the "by invitation only" party thrown by SYL every year on May 15 to celebrate the founding of their party. We ate cakes, drank tea, milk and grapefruit juice, and listened to guys go on and on. Warsama Aden talked, then Shekh Somebody talked forever about the goddamned religion (with a few anti-*gaal* remarks certainly thrown in). Alio talked about our glorious town, then left. We figured that we were maybe semi-expected to say something (it would have really been the PC [Peace Corps not "politically correct"] thing to do), but our cold feet and our lack of eagerness to address a political meeting got in the way.

Dinner was as usual; it's never much fun because of the interminable hassles. [Last night, however,] we learned from Olat some of the ways that Somalis look at stars. There is the Great Camel (*Aur Er*) near the Southern Cross, which was very hard for us to see at first, because the camel is formed by looking only at the dark spots; the stars are not considered at all, only the dark places. He also told us about the Somali interpretation of what we see as Orion. It's *Sed Ali*, who is holding up the head of a *gaal* he's just slain. Good for him.

May 16 journal entry. Alio came over ... and we had a very Peace Corps conversation about our garden and our house [that we were planning to build]. We're setting everyone up for the idea of bringing girls out here. When they tell us that we should get Somali wives, we tell them that that's what we're going to do as soon as the house is built. He also told us about the *barone* (local version of the Saturday night sock hop) [townspeople] held last night. Everyone jumps around, hyperventilates, freaks out, then, according to our source, heads off into the bush in couples for a little sex ...

[Since getting back to Kansahdere] things have not been bad. We hang around home a lot; we haven't had too many callers, but have sat and talked with those who have come by. John is much better at the superficial BS than I am. After a little difficulty when we first got back [from Baidoa], I've gotten so I just answer their ridiculous questions truthfully rather than sarcastically and go on about my business. Sometimes the ridiculous can be bent to the humorous. A few *runtees's* ["he's right," literally "his truth"] and *sassu's* [as I recall, a Rahan Weyn word for "that's the way it is"] can loosen things up a little on occasion.

We worked on our own little farm after tea, needless to say getting all the help we needed ... It's going to be really nice handling the crowds when we start making bricks and building our house. They all know so much.

May 18 journal entry. The rest of yesterday was very average. Dinner was, as usual, a hassle, with the whole family present and [the usual foolishness] going on. Olat saying, "No, you want more *ghee*." Jamila complaining about a million different things. All normal. We listened to the usual Saturday night ball game.

May 19 journal entry. Then we listened to the blast-off of Apollo 10. Of course, there were no hitches and I was soon asleep. Nothing could seem farther away from our experience in this place, but that certainly does not diminish the magnificence.

We had a dandy conversation with Olat this noon that really showed how this religion screws the people over. Everything is *"insha allah"* or "If God says," but I never would have believed what Olat would say to us. The conversation got started by our suggestion to Olat and Jamila that they eat something. Olat was having dizzy spells and Jamila is always complaining of something. Jamila said she didn't like ... (everything). I stated my opinion that if something doesn't eat it will die. Reply: "If my time is up, God will take me." How do you deal with that?

Olat told us about people drinking rubbing alcohol and gas. Of course, it makes them better and nothing we could say could change his mind. Then Olat talked about how much he prays, for such things as Mukhtar [their son, about 5 at the time] being independent by his 20th year. We said that Christians believe individual effort can make a difference, [whereas] here it's all up to God. Olat had examples of the benefits of prayer, e.g., the time the doctors saved a man by removing 5 ribs. (The doctor, of course, had nothing to do with it; it was all Allah.)

Then we talked about who has the financial responsibility for marriage and divorce, and we learned that Jamila is really pissed because the kids are too hungry [meaning that they want too much to eat]. There is no understanding of anything.

Then Olat began to talk about the people of the Upper Juba. He doesn't like them, and he's lived here for 18 years. He says a lot of the same things we do: people are suspicious, ask a million questions, and the people here have cursed him with wizards. And he's one of the most civilized guys out here. How do you come up with anything [productive] when you cross Islam and voodoo? He's the guy who has been sick for 8 years, has never been assessed at a hospital, but has spent hundreds of shillings on smoke, slaughtered goats, and Koranic readings.

May 20 journal entry. Today Miriam [their daughter, about 4] had a new dress and was easily the cutest girl on the block. No work for her, though; today was her day off. After dinner Mokkai asked us for spray. It seems she's troubled with fleas. We suggested that she wash her clothes and her bedding, but she insisted that we just give her the poison and she would spray herself. No one will ever listen to us. *Gaals* can't possibly know things. They just have things. After all, hasn't God smote them? Even Olat is talking about going to a healer in Dinsoor. Man, go to the doctor.

May 21 journal entry. We got some interestingly intolerant propaganda and a legend from Olat at dinner. Jamila was feeling bad a few nights ago, so, instead of having the soup John brought her, she sent Aimoy downtown for 7 bottles of grapefruit drink.

[Conversation tonight]: If one gets bitten by a spider 7 times, he is doomed to misery. A spider saved Mohamed and 2 of his friends when they were fleeing Mecca and the evil Christians. He weaved a web over the hole the guys hid in and Mohamed blessed it. "Hell is a very bad place, Jim. We all pray we not go to hell. If Christian man says '*bismillahi*' ["in the name of Allah"] before he dies, he will go to heaven. Hell is very bad place." Apparently, a convert is supposed to have no trouble getting to heaven, being admitted before those born Muslim. I don't think my answer of "Yes, but no one has been to hell and back to tell us whether it's true or not, have they?" was appreciated. I'll have to keep quiet.

There are 12 days when people can enter Mecca; 4 of them during Eid-Aareff. Haji Ali Aden, the deputy [the local representative to the national assembly], is the only local to have been there, and he's been there 4 times. "He wants to go 7 times. He not want to go to hell. Hell very bad place. Haji Ali pray God he not go hell." It's interesting that Olat prefaces a lot of things with "our religion say," but occasionally he slips into the attitude of speaking the truth. They're always right. A real jerk out at our place today told John, "Why don't you go to the mosque. It is done. You are in Somalia. You must go to the mosque."

[We had a couple unwelcome guests.] They just weren't wanted. I tried to be as rude as I could, but to no avail ... Then we got to [discussing] how far the US is from here. They couldn't believe it. They wanted to know the directions of Rome, US, Mecca, Lugh, Dalo, Mandera [in Kenya, near where Kenya, Somalia and Ethiopia meet]. Then they decided they could take the Lugh road. "Can we go in your car?" "No. there's an ocean." "Really! No. There's no ocean near Mandera." Later: "Will you pay for our plane ticket?" "You want 5500 shillings [about $800] *baksheesh*?" "Oh."

The old routine has definitely taken over this week since we got back.[135] The time for thinning our demonstration plots is coming up, but other than that there is very little that falls under the officially-recognized category of Peace Corps work in agriculture ... We have a small plot of vegetables we're growing for our own use. (Incidentally, the radish seed that I purchased in Warsaw,

NC [where the letter's recipient was serving in VISTA] has turned into young plants with a future. We're waiting for a little more rain before we pass final judgment on the tomatoes, carrots and lettuce.) We carefully look after our morning glories and zinnias. Anything to fill the hours. We put in a little time on public relations, rubbing elbows with the local gentry. We make lists of anything, just so long as the list has some application and the making of said list takes a little time. We have lists of money we spend, radio schedules, shopping lists for Mogadishu and Baidoa, dates on which we have wet dreams. [Could this really have been true?]. We have all sorts of lists.

    ✍   *I wrote to my college friend in Peace Corps/Nepal.*

It's amazing that the last 7 months have been the best of your life when for me just about the opposite has been true ...[136]

Right now, supposedly we're in the middle of a rainy season, but it's been one of the weakest excuses in years. It was a month late in arriving, and people and animals are reportedly dying in northern and central Somalia. There were even tribal wars around here over water rights. When the rains finally did come, there was actually very little rain, and the chances are good that there won't be enough to get any sort of a crop. (But that's Allah's will and our luck and all that.) The first and by far the wettest half of the rainy season is over, and I don't think we've had more than 4 inches. Under ideal conditions, 8 are needed to get a sorghum crop. It could be big trouble before the next rainy season (and the drier of the two at that) arrives in October. Right now, the only effect that the rain is having on us is to make the roads impassable to trucks carrying mail and ourselves and to occasionally make things a little gooey, humid, and moldy inside our hut.

... The average Somali combines intolerance for outsiders; religious, national, personal and tribal pride; a desire to take advantage of anyone to get something for nothing; all in a combination such that few of them are bearable to people from our cultural background. I'm trying harder, but it's difficult to work up much interest in the culture or affection for the people when we have to cope with a lot of BS and feistiness that seems to come in an endless stream. As a result, we're happier when we can keep the rabble off our backs, keep the irritations to the bare minimum, and work on the few relationships that we find enjoyable.

> ✍ *I wrote to Conn Price, who was in charge of our training in South Dakota. By the end of training, we all loved Conn. He had done ag extension work at BONKA in Baidoa.*

May 23 letter. Our group in general seems to be faring alright, although when we get together our conversation seems to be dominated by such topics as the amount of time on our hands, the seeming lack of genuine local enthusiasm for change, and the strained quality marking our average relationship with the individual Somali.[137] You must know that Zak has left for the U.S. We'll certainly miss the guy, but he just wasn't happy here, feeling that he was getting very little out of his experience. Don in Baidoa wishes there were more farmers within reach, but Zwinko in Dinsoor (working at an incredible pace with Big Abdi), Phil in Bardera, and Dan in Lugh seem to be getting along as well as can be expected.

May 23 journal entry. This morning at breakfast Olat told us that Aden, the laundry boy, was married last night. He apparently married one of the 2 hookers we saw here a while ago. Olat was not too positive: "public woman, stupid absolutely." He said she'll probably keep on doing it after the marriage. John placed some groundwork [for our plan to bring 2 women with us from Mog after we built our house] by saying "Some, though, are very good." I just sit and say nothing.

We had a very interesting conversation with Olat. He wanted 25 shillings to buy a goat to be Koranically bled and eaten on the 12th of this Arabic month. The *shekh* told him that his dreams told him Olat should do it. Olat is really down on the Upper Juba people, because no one helps anyone else, everyone tells him to go to the market [sic]. [He says] they're probably just afraid he'll put a wizard on them. Olat has visions/dreams that accurately predict rainfall, but few people will listen to him.

[Olat continued:] A lot of people who become successful also become very bad; they forget about praying to God. Olat says that he has had a lot of wizards put on him. He has seen things in his house. The people in this area are especially good at "casting spells," because they are "slave people." [By "slave people" he meant people who looked more African than Somali. Many ethnic Somalis were careful to distinguish themselves from people whose ancestors were from other parts of Africa.] They make wizards out of *hidheet*, the root used for building *dersis*, etc.

Earlier today we talked to Olat about Somalia and emerging nations. "Much money is needed, but Somalia is young." His views on the relative merits of the country are pretty enlightened. He also said there are many religions that think they are right. He could have said that Islam is right, but he didn't. He said God knows for sure [which religion is right]. A very surprising statement coming from him. It's interesting to listen to him, but there can never be any discussion. No such thing. He also said that the "slave people" are almost as evil as the "*yahood* people [Jews]," who are absolutely the worst when it comes to making wizards.

May 24 journal entry. At breakfast, Mokkai said there will be no more rain because some sort of insect was heard crying. They have a million ways of figuring things out.

May 25 journal entry. This afternoon I gave Aimoy an English lesson. It goes slowly, but he learns. It was interesting to compare his attention span, etc, to ours [when we were learning Somali] in training. At the end of 3/4 hour, he's through. Just like we were.

We butchered a baby goat this morning and had goat and rice for lunch and barbeque and *ma'ashuiro* (doughballs—tremendous) for dinner. Real good grub. Truly fantastic.

Olat has really been praying his ass off lately. It gets a little distracting, as he performs the ritual on his bed, whispering his *bismillahi*'s in our ear. Or else he sits next to our table and twirls his prayer beads and mumbles his praise of Allah, alternating mumbling with conversation with us. [We had our meals in an enclosure adjoining Olat's and Jamila's *mundel*.] Olat is even going to the mosque. We're kind of at a loss to explain his sudden devotion. Some Haji probably told him that he'd better start shaping up or his health will get even worse. It's ridiculous. The object of prayer seems to be to see how fast one can finish.

May 27 journal entry. Yesterday, Olat told us that he's going to slaughter a sheep for Mohamed soon. Shekh Sapri, Ibrahim Issak and some other cat came over. He added that they might even have a big-time *shekh* over for festivities. These 4 are all "Shekh Abdulkadir people," and they had to celebrate their meeting with a little song. The evening before Olat had taken part in a *dikhri* at Mokkai's and was very hoarse. He's gotten so involved in his newly-found devotion that he's not around much. I guess he spends all of his time in spiritual consultation.

May 28 journal entry. Aden Bota arrived from Baidoa last night. Unfortunately, he's going to Dinsoor [instead of back to Baidoa]. We've decided we can take off as soon as we check all the plots. The word is that *gu* [the rainy season] is over. After 2 weeks of rain—maybe 4 inches. Things shouldn't grow too well after a while. We're starting to get extra sleep, trying to save up for an imminent trip into Mog.

May 30 journal entry. Happy Memorial Day. We thought maybe we'd be taking off today. Two Land Rovers came from Dinsoor, bringing such celebrities as Aden Buutan, Mad Maalin, and our old buddy Shekh Hassen Alio, who was supposed to be the ag man here. But John had seen him once in Baidoa, once in Dinsoor. I met him when we gave him a ride from Dinsoor to Baidoa when we were first in the country. [He must have been the guy who did the talking when we visited Gorisane the first time.] He came over for a little visit during the afternoon, and what a bull shitter! He can really sling it. He was reassigned to Dinsoor, where he's working with Abdi and Zwinko. Of course, he told us just how much he knew about ag in this area and how much the place would improve if he weren't so old and tired …

About 4:00, working through Olat, we heard that Aden Buutan might have room for us going to Dinsoor. We raced around, got our stuff ready, thinned Abdulkadir's sorghum, and got ready to take off. After several hours of waiting, dinner, more waiting, we found out that there was no room. Mad Maalin, a friend, is coming back and going on to Baidoa and Mog within a few days. We should get space in his truck. It'll be good to see Fritz, talk to the trainees (due in Baidoa tomorrow) [Somalia 9's, the next group of PCVs], and get on into Mog. [This was for a break; we had not yet decided to leave Kansahdere.]

May 31 journal entry. We watched 2 papayas sprout. We had Shekh Hassen Alio over to lunch. What a *shaydun* [devil]. We did nothing all day. Aimoy goofed around all afternoon, and we finally ran him off when he was deliberately screwing up his English lesson. While I was showering [out of a bucket], Mohamed Alio came over to ask again for some money to get married, to find out which of the doors we are going to leave behind (he did thank John when he told him we were leaving him one), to ask us to build him a new door for his *mundel*, and to ask John to buy him a new bed. Sure, the white guys have an endless store of money. Hit them up for anything. Next time I think we'll ask Mohamed concerning the whereabouts of his manners.

Last night at dinner Jamila told us about the crap people give her when she goes downtown. "Why do you work for the *gaals*?" "What do they eat?" "What kind of clothes do they have?" "What do they have in their *mundel*?" Etc. She says she doesn't say anything except "I don't know" and goes on about her business. Both she and Olat, despite being woggish, certainly have our best interests at heart, and we sure as hell appreciate that. It's too bad they have to take shit for trying to pick up a few shillings [by cooking for us].

During breakfast, we paid Olat and he gave Jamila 50 shillings. Her reaction was really something. She didn't know what to do with it. At dinner she said she wants no other man and seems to be storing away good clothes for when she figures Olat will leave her. He is talking about going to Mog after John and I leave [after we complete our PC service].

Last night John and I talked about our relationship with this country. The people are so suspicious and feel so superior. And when we compare what they have with what practically every other country in the world has, we wonder where they get their idea of superiority. A lot of it must come from their religion. [In our situation] there's no such thing as discussion or friendship, since relations are founded on such bases as the desire to ogle the white freaks and the desire to take them for whatever is possible. After all, what can *gaals* possibly have to offer someone who already knows everything? The culture just cannot be dealt with in any way that is rewarding to us. The only way for us to enjoy this culture would be to shrug off everything we've learned and learned to enjoy and respect in 23 years and become a wog. Then it would be enjoyable. As it is, so much just has to be discounted, shrugged off and ignored that it doesn't leave much of an experience.

June 1 letter. We just got through eating a truly delicious (no facetiousness intended) lunch of *sor*, which, when cooked correctly, consists of an oatmeal-like mixture made out of ground sorghum.[138] While still piping hot it is spread up on the sides of a big bowl, and the hollow in the middle is filled with a wonderful soup made of bits of meat and *subakh* [*ghee*]. When cooked right, with *subakh* that isn't too rotten, it tastes damn good. When cooked wrong, it ain't too tasty. It's eaten with the hands, breaking off pieces of mush from the edges of the bowl, sloshing them around in the soup, and sucking it down by the handful with a slurping sound. It's truly a meal to look forward to.

... Because of the muddy roads, the food situation is the worst it will ever be, but we still get meat practically every day (sometimes 2 or 3 times), have rice, spaghetti, plenty of fresh camel's milk (which, like *subakh*, isn't bad at all when it's fresh), beans, a local spinach-like vegetable that is little more than a weed that grows in the sorghum fields but isn't too bad if you keep reminding yourself that it's something green to eat, and occasionally papaya. We're not hurting a bit.

The rains have really screwed us this season ... The next rains aren't due until October. Things could get a little tight for the average nomad, who is dependent on green bush to feed his camels and on watering holes to get water for himself. Normally, by the end of a dry season, things are pretty tight. This year they should be much more so ...

Big Plans to Build a House

    ✍ *Notwithstanding our complaints, we were still optimistic that we could accomplish some things. During training we had experience doing construction with a cinva-ram machine, a simple metal form for making bricks out of rammed earth and cement. We were going to build our own mansion out of cinva-ram blocks.*

April 25 journal entry. We're also fired up to get going with the construction of our cinva-ram palace.[139] We drew up the floor plan, figured out the materials and the costs, and covered just about all the details. We figure we'll need 1500–2000 bricks. There are a million logistical problems, but, if it is at all possible to pull this off, the end product will be a classic, one of the biggest jobs ever undertaken by vols in this country. We're busy trying to organize our approach to the hassles. Today we're worrying about getting sand. We're going to talk to Calija, who is in charge of construction of the new mosque, to see what sort of deal we can arrange. We also have to see the city about getting some land, get someone to build a fence and *muskosha*, figure out a place to mix the dirt and cement, get a couple of *akals* [the temporary huts the nomads use, made from mats and curved sticks] to keep the rain off our bricks and figure out a way to get water to work with.

If things get too tough, we're going to build a *barako* to specifications. [This was a rectangular house, bigger than a *mundel*, made of mud and wattle with a corrugated metal roof.] It would be disappointing, though, after how excited we're getting about the brick house. We plan to work until our materials run out or the rain stops, whichever comes second. Then we'll go into Mog and our young lady friends. We pick up a PC truck and some materials, come back and finish our house. Then we go back into Mog, sign a year's contract with 2 young beauties of our choice, and come back for the rest of our stay. (We may even be partially reimbursed by the PC because of their position as "language informants.") If everything goes perfectly, what a comfortable set-up: Fadumo and Abdia to take care of us, and a fence to keep the locals out. I may stay here the rest of my life.

May 13 journal entry. Today was the day. We bought our own plot of land—30 by 32 meters—and the Bis Corpis [Somali for Peace Corps] is in the land business. Olat was indispensable as we worked through him, picked out a spot that had no owner and paid the municipality, in the person of Warsama Aden, the grand sum of 23.50 shillings [about $3.30]. Then we squared up the corners, using the old method of bisecting arcs. Then—things were happening so fast our heads were spinning—again with great help from Olat, we arranged for construction of a fence of *dana* trees and a *muskosha* [drop toilet]... We originally wanted a fence like the one we have around our present long drop, but the whole package would have come to 700 shillings. Too much for even the *gaals'* wallets. So, we're paying for a fence of tall *dana* trees, with a gate big enough to drive a truck through. Also included is a 3 meter deep *muskosha* with a fence around it. We are going to carefully watch the workers to make sure that everything comes out the way we want it, but everything might be hunky dory.

We'd no sooner made arrangements with one guy to do the work when another guy dropped by to tell us that we were shits for not having him do the work. Sorry, Jack. (John just said Olat doesn't like the guy, says he's a *bon* and he thinks he's a wizard. Luckily he's not one of the hyena people or he'd really be on the black list.) [*Bon,* pronounced "bone," means "slave" and was an insulting term for a person who looked more African than Somali.] To celebrate we finished off the rest of our wine.

May 14 journal entry. We checked out the construction of the fence, and the two guys seem to be working hard and doing their best to please. We told Olat to tell them that, if we are very happy with their work, we will have more work for them. Perhaps that will be their inspiration. We're really hopeful that things will work out for the very best. Yesterday John received a visit from the landlord, who was letting him in on a secret. He didn't want him to tell, but he was going to get married. And, of course, he could use a little money.

May 15 journal entry. After eating we checked out the fence, which is coming along very well. We're pleased. Knock on wood.

May 18 journal entry. Today we checked out the work on the long drop and thinned radishes. We also came up with a great new plan for the house. We did a lot of figuring and came up with a total of 2500 shillings, with quite a bit of material still left to add in. The squeeze on our money could be considerable in the next 4 or 5 months—especially when beer and a refrigerator are thrown in. If by November 1970 [when my two years in the Peace Corps would be up] I've had 7 weeks of good vacation, bought a decent camera, and lived an enjoyable year in our house, I'll be happy. It should work out ...

Khalif came over Friday night and we talked building techniques and his own building experience, as well as his personal history. He has no transit, but he says that the foundation of the DC's office [which he must have built] is level. He also says that we should get sand from his truck. (He says Mad Shaffy is a thief.) He's a damn good guy, who actually accepted the fact that he's had no experience with our blocks. He's going to be a lot of help, especially when it comes to the foundation and roof.

Yesterday John and Warsama Aden shifted the location of the *muskosha* and the 2 guys [workers] got right on it. The fence, except for one spot near the gate, looks very good. We're still going to ask for a garbage hole and "chicken brush" along the bottom of the fence, as well as repair of the one weak spot. They're being paid for 20 days' work and it's been 6 now. They can squeeze in a little *baksheesh*.

May 19 letter. It'll be the nicest house in town, and we're going to build it all our selves.[140] I know a little about building, John knows quite a bit, and between the two of us we're going to turn out a beauty. It'll have a living room/dining room, a semi-hallway, and 2 bedrooms. There will be a covered porch and an adjoining kitchen, built not out of cinva-ram but out of sticks covered with cow shit. Right now, we're waiting for the roads to dry up so we can bring in some sand as well as get into Mog to buy lime, metal sheets for the roof, and a million other things. If we bust our asses, we figure that the whole thing can be built by the two of us in less than 6 weeks, allowing time for making and curing the blocks. The outside dimensions will be 14 X 26 feet. Right now we're having a fence built to keep out prying eyes, dimensions approximately 35 yards square ...

We're ready to get working on the house itself. Then we figure we'll get into Mog (after the house is ready) and hunt for suitable living partners. We think we've found them (named Fadumo and Abdia), but we've yet to sound out the two lovelies on the idea.

Having two beautiful girls around full-time would brighten things up around here. Wonder how our town will take it? Hope things work out so that we get to find out.

May 20 journal entry. I got up early to get letters to Khalif before he took off for Baidoa, and also to get his level. We probably can't get sand until he gets back with his truck, but we can dream and maybe something will come up. We had a long talk through Olat with Aden and Abdio, the 2 guys working on the *moskosha*. It was agreed they would provide the wire for the fence—only 75 shillings, but the principle involved was tremendous. [Presumably, this was because we had agreed on a fixed price for the job, and they did not ask for additional money, instead providing the work *baksheesh*.] Later they hauled in the logs to go over the [toilet] hole and really wore themselves out. (There were no donkeys available.) They like the idea of getting more work from the *gaals*. We made a few more lists and planted our papayas. No rain for a week—a real bad season.

May 21 journal entry. We checked with the construction crew to see that the rocks were piled over the layer of logs and that the walls around the toilet had a good start. They're eager to please and we're eager to be pleased.

May 22 journal entry. I got cramps and the shits. Not good. In the morning we marked out the foundation for the house and checked out the work on the *muskosha*. Work on the foundation went well. We laid out corners using 9 X 12 X 15 right angles, and things check out pretty close. We contracted to have Abdio and Aden get crushed rock for walks. We're getting the garbage hole *baksheesh*. Very nice. We're pleased with their work. All is going well.

We had the usual amazing number of savages drop by just to quiz us. They asked if we were weeding our farm, told us we don't know what we are doing, told us the house is too small, etc. It's been 9 days since the last rain. Crops sure seem doomed.

May 23 journal entry. We scratched out pathways for the house, found out the *muskosha* is going to have *dibe* [mud/manure mixture, put on the fence around it], and set the wheels in motion for the paths. Things are going smoothly so far … We need the truck to go get sand and other stuff, and also need things like doors and windows before we start.

May 24 journal entry. We worked on the house until noon, setting up batter boards, using our long board as a straight edge. [Batter boards are the temporary wooden framework to which strings are attached to lay out trenches for the foundation.] We also cleared the bushes from inside the house and the rocks from the porch. Of course, we had a million guys show up, none of whom had any idea what was happening. It's kind of strange. In the traditional PC sense, we should be working as educators. But here the people feel they know everything. It makes teaching something new sort of difficult. No one has asked us to tell them what we're doing. They just come around and laugh.

May 25 journal entry. We worked on the house, finished the batter boards and started digging the foundation, using the local style pick and our shovel. It was hard work because of all the rocks (some of them huge), and our hands took a beating. It got hot, so tomorrow we're going to start at 7:00. It feels good to have something physical to do, and, by the time the house is done, I think I'll have relearned how to work.

May 27 journal entry. Yesterday and this morning we worked on the foundation. Tomorrow it should be finished … Yesterday Abdi and Aden finished the walk. All that is left is to *dibe* the long drop and dig the garbage hole. We'll be all ready. We paid the boys off, and now we'll have to see how fast the rest of the work gets done.

May 28 journal entry. This morning we finished the foundation, under the watchful know-it-all gaze of Saass and Aden Maddy. The people here ... never get tired of telling us how we should do something. Aden finished the garbage hole.

May 29 journal entry. A real slow day. This morning, the day's only excitement came from the mouth of Mohamed Ali, who told us that Aden Buutan didn't like the idea of our building a house on land bought from the city. We immediately checked with Olat, who was "goofin' on the Koran" over at one of the local *shekh*'s. Needless to say, we'd formulated good arguments (e.g., if you don't like it, bye). Olat cleared up the problem. Aden Buutan, who is rumored to be an asshole, was very upset at Warsama Aden for having sold land to us (as well as to a couple other people) before "the government in Mog was all set up [after the elections]." As far as the 2 of us and Olat were concerned, there was no real problem. We'd paid our money and had the sheet of paper [proving ownership]. *Bis* [that's all].

June 1 journal entry. Jamila told us it's all over town that Aden Buutan doesn't want us to build. Everyone's wondering what the *gaals* are going to do about the actions of the all-powerful local government. We're going to ignore it and wish the small-minded townspeople would do the same. What very possibly happened is that Aden B saw our fence, asked Warsama what was going on, was told that some land had been sold (to the *gaals* among others) without the prior permission of the higher-ups. The little stuffed shirt got all up in arms, because his irrefutable authority had been threatened— after which he sold some land himself. The locals don't know this, I'd imagine, and I'm sure they don't know we've paid for the land. (Hell, they don't even know we pay Olat for working for us.) They just want something their small minds can gossip about and, after all, *gaals* are prime material.

June 1 letter. We're planning on talking the PC into loaning us a truck to haul in materials for our house—metal sheeting and wood for the roof, more cement, nails, lime, etc ... [141] If enthusiasm is a forerunner of success, [the house is] in the bag ...

Now the word is all over town that Aden Buutan doesn't want the *gaals* living in town. Everyone is asking what we're going to do—as if we're supposed to be trembling in our boots at the thought of tangling with their incredibly inept municipal government. We ain't gonna do nuthin', Abdi. They just don't understand why we're not sufficiently cowed.

A Final Rant About Life in the Bush

June 1 letter. A familiar song. Somalia is by far the best and cannot even be approached in any way by any other country, be it the US, Italy, Russia, Kenya, or whoever. The religion here is the best, and anyone who is not Muslim is vastly inferior and is doomed to the fires of hell. White guys have a lot of material things, and, since they're not of the same religion, they are to be taken advantage of. But Somalis mustn't be fooled by the white guy's material advancement—he really has nothing to teach us. [Somalis] know everything, and mustn't listen to anyone else. And this is no exaggeration.

This basic approach typifies our relationship with every single person. As a result, no one believes us when we tell them that people are going to fly to the moon. They won't listen when we tell them better ways to farm. They know. They've got all the answers. The reason that American farms are so much better than those here is that the farmers have insecticides and tractors, not because they know anything that the Somalis don't. Damn it. You get tired of it. Every single person acts as if he knows absolutely everything that there is to know. As a result of this approach, any sort of real discussion, any real cross-cultural exchange, any real friendship is impossible.

We don't discuss anything with people, instead just listening and silently comparing the two cultures. And some things are interesting. For example, there are people in our neighborhood who by night turn into hyenas. No one knows exactly who they are, but everyone knows of their existence nevertheless. There are also a whole lot of people who can make "wizards" that take hold of people's souls and make them do strange things. When someone gets sick, he could go to the doctor in Baidoa, but it makes more sense to have some old *shekh* read the Koran over you, pay a lot of money for witch's brews, or pay money to slaughter a goat and drink its blood under the beaming eye of some *shekh* or another. And these practices are by people who are not pagans; they are Muslims. I guess—well I'm sure—that it's the African influence. And it sure screws the people up. They'll never improve if their educated countrymen (and there are some—all in Mogadishu) continue to ignore them. After all they won't pay any attention to an outsider. And they have a hell of a long way to go ...

I have reached a conclusion of monumental importance.[142] The Peace Corps, as an organization, is worth no more than a big pile of crap. Originally, I'm sure, the goals were noble, the aims admirable. Now, there are so few people in the hierarchy (from in-country staff [in other countries] right on up) who give a damn about what is being done overseas that it makes you want to puke.* For the most part, the people who serve as administrators seem to be little assholes who are in the Peace Corp game not because of any burning desire to cure the ills of suffering humanity, but because of the desire to see how far up in the hierarchy they can climb. When one makes a reasonable complaint, no one listens.

For example: Our training program was run by a group of returned volunteers who had formed a corporation to help train people preparing to serve overseas, primarily PC. They botched the job badly, and it was a unanimous recommendation on the part of the trainees that they not be hired in the future. So who is training the group that is due here any day? The same incompetent bunch.

---

* I'm not referring to in-country staff in Somalia, all of whom, particularly Bill Thompson, were responsive, easy to work with, and very supportive of our program.

The head of language instruction, who did his absolute best to destroy our training program and fell only about a foot short, was even signed on to try it again. I mean ... the hierarchy completely ignores the [opinion of the] volunteer.

There is absolutely no reason for the PC to be in this country. The majority of the PCVs come home having had only-OK to miserable experiences. The great majority of Somalis are anti-Peace Corps, including key people in the ministries of education and agriculture. There seems to be little of the traditional Peace Corps job success. Official papers have been filed by past staff members, carefully listing the problems and the inevitable conclusion that the Peace Corps doesn't belong in this country. But that doesn't mean anything to the big shots. What do you mean Somalia is not a place for the Peace Corps? You're just saying that. All countries are the same. And besides, we have to keep up the number of Americans in the country, so that the Ruskies don't get in there and take that little country away from us (wherever it is—near Tahiti, isn't it?). Nobody listens.

✒ *In my last letter from the bush to my family, I said:*

Our morning glories have just about covered one section of a wall of our "porch," the first signs of germination are showing in our bed of papayas, and there are flowers on the melons and beans.[143] The radishes are just about ripe. We've read a few good books apiece and aren't making too many enemies. Things are OK.

Leaving the Bush

July 13 journal entry. It's a new era. I'm now in Mogadishu, working in sports and recreation. Over 6 weeks ago, John, Don and I came into Mog to get drunk, laid, etc. We were really a sight, I remember, rolling into Capo's [an Italian restaurant] after 13 hours on the road. John and I had left KD on the first truck out, ready for the big city. It turned out that Thompson was in Hargeisa with Randy and Bakes on their "parasite tour." We hung around Mog for about a week, spending half our nights at the Lido (Fadumo still being the love of my life, of course). Bill showed up, and a few days later we were off in the red truck filled with tin sheets [for the roof], cement and wood for our house.

It had been a very unsettling ten days psychologically, as the 3 of us [John, Don and I] tried to figure out what to do about our relationship with this country. We talked to Sol Siegel [one of the 8s remembers he was a psychologist, who would have been in Mog only temporarily], [Dr.] Parsons, Bill [Thompson], and others about the many areas of dissatisfaction. The state of being undecided was very unsettling, changing my mind a dozen times daily [about whether to leave the bush or leave Somalia entirely]. We left for the Upper Juba with Don having decided to leave for home, John having decided to stay in KD and build the house, and me still being completely up in the air.

Don stayed in Baidoa to get his stuff together, and John, Duane and I left for KD. By then, I think I'd decided to leave. I remember being very unenthusiastic about the prospects of working on the house, which had once meant so much. It was with almost a feeling of terror that I returned to KD. The bush just had too many uncomfortable moments associated with it. We got into town about dusk, in time to unload the stuff from the truck, eat something, and realize that everything was exactly as it had been before—certainly no better. What a miserable existence.

The next morning we fired up the pickup to go get some sand. After getting the run-around from our buddies we finally had to scrap our plans. We had a couple flat tires and couldn't really take a chance on cruising around the bush with no spares. It looked like we'd have to get back to Baidoa and have the tires fixed before we could do anything. But first, we thought we'd check our new home site. What we found made John's mind up for him [to leave the bush]. And with his decision, I no longer had to consider what it would mean for me to leave him out there alone. We were ready to go.

Cows and goats had been allowed to graze unbothered, traipsing in and out and through the fence, knocking it down in a number of places. The local jokesters had felt it necessary to tear up all the batter boards, bust them into their original components, and pile them in one of the trenches. Boy, were we pissed. Bye, KD.

The next step was to move all of our stuff into Baidoa, telling people that we'd be back in a few days. Parting was no great sorrow, as the little laundry guy Aden had to hang onto the truck door as we rolled out of town, demanding more money. John damn near hit his first host country national [a common phrase in the Peace Corps for residents of the host country].

Bill [Thompson] got back to Baidoa about 2 days after we got there. We explained our situation, and he wasn't too thrilled. Next we went to Dinsoor and Bardera, checking things out in general. I knew that I didn't want to stay in the Upper Juba. That much I knew for sure. Bill and I talked about the alternatives and decided that we'd have to let things sit until after the conference, scheduled for July 2 and 3 in Mog.

After a couple really rough days, the cement had been sold to Zwink and taken to Dinsoor, and we were out of KD. Our final departure was typical of our relationship with the town. Nobody really gave a damn [that we were leaving]. Everyone was demanding rides. Alio Buro was pissed not because we were leaving but because we hadn't told him. Olat and his family got good [and deserving] *baksheesh*, so he wasn't too upset. The entire experience had been just a little too big and too strange for anyone to handle—ever. It was goddamn good to get out. Unlike with Gorisane, there was not a single doubt. No regret whatsoever. The bush and I were through.

I came into Mog about a week before the conference, ostensibly to check out the possibilities for working in recreation. I did a little of that, but mainly worked on a presentation for the conference, drank, and got rid of Fadumo, who had proved to be too much trouble. A lot of BS with no compensation. I found Ardo, who isn't exactly working out either. She has dollar signs in her eyes and has a couple rich ones [customers] that she hangs over my head. It just may be time to keep moving on. Too many other fish in the sea and all that.

[The 8s' conference was held on July 2.]* Bob Bonnewell wrote in a newsletter at the time:

> As a basis for discussion the Eights filled out a Completion of Service form. When the conference opened ... these tabulated results and a paper written by Jim Douglas [this is below] became the basis for the discussions.
>
> The main complaints were aimed at the original programming of the group along with choice of posting sites, lack of support by the Ministry of Agriculture, the attitudes of the farmers towards agriculture, and the attitudes of the Rahanweyn towards the white man in general. Faced with a combination of an unpleasant living situation plus no opportunities to make what they felt would be a meaningful contribution to agriculture in the next two years, four of the Eights decided to leave their original posts.
>
> In the other cases, with three exceptions, the Eights felt that, although their work was not particularly significant, they would return to their posts, as they had a comfortable living situation and hoped to find some other areas of work to augment their efforts in agriculture. The three exceptions felt that they were making a meaningful contribution to agriculture in their areas.

In general, however, people ended up happier. John Marks is going to teach in Beled Uen, and Fritz [Don, who had been in Baidoa] is taking off for home. He's making the right move, but

---

*   My sum total description of the conference was that "I and others made presentations, and Leo [Gallarano, the director] and Kelly Coleman [none of us remember who he was] made certain un-understanding statements of their own." A longer excerpt from the newsletter about what was going on with the 8s is in Appendix D.

they're really breaking up the Yankees. [Zak had already gone home. Baker and Duane would be gone by mid-August.] We've done a lot of things together, but Fritz is going to be so much happier at home that I can't wait for him to get out of here for his sake. With Zak and him gone, the place is going to take on a different look. The good old days of wine, women and song on a grandiose scale will be damn near gone forever.

Mogadishu—the Big City

My Reasons for Leaving the Bush

✎ *I submitted the following to the Peace Corps as the expla-
nation for my decision to leave the bush. This must be the
paper that Bonnewell was referring to.*

An Analysis of My Experience as a PCV Working in
Agriculture In the Upper Juba—July 1, 1969

After having spent approximately six months living and
working in the Upper Juba (specifically Gorisane and Kansahdere),
I've reached the conclusion that to continue in the same capacity
would be unthinkable. My general reaction to living and working
with the Rahan Weyn people has been one of overall dissatisfaction. There have been many factors contributing to this feeling,
including my relationship with the Ministry of Agriculture as well
as my relationship with the inhabitants of the Upper Juba. It is to
be made clear from the outset that I have absolutely no criticism of
the members of the staff presently in country. The individual and
personal support, specifically as provided by Bill Thompson, has
been excellent. In many cases this encouragement and support by
the Assistant Director has been the only bright spot in what has
otherwise been a fairly bleak experience.

Although certainly well-intentioned, the entire agriculture program was obviously ill-conceived and poorly thought-out in virtually

every respect. The potential relationship with the Ministry of Agriculture (to be discussed in greater length in the next paragraph) is a factor that seems to have never been sufficiently considered from a practical standpoint. Presumably, there were brief looks taken at potential posts, but an encouraging word from a glad-handing DC [District Commissioner, the head of local government] would seem to have been virtually the sole criterion for the decision to post an Eight in a particular location. A closer look at the posts might have revealed that a prospective volunteer would have an extremely difficult time trying to live in the area—attempting to develop agricultural techniques. From my perspective it seems that someone decided that "Ag sounds good. Let's send some aggies to Somalia," without any knowledge of the situation in the Upper Juba or any real concern for the fate of the individual volunteer. The philosophy, "Let's get some more American bodies into this country and get them out in the bush where they can groove on the culture," seems to have prevailed.

There are definite reasons why the job situation itself has proved to be unsatisfactory. At no time has the Ministry manifested any real desire to work with the Peace Corps. (Lip service excluded, of course.) In fact, there have been criticisms concerning general incompetence of PCVs, their lack of appropriate training, and their tendency toward laziness. (It would seem that the shoe might be on the other foot.) In addition, from my personal vantage point as a volunteer in the bush, the Ministry has proved to be a virtual nonentity—and a very poorly organized and inefficient nonentity at that. During my four months in Gorisane, for example, the local agriculture agent deigned to show up a total of three days, during which time his activity was limited to drinking tea in his pal's *mundel* and spraying DDT on the same man's demonstration plot—the only demonstration plot in the area, subsidized heavily by BONKA and the Ministry in Baidoa. The man in charge of agricultural extension in Kansahdere appeared locally for two days, during the seven-month period that a volunteer was stationed in that village.

These extension agents are considered to be our counterparts, but in the great majority of cases they do nothing to further the development of agricultural methods in this country. Although not lacking in knowledge, these men employed by the Ministry exhibit a lack of commitment to the development of Somali agriculture and seem concerned primarily with personal advancement gained by saying the appropriate thing to the appropriate superior. There has been no visible disciplinary reaction by the Ministry to this lack of constructive output, although rumors are currently being bandied about that "by God, heads are going to start rolling if somebody doesn't stop goofin' off." Such disciplinary action remains to be seen.

On the whole then, the Ministry seems to take no real interest in the advancement of national agriculture. Admittedly it is a poor Ministry from a financial standpoint. But if those guarding the federal purse strings would recognize the resources of the country and modify the fiscal policies accordingly, the potential of the Ministry would be considerably increased. As the system presently functions, gasoline for government Land Rovers is virtually the only thing provided (and much of it is not used for job-related travel). Such crucial items as seed, pesticide, and farm implements are unavailable in Somalia outside of the USAID stations at Afgoi and Baidoa, and the Ministry seems to be in no real hurry to rectify this situation by making these items available for sale or rent. But this would involve logistical issues that perhaps the Ministry is incapable of handling at this time.

My general conclusion concerning my relationship with the Ministry: Due to the particular nature of the legendary "typical Somali personality," even exceptionally competent white non-Muslims are incapable of dealing with Somalis as well as the average Somali is capable of dealing with Somalis. Although admittedly lacking in resources, the Ministry of Agriculture is capable of overcoming resistance to change far more effectively in a given location than a Peace Corps Volunteer is. There are men in this country who know what can be done in the field of agriculture. They just don't care to do it. And in view of the particular setting, if the host country government doesn't care about progress in agriculture, I don't see how I can possibly care.

Having discussed my relationship with the organizational hierarchy, the next step is to deal with my experience at my post. This has certainly contributed the most to my feelings of general disappointment. Many of the earlier criticisms of the job situation would be generally recognized as "fact," as it were. The following analysis of my experience deals with much more personal elements. As a result, I expect that someone reading this who has not undergone the same experience will be quick to explain away the problems. But for another person to gain any insight into my experience, it will be necessary to accept my analysis as including possible elements of truth. Although more emotional and personal in nature than those discussed earlier, these problems were no less real.

I found virtually no satisfaction or gratification living in the bush of the Upper Juba. Of course, certain problems with the language contributed to my general feeling of dissatisfaction with the experience. Upon moving to my post, my initial enthusiasm was great enough that I learned a considerable amount of Rahan Weyn. This was a necessity, considering the fact that no one in the village spoke Somali or English. For several seasons, however, this did not favorably affect the experience to any significant degree. The number of dialects of Rahan Weyn is formidable, and each differs in pronunciation, verb conjugation, and vocabulary. This frustrated any communication across sub-tribal divisions.

Even more important was people's predisposition concerning my ability to speak their language. Having had no contact with white men before, they assumed that I was unable to speak their language and could not understand even the simplest thing I said. Admittedly, there had to be minor differences in pronunciation when I spoke the language, but when speaking with people with whom I spent considerable time I had little difficulty being understood. This unconquerable predisposition on the part of the average bush inhabitant turned any attempt at communication into a frustrating and fruitless experience. It is, after all, nice to be able to talk to the people around you.

In addition to the problems in dealing with the people using their language, there was the problem of boredom. Agriculture in the Upper Juba is regarded by the inhabitants as an activity that does not warrant too much work. Even if the proper techniques were utilized, the entire process of field preparation, planting, cultivation, and harvest includes a lot of time when the primary activity is watching the sorghum grow. Other projects might be initiated, but the complacency of the people makes many of the ideas unthinkable, with failure and utter frustration the only possible final result. One's personal projects can only keep one busy for so long since, after all, one can build only so many tables. Generally keeping oneself busy helps, but it does not compensate for the negative aspects of the experience. Just living with the relationship that one has with the culture becomes a 24-hour-a-day job and one that is not particularly enjoyable at that.

Moving to the bush for the first time, my expectations were, indeed, minimal and my enthusiasm was very high. Perhaps my only predisposition was the desire to participate in some small way in a foreign culture. This participation—at least on any level that I could find rewarding—proved to be impossible. I wanted to learn about the bush culture and develop a few mutually enjoyable relationships. Because of the strong predisposition on the part of the people, the possibility of establishing such relationships was impossible.

The two cultures are so incredibly different and white men are so incredibly strange that the possibility of becoming anything but a freak in the eyes of the people is precluded. The people have heard of white guys, but the idea of one coming to live in their village makes no sense whatsoever. Because of his total strangeness, the white man is nothing but an object to be laughed at, talked about, toyed with, "*baksheeshed*", and instructed concerning the benefits of planting in hills rather than rows. The things that the white man does, the things that he suggests, the things that he has, are so totally different from anything the local inhabitants have ever seen. The *gaal* does not fit into any framework known to the local people. Anything goes as far as relating to him and dealing with him are concerned.

All efforts to relate to the people on their own terms, at their own level of sophistication, failed because of the ridiculous position to which the culture assigns the white man. What kind of a life is it when one of the people I know the best after six months has to repeat my every word to the entire neighborhood because no one else understands what I'm saying? One tires of relationships in which one is always an object, never a person; in which he is always on display, never allowed to merely participate in events as they go on around him. I have concluded that I don't enjoy living and working under these conditions.

There are certainly very understandable reasons for the inability of the people to see the outsider as a legitimate entity. We are white and non-Muslim. How can a Muslim react even semi-normally to someone the likes of whom he has never seen—someone he has been taught from the age of 4 to regard as inferior, unclean, damned to hell? It is obvious why we are not to be regarded seriously, worked with or learned from. The people in their relationships with us invariably feel that we are the ones who should be instructed—in virtually every aspect of existence. (Needless to say, this makes one's position as an agent of change a little tenuous.) Allah is responsible for changes in life's patterns, and it is only too apparent that a non-Muslim PCV is not an agent of a Muslim god. Tradition is such that, regardless of the type of existence they lead, the people are basically content. This life doesn't count; it's praying and being faithful to insure a better life to come that scores points. A white outsider is not going to be able to relate to or affect a society like the one found in the Somali bush.

In evaluating my experience I have tried to find something from which I could say I gained some feeling of satisfaction. I've not been able to. I have certainly gained none from my work. I've found none in my relationship with the people of the Upper Juba. I was eager to participate in some small way in a totally different culture, to form some rewarding personal relationships, but, seen from the point of view of my experience, the opportunity simply does not exist. I understand this relationship with the culture. I realize why I have been given the reception I have. I have been allowed a very close and interesting look at a culture extremely different from my own, but to continue living within the framework that has been established would be ridiculous. It would be possible to endure, as it were, but I feel that it is foolish to see "how much I can take" or whether "I can make it." In terms of feeling any personal satisfaction or happiness, my experience in the Upper Juba has been a decidedly negative one. And in the words of one of the great early philosophers: "Ain't no sense in kicking a dead horse, man."

Starting Out Well in Mog

🖎 *I summarized the changes and my improved attitude in letters to friends and family.*

August 30 letter. From our original group of 15, 4 have resigned [and gone home] and very few are generally happy ...[144] We had a conference of our group at which we took a pretty good look at the way things have gone. I, for one, was pretty talked out, the topic of our individual discomfiture [meaning discomfort] being the sole topic of conversation for the preceding 2 or 3 months. After the conference, 3 of the 11 remaining switched jobs and posts [including me].

I'm in great shape—a whole hell of a lot happier and generally more satisfied than I've been since I arrived in the country.[145] I just wasn't happy with the bush. I was tired of trying to deal with people who found it impossible to regard me as anything other than a white object, to be toyed with, taken advantage of, and laughed at. Also, I was dealing with people, trying to change people, who had absolutely no interest in changing and felt that we—not they— were the ones to benefit from any instruction in agriculture. And it just didn't do the job as far as filling up the hours of the day were concerned. Not exactly my idea of the fulfilling PC experience.

Our ag program, in retrospect, had to have been conceived by a bunch of air-headed idiots, if they had any thought that we'd affect local agriculture in any way.[146] The people, at least everyone I came into contact with, could just give a big rat's ass about any sort of change. They're completely happy, and the Somali government does absolutely nothing to help move along the change that everyone knows is completely necessary if this place is ever to exit the Stone Age.

> *I started to work almost immediately, supervising recreation at the juvenile section of the prison, building basketball courts and a playground, and teaching basketball. More on all this a little later.*

July 22 letter. I think I've found a place where the happy moments are going to outnumber the unhappy ones ...[147] One day I work one place, the next day, another—hustling, arranging, attempting to introduce a little coordination and planning into a society that has absolutely no concept of what it is to coordinate and plan. I've been working for about 2 weeks and have been the happiest I've been since getting into the country ...

In Mog the people understand my Somali, unlike the bush, where every village spoke a different dialect and no one had ever heard a foreigner try their language.

A lot of the daily scenes are probably pretty similar to those in other Arab countries or any developing country anywhere.[148] There are the dirty market places, the small restaurants, the crowded streets, just like in a small Mexican town. Because Mogadishu is the capital city and because there has been a little European influence, it is quite a bit different from the rest of the country, where the people are so primitive that they're virtually impossible for a foreigner to deal with. They've just never seen anything like us.

Here in Mog there's quite a bit of anonymity. Crowds will occasionally gather to see what the crazy white guy is doing, but not nearly as frequently as happened in the bush. I've discovered that I don't really like being the center of attention. So, Mog is nice. For example, a PCV here can go into a local-style restaurant and not create any stir whatsoever ... The local food is not too imaginative. The basics are rice, goat meat, tea, milk, bread, and bananas. The Italians have, however, had a certain effect on the local cuisine, and you can get spaghetti almost everywhere. We have a house girl who takes care of the cooking, so the number of possibilities increases. At home we eat potatoes, different types of meat, papaya, beets, carrots and eggs. Although our girl could be quite a bit better, we generally get plenty of food and it is warm.

Getting Settled in Mogadishu

July 15 journal entry. Right now, I'm still sponging off Thompson. It's been saving me money, but I've got to get out of here. I'm supposed to meet a guy tonight to look at some places. Bob Love is going to sell me some furniture as well as leave me his *boyessa*. A damn good deal in both respects. I also expect to pick up some really worn out PC items and should be about set.

I think once I get settled Mog will work out well. I dig the relative anonymity and will also enjoy the minor luxuries—beer, girls, hustle and bustle, etc. It's possible that I'll be *very* happy—especially if I can accomplish a few things on the job, which I expect to since I'll be doing them myself. If I do things right, it will take quite a while for the locals to destroy them.

July 20 journal entry. Surprisingly, I have to say that I'm really enjoying Mog. There are bad moments, but, in general, I have to say that I actually like it. Just walking around by myself has ceased to be a chore. The language is coming more easily, and once I get settled I think I'll use an informant [one-on-one language teacher].

I still haven't found a place. I have everything else, but no house. I looked at a bunch of places in Shangani [a very old section of Mog], but none [were OK]. For sure I don't want a place on the ground floor. Mohamed Hashi says there is a place like his near his and is going to look into it for me. His is a nice place, and it's sort of a good location. It's near the prison and PYA [Police Youth Association] but far from Shangani, the Ministry of Ed, and the PC office …

Fritz left Friday morning after all night at the Lido. What more can I say. We celebrated his departure with an Oranjeboom [Dutch beer, pretty low-grade] at the airport.

August 1 journal entry. This may be the first Friday since I moved into Mog that I didn't have to recover from the Lido. After what happened Wednesday I think I'll pass for a few days. Another one of those "drop by for a look" nights turned into a horror movie. I ended up with Udbi, having a pretty good time. We headed back to Thompson's for a little relaxation. [After a while] my dear girl announced that she had to get home. Fine, we'll go in just a minute. She started getting huffy, and then I must have said something. I don't know what, as the details are far from clear. She went crazy. Before the encounter was over, she'd thrown just about everything in the room at me. I kept trying to calm her down, then I'd let her go, and off she'd go again. She woke up the entire building, Thompson making his entrance with "What in the hell is going on in here?" The cops were outside but didn't come up, thank God. Lul [Thompson's girlfriend] finally cooled things off. What a night.

Yesterday Randy and I started to work out with the Russians at Benadir School—volleyball for the first time in over a year. A couple of the Russians were good and several were adequate. After the game we went to one guy's place for Bavarian cognac. A real fine afternoon. Thursday we play at the Russian Club, and I'm really looking forward to it.

August 19 journal entry. [I've gotten some letters from college friends, and] it's amazing how difficult it is to communicate my experiences here. Their reactions, most of which I have to read between the lines, are not completely understanding ... [I realize now that I was awfully candid in my letters to friends.]

I've signed on to help with a sewage and paving project in Hamar Weyn [a neighborhood in Mog], which has taken a year to get to the stage where a contract was drawn up. After meeting with the Hamar Weyn committee head, the next step is to wait for them to put 8000 shillings in the bank. [There's no further mention of this project.]

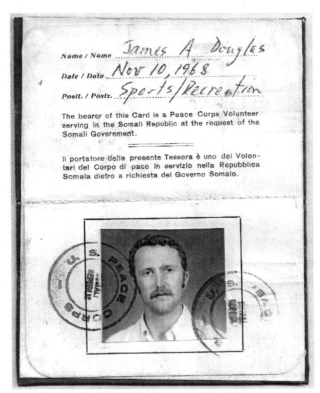

My ID card during my time in Mogadishu

Our apartment, upstairs with slanted roof—photo by Randy Meyers

Famous doorway in Shangani, not ours—photo by Randy Meyers

Fisheries Ministry, former fortress and lighthouse—photo by Randy Meyers

Living in Shangani, the Oldest Section of Mog

> *I moved in with Randy, replacing Baker, who went home after a serious car accident.*

August 17 letter. Things are really pretty peachy.[149] Since I last wrote you, I've accomplished a few things, more or less, and I've found a place to stay. I took a spot in a relatively nice apartment (by PC/Somalia standards at any rate), replacing a guy who gave up on the idea of staying here after a dandy car accident, in which he piled his Land Rover into an army truck that had chosen to stop in the middle of the road at dusk without any lights. He got a real fine gash across his forehead and was lucky he didn't get completely cleaned out.

... We have a pretty nice place, each with our own room over-looking the ocean. It has to be the coolest place in the entire city, which should be handy when the hot season starts. It's pretty looking out at the ocean, over houses that are certainly hundreds of years old (we're in the oldest section of town), watching the breakers (which are wild this time of year), and checking out the ships that are lying at anchor off-shore. It's very nice. We have a good *boyessa* who doesn't have any variety at all from what we've been able to see. But when 2:00 in the afternoon finally rolls around, we're willing to eat just about anything that's hot.

Our abode is graced by the presence of Fadumo, one of the lovelier host country nationals, who somehow seems to have come to appreciate my particular brand of social grace.[150] [This is a different Fadumo, neither our *boyessa* in the bush nor the young woman from the Bar Lido.] Needless to say, having a girlfriend helps make one forget some of the problems inherent in dealing with the locals at large. She's sort of a recent acquisition and is different from the previous selection in that she's not a professional [meaning a prostitute]. She is one of a small group of girls from well-to-do families who like a good time but are more selective in who they spend time with, because of the fact that they don't have to work for a living.

August 19 journal entry. She's a damn good girl, but I get short-tempered with her sometimes. It's my fault, because I just get tired of trying to communicate. When Gilles was in town, he and Zenab, Fadumo and I had some really enjoyable times. I remember digging Fadumo the first time I saw her, and with her wig (paid for by guess who? What a soft touch), she's beautiful. [She was also beautiful without her wig.]

August 30 letter. Fadumo has run into a little trouble with her family because of the color of her boyfriend's skin.[151] She's been disowned, and her cousin has threatened to kill both of us (which is crap, since the men here are nothing but a bunch of pussies, completely undeserving of the incredibly beautiful women). Her brother stuffed her things in a suitcase and threw everything out in the street. She's also damn good to live on a PC salary, since, if one wants to ever enjoy himself here in Mog, he has to watch every cent about 90% of the time. She's had a couple previous white benefactors who had a hell of a lot more from the financial point of view than the old Goose does. [My nickname in college was Goose.] (The word *goos* in Somali, incidentally, means your dick—thought you might get a chuckle out of that bit of information.)

September 14 letter. Here, with the tribal traditions and all that, to get bounced out of the family is not too good.[152] So now, I guess she's all mine. And, one thing I've discovered is that PC salary does not stretch too far when I'm more or less providing for 2 people. As a result, I've cut down on certain things: one meal a day, not too many exotic evenings out on the town, etc. This austerity program is a grim necessity, however, if one is to be able to save up enough money to really throw a good one every so often.

This idea of having one girlfriend for an extended period of time (which looks like it's going to be the case) is kind of a new experience after having been a frequent customer out at the Lido— the wild-ass joint where the hookers, all beautiful girls, hang out and a band plays twice a week. When I sit down to think about it I miss the all-nighters out at the Lido ... It's a place that cannot be adequately described. It has to be seen, savored, and enjoyed before it can be understood.

September 7 journal entry. The biggest single problem is financial. There just isn't enough money to support myself the way I want and Fadumo, too. I really enjoy her company, but she shows no under-standing whatsoever of our financial situation. There's a rumor that we're going to get a raise of maybe 200 shillings per month, which would be a real boost. Right now, with paying all of Fadumo's expenses, just living, and trying to keep my thirst quenched (a real bad habit—I guess I just like to drink beer and shoot the shit too much), it seems like I'm always worrying about my financial situation. In addition I'm trying to save 150 shillings a month: 100 for the last week or 2 in the country, and 50 for Fadumo when I leave. It's tough. I think I'm going to have to cut down on the number of days/week I drink beer. Perish the thought ...

Right now I have plans for fixing the house up. Randy [will not be too interested], but that's OK. I'm going to start with curtains and an overhaul of the old PC table. I'll get another set of box springs and use it as a couch out in the other room. I'm also going to buy Bob Love's cabinet and a couple chairs. It's going to be a project that will take a long time, because of the financial angle, but the place will be a lot improved in the end.

Charley's bar has been fixed up real nice. We had a great night out there with the Germans. They really go to town. Jimison and I had a great talk about a basically hedonistic approach to life. I think I surprised him with a philosophy that seems to reject any overwhelming concern for the people of the world, because of their determination toward self-destruction. [As I matured, this attitude changed completely.]

[Last night Fadumo and I went to the Lido.] Momina Hot Pants (with Jimison) was accosted by cops outside, because she was wearing pants. A healthy conversation ensued in which Fadumo and Momina kept their cool and tried to explain what the best solution would be. Interestingly enough, the solution came when a police lieutenant, not in uniform, got out of his car and approached the discussion. The result was that Momina was let in—because she was there with me! I think the guy had seen me at the Police Academy or something. VIP!

September 21 journal entry. Fadumo is still here, behaving nicer than ever. I plan on spending part of the clothing allowance on her. She should like that. The last time, when I gave her cash instead of a gift, she went out and spent it on booze for her buddies. I have to say I learned something from that experience. Now I give her alternating 5 and 10 shillings per day, plus about 50 shillings once a month (in goods, not cash). My hope is to prepare her materially for bagging a decent man when I leave.

I took Mohamed Gebril to the hospital yesterday. He was really sick, and it was very scary. The [new PC] doctor was not really being too much help. (It's the end of an era [with Doctors Parsons and Shirrar gone]). He just told Tom Quinn to take him to the hospital. The preliminary diagnosis was tetanus (probably not the case), and he was having facial convulsions, drooling, generally feeling and looking like warmed-over shit. We spent about an hour getting refused admission by the capitalist-hating Chinese at their hospital and another 2 hours waiting at Digfer [must have been another hospital] for the appropriate doctor to show up. But eventually Mohamed settled in. The last report was that he was in better shape. I hope so, because he was really sick.

October 1 journal entry. We have no water in our house, and when it does come, the barrels leak so bad that by nightfall there is none left. No sense telling the [landlady]. That won't do one damn bit of good and we know it. The place also has fleas. Now we're just waiting to get into our new place.

October 2 journal entry. Fadumo has started a savings plan and the PC is reimbursing me 10 shillings per day for language instruction. Everyone is perfectly happy. I'm learning the language. Fadumo is getting her money. I have more money to let us do what we want.

The week is over. I'm eating at the Hayden's tonight, and a bunch of us are going to Gezira [a club] after that. Very good. Tomorrow we play Police [in basketball]. I'm 10 feet tall.

Starting to Work

> ✍ *I started to work almost immediately, first supervising recreation at the juvenile prison.*

Now I'm living in Mogadishu, working on a pretty generally free-lance program in sports and recreation.[153] I don't kid myself into thinking that I'm shaking up the entire culture with my efforts, but I have been generally pleased with the way things have worked out. I usually enjoy the work I'm doing now and generally enjoy the way life goes in general.[154]

Five days a week I work 7–9:00 AM at the juvenile prison, supervising recreation for the little devils. [I replaced a guy who was a teacher and went to the prison on the side.] It's the only definite schedule I have.[155] But sometimes the 6:15 rising hour and the 20-minute walk aren't the most appealing.

The kids are in the jug for anything from vagrancy to theft to arson.[156] Some are damn nice little kids, others are out-and-out shits. I supervise soccer and dodge ball (which they love because they get to try to clobber each other) and have worked at introducing exercises.

July 20 journal entry. Things at the prison are working well. Although it would be ridiculous to expect anything but gross confusion and disorder, the kids and I are getting along well. I really enjoy a lot of them. Ali Guli is starting to behave himself and stop pouting (knock on wood), but Mohamed and the other Ali are in isolation for fighting. That was a really wild day—I had to break up 3 fights. Volatile little devils.

August 1 journal entry. Ali Guli was released after having been in a year. He said he'd come to see me. I sure as hell hope so.

August 20 journal entry. Things are OK at the prison. The kids are learning to do jumping jacks, toe touches and pushups. The kids aren't too well-developed or too well coordinated, so it gets pretty humorous at times watching them try to struggle through 10 pushups or to get all 4 counts of toe touches in the right sequence.[157] They'll learn.

September 7 journal entry. The kids are just piling in—over 40 now, I

205

think. I've had several pretty rough days trying to handle so many of them. The leaders are gone. Ahmed Dufle got out, Issa is gone, and The Arab is leaving in a few days. It's good for them, bad for me. The athletes of the place now are not leaders and there are too many crybabies. Billeh is the only good kid left. We're still doing exercises, and they're getting better. I've just about given up trying to introduce volleyball, although maybe I will get parallel bars and chinning bars. Volleyball is just too difficult to teach 40 energetic kids who never play games with their hands.

Some days things go great.[158] Other days I get a lot of crap and end up dishing out a lot of it as well. One minute [the kids are] having a hell of a time, the next minute it is gang warfare.[159] Several of my very favorite kids got out—one after having been in for a year.[160] It's great for them to be out, but most just go back to the streets—where they don't eat as well, don't have opportunities to wash their clothes or themselves, and don't have classes in English or supervised recreation periods.

September 16 letter. Work at the prison has gotten very routine, although the little bastards manage to be unpredictable enough in their behavior that I never know from one minute to the next whether I'll be loving them to death or threatening them with group extinction.[161] I had fallen into the rut of never introducing anything new, just sticking to soccer and dodge ball, which made them know generally what's coming next. Now, we do those, but also do calisthenics and other stuff, trying to have something more or less new every day or two. It's been working out well. Last night, I showed some films, one of California and one of the Apollo 9 project. The one about California was OK, but the one on Apollo, which I'd never seen, was truly fantastic. The kids, unfortunately, know so little about space and what exploration has happened that they had no idea what was going on. I'm not even sure they understood when I explained it [in Somali].

September 21 journal entry. I've really settled into a routine, and sometimes it's frustrating … After one horrible week, prison is going very well. The kids were really acting up. The captains (especially Owezz and Hassen Ali) do very little to help things. One day, I got so ticked off because of their lack of enthusiasm, I just left. Boy, were they contrite. After I explained the situation, a couple of them must have spread the word, because the next time I went they were little angels. They've been damn good ever since. I had been letting them get to me a little bit too much. They wouldn't obey or would start fighting, and I'd get all worked up. Now, I usually let them work out their own problems, unless they're disrupting the game or one guy is bigger than the other. And when they talk back, I just ignore them or quietly tell them to be quiet.

I've also started introducing a little variety, where before we had just been playing soccer and dodge ball. Now we have *buugleh* [which may have been our name for dodge ball], exercises, ropes, chicken fight. They always piss and moan when I decide it's time to stop *buugleh* and do something else. But they end up loving it.

October 1 journal entry. I'm not at the prison this morning, because the little bastards acted up so much yesterday that I quit early, cancelled the plans for the movie last night, and am not showing up today. Maybe they'll learn what is considered acceptable behavior by the teacher. The way I look at it, if they make things tough enough for me, I don't owe them anything. When they get to the point they take things for granted, that's when they starting being shits.

It's starting to get hot again and by 9:00 the entire city is absolutely scalding. [162] And I get to work outside!

> ✍ *Working with kids at the prison had parallels with our relationships with the Somali people in general.*

The experience at the prison parallels my overall experience in this country, at least since moving into Mog …[163] Somalis are amazing, and I'm beginning to get a little greater appreciation for their differences. The people in Mog are completely different from those in the bush. They're a little more sophisticated, they know a little more, a lot more of them get a semi-decent education. This doesn't mean that they necessarily dig the white man too much, but the chances of having some sort of worthwhile communication are considerably improved. But they're also incredibly emotional and unpredictable. They can fly into a completely unforeseeable rage at the least provocation—or no provocation, as far as a foreigner can see. The next minute all is forgotten ... This trait seems to have rubbed off on me.[164] A lot of my emotional fluctuation, I'm sure (or at least I think I'm sure), comes from having to deal with it just about every second one deals with Somalis. You never know what's going to happen next.

I vacillate, virtually from one moment to the next, between real affection for the place and the people, and total contempt and hatred.[165] There are very few volunteers who don't have this sort of love-hate relationship with the place. (There are exceptions in my group: guys who pretty generally hate the place all the time.)

Constructing Basketball Courts and a Playground

✍ *In addition to riding herd at the juvenile prison, early in my time in Mog, I worked constructing two basketball courts and a playground. The basketball courts had been started by previous PCVs but never completed.*

August 17 letter. The job has gone well.[166]

July 20 journal entry. Last Thursday, with the help of 3 literally witless students, I started to work on the Ministry of Education's basketball court. The kids weren't too creative, nor did they do real good work. But we did get all the lines down for basketball; now we need a different color paint for volleyball. PCVs, by ourselves, [will have] to set up the standards and baskets (donated, interestingly enough, by the Red Chinese).[167]

At least now we have a place where we can play whenever we

want.[168] It was a little infuriating, though, to be working in the midday African sun, hung over as hell, with these wise-ass Somali students standing around making comments to the effect that we were wasting our time—building *them* a basketball court!

Yesterday Bonnewell and I put one of the rims on the backboard and then discovered that the standard at the other end of the court was completely screwed up.[169] The base is level, but the bolt holes for the backboard are about 6 inches higher than at the other end. It puts the basket on the very bottom of the backboard—and that just won't do. I'm going to have to square things up.

August 17 letter to family. The other court, in Afgoi (a town 25 km [15 miles] from Mog), was a completely different story, mainly because I worked with a counterpart from the Ministry of Education [Iman], and one of the teachers [Kassim] mobilized his students.[170] We crammed a hell of a lot of work into 4 or 5 hours, as Kassim, who wants to turn Afgoi into the best sports center in the area, did a great job organizing our labor force.[171]

We should have had a photographer from the PC press out there, because it was the model self-help project.[172] I had organized everything (usually necessary here), rounded up nuts and bolts, paint, nets, rims, etc, and the students went berserk. It was a gratifying experience to be directing a group of maybe 25 pretty intelligent students who had a fairly good idea what they were doing after being told and shown once. I had to do a lot of yelling, but things went very well. Like I say, I wish I would have had my camera. It was a 13-hour work day, but it felt damn good when the court was finished.

August 19 journal entry. I [put up the rims at] the court in Afgoi. It took a few hours, and the kids were genuinely grateful, although they have a hell of a lot to learn about the game. Not like the smart asses in town here.

> ✎ *Because it involved coordinating with other people, the playground project was more complicated—and frustrating.*

I'm working on a pilot project that will construct playground facilities for one of the lower class sections of town.[173] It's paid for by USAID [US Agency for International Development] cash and directed by the National Police.

July 15 journal entry. I'm working with the Police Youth Association, sort of hustling in general—designing playground equipment and concrete courts for volleyball and basketball, trying to track down a bulldozer, etc. Right now I'm trying to manage to run into Mohamed Hashi to give him the shopping list for pipe for swings and bars and things. He's stood me up 3 times. I'm trying. At least it's not my fault that things aren't getting done. We have to wait for the workers to finish the walls anyway.

July 20 journal entry. The PYA is moving along, despite the fact that I didn't run into Mohamed until today. They've already got the bulldozer working, and all the walls are just about done. Tomorrow we go buy pipe. Maybe! The place should really be nice.

August 1 journal entry. PYA has really slowed—no pipe in town, and I've been busy with the courts at the Ministry of Ed and in Afgoi.

August 16 letter. I've designed playground equipment, rounded up pipe for their construction, will supervise the construction of a basketball court as well as the construction of the swings, etc.[174] So far I have generally tried to keep my foot in the general vicinity of my counterpart's ass.

August 17 letter. The police playground project is more or less sputtering.[175] A week ago, my counterpart said that he had to get a bunch of signatures from assorted brass before the workmen could start welding the playground equipment. He said that he would let me know just as soon as they were ready to begin welding and that it would be a day or two. I haven't heard from him since. Tomorrow I go tracking. It's definitely time to get going, since the rumor is that the three months allotted to the project end pretty soon and that the guy in charge of USAID funds for self-help projects is kind of tough when it comes to extending deadlines.

August 19 journal entry. I've been waiting to hear from Hashi about starting welding. I found out today that he's at a sports conference in Kampala. No wonder I couldn't find him. It's time to get cracking or Gould [who must have been the guy at USAID] will cut off the money. I have the plans all drawn up. (Come to think of it, I wonder if the guys at the Police garage have lost them yet.) All we have to do is get going.

> ✍ *Two weeks later, frustration was building.*

The pilot playground project [is] something completely new and different to people here.[176] USAID is the financial backer, and the National Police provide general guidance on a more-or-less basis. They are easily the most efficient group in the country, but one that still on occasion more closely resembles a group of [slobbering] goofs. I'm sort of a top honcho, general and technical advisor (in that I've designed swings, teeter-totter, etc) and will be in charge of their construction as well as the construction of a basketball court.

Unfortunately, my Somali counterparts don't regard me in quite the appropriate light. For example, at a meeting the other day of all the big shots involved, we agreed to build the basketball court my way, considering minimum specifications, amount of cement, etc. I appeared this morning to discover that, somewhere between the time of the meeting and this morning, the guys had decided that it would be a great idea to pave the entire area, instead of just the space for the basketball court. Any idiot could immediately see what was wrong with this brainstorm. But these guys don't quite have the quickness of idiots, I guess.

Anyway, they were preparing to spread a layer of concrete maybe 2 inches thick over the entire area and call it good. I just about went berserk, but realized that talking was going to do me no good. I got up to the AID office as fast as I could go, reported what had happened to the guy who is controlling the fiscal flow, and we set out to round up the Somalis who had a little authority and had decided on the change in plans. Well, when the important white guy confronted them with [the change in plans], of course they said I hadn't understood what they were planning on doing. They said they had been planning to pave only the area for the basketball court all along. You lying pieces of crap. Small thing, but typical.

🖎 *And the next day ...*

August 31 letter. Yesterday I went over at 9:00 to meet with my counterpart. [177] (He eventually showed at 11:00.) Waiting were 3 or 4 laborers (we'll need at least 15 to even come close to the deadline), who had started on the foundation to pave the entire area. I had a little talk with them, discussing the problems that such a plan posed, and we switched to doing things my way. We set out a rectangular area, using awesome little tricks (to the Somalis, at any rate) like a 3/4/5 right triangle in order to make square corners. While we were taking a breather, up rolls my counterpart. We then proceeded to have a conversation (too complicated to go into in too much detail) that was pretty damn interesting. He just went crazy at the thought of following an idea produced by someone other than a Somali. (This is a guy who has had 2 or 3 years of education in the States.) I have to admit that at first I didn't respond too well, but then I calmed down, and he kept on going.

Quite reasonably I suggested that, since AID had donated over $3,000 to the project, perhaps they should be allowed some sort of token supervision so as to preclude any monumental screw-ups. He responded by saying that this was BS, that the US government had given the money directly to the Somali government to do with whatever it saw fit. US foreign aid is a pretty confused business, but it sure isn't that confused. Then, in Somali, which I assume he didn't think I would understand, he started presenting his spiel to the others—who I'm quite sure were sort of on my side, or at least as much so as they could be in an argument between one of their superiors and a white guy. He told them that I was trying to screw the project over and that his ideas should be listened to because he and the others would be living in the country long after I left. He told them that there are plenty of other governments around (such as Russia, China, Italy) that would be only too glad to sink a little money into the project if the US wasn't interested ... And so on and so forth.

I saw that talking would do no good and was proud of myself for settling down after the initial little spark of anger and just listening to this guy rave on. There was an engineer from the police there who wasn't a bad guy. He said that he had built a court 5 cm [about 2 inches] thick (half the thickness that I proposed) of un-reinforced concrete and that it was still in fine shape 8 years later. My conclusion, which was a pretty rational one (again, I'm kind of proud of myself for staying more or less logical), was that, by themselves, they would probably be able to come up with a reasonably good facsimile of a basketball court. It won't get done nearly as fast as if I was working with them, and it won't be as strong as if they followed my plans (that's my conclusion not theirs), but they will have a court. The playground equipment is just about finished, and any idiot (I think) could get the stuff anchored in the ground. My conclusion was that they didn't actually need me anymore. As far as they're concerned, they don't need my advice, and my supervision would be meaningless, since they're going to do it their own way. And it will be a completely Somali project, which, despite the reason for its having turned out that way, is a pretty good deal.

September 14 letter. In the end, my 6- or 8-week connection with the project contributed plans for playground equipment.[178] Now all I do is check by every few days to see that things are moving ahead and let the guy at USAID know what I've seen. No supervising at all.

Teaching Basketball Skills

> ✍ *I spent most of my work time in Mog teaching basketball skills to school kids and trying to help Somali organizations with their basketball programs. Like seemingly everything in Somali, it came with significant ups and downs. There were moments of great satisfaction mixed with extreme frustration.*

July 15 journal entry. I'll try to rejuvenate the idea of interscholastic competition started by [an earlier PCV]... Other possibilities involve clinics for both school kids and pros, as well as referees. There is a lot to be done. Just a matter of finding time.

> ✍ *In mid-August I wrote to college friends.*

This country has just been introduced to sports in about the last ten years, and they really eat it up, both as participants and as spectators. [179] Possibilities for night-time entertainment are extremely limited, and they go for anything that they can get all fired up and holler about.

August 19 journal entry. Today I started organizing my thoughts concerning interschool sports here in Mog. I'm going to try and work through Kassim in Afgoi at first, then form a committee and see what they think. Possibilities include clinics at the individual schools after games. There is also the possibility of hand-outs in elementary English ...

I sat in the office, learning Somali from Ii Warren [the PC newsletter, copies of which are in Appendix D]. I then worked compiling lists of schools for an interschool sports program and drew up sample schedules and tournament charts. It was a pretty full day. Now I have to prepare letters to schools concerning the possibility of forming leagues ...

I wrote to People-to-People Sports Committee in NY regarding their gifts of sports kits to Somalia.

September 7 journal entry. I got a completely innocuous reply to my letter to People-to-People Sports Committee. "We'll keep you in mind, etc." I've got to get into see Dan Hargat very soon and see about the stuff he has. [I think he worked for US Information Service (USIS).] He's doing things like giving sports equipment to SAFO [Somali American Friendship Organization].

My recent attempts to get hold of Mohamed Omar have failed. [He was the head of PE at the Ministry of Education.] He's stood me up twice. I have lists of the schools in Mog; all I really need from him is a list of the names of PE people. He's such a bull shitter. He's even said that he's planning on going around to schools with me. BS ...

I got a pretty good response from PCVs to my letter concerning sports assistance. Fred VonSaal wants a basketball court built in Borama. Several people asked for rules, suggestions for games, etc. I have a handout on soccer that I can send out. My big project recently has been writing a pamphlet on volleyball rules and skills. It's been a lot of work, but I'm just about finished typing the stencil. It could be much better in truly finished form, with pictures, etc. But this is a start. I've also asked Marks to work on a soccer skills handout. It just occurred to me that I should send out information on dodgeball [because it was so popular at the prison].

September 14 letter. [Interscholastic sports will be] a worthwhile project, I think, and once it gets rolling there'll be a lot of work.[180] Lately, I've been sitting on my ass waiting for return phone calls from people who never call and going to appointments with people who don't happen to be in the office at the time. That's OK. I have no real expectations. Just like to stay busy ...

Things go goddamn slowly here, and the results, if any, aren't too earth shaking. [181] But things are generally OK.

September 21 journal entry. I finished my opus on volleyball and sent it out, along with one on *buugleh* [dodge ball] and the earlier one on soccer. I've sent stuff to Krall and Bob Harley and given rims and nets to Riedy. I think I'll be able to help PCVs in the bush; some seem to be anxious for some help ...

They fired Mohamed Omar [as head of PE]. *Alhamdulilah!!!* [Thanks to Allah.] His replacement is seemingly quite the ball of fire. Old Mohamed had sold all the balls and other stuff, so I got a couple from Dan Hargat and gave them to the Ministry. The new guy anticipates forming a tournament of maybe 15 boys and girls [basketball] teams. He's really a mover. He sent out a circular to all the schools, singing the praises of a strong body, etc.

Today we started basketball classes. Eventually, we'll try to have a schedule worked out so that as many teams as possible can be included. Today went very well. Two teams were there. The guys had played a little, but not too much. What really pleased me was that they seemed to want to learn and didn't think they knew it all. No smart asses and a lot of kids who tried what I told them. I'll be working 9:30–11:00 and 4:30–6:00. It should be OK.

[Later that day:] I just got back from an afternoon at the Ministry teaching basketball. It may not work out like I was hoping. Yesterday, I went at 4:30, waited 20 minutes. Abdillahi showed up 5 minutes after I left. This morning, they gave me one of the balls that we'd gotten from USIS. They'd screwed up the bladder not knowing how to fill it up. I took both the balls, succeeded in filling one up, but the other one was screwed. I left them both at PC.

This afternoon there were 50 kids from 4 or 5 schools, with one ball for 3 of the schools! I learned something from watching the one school that "knew how to play basketball well." There are going to be kids who think they know it all. Hell with them. I'll work with the ones who feel I have something to teach them—and hopefully whip the pants off the smart asses when the time comes.

 ✍ *Slowly, my role with interscholastic sports took shape.*

September 22 letter. My energy level has been sort of low.[182] The hot weather is starting and, at the same time, I have to do a lot of walking. [Mogadishu is 2 degrees north of the equator. During the dry season it got so hot that, while walking, I would cross the street to get into the shade.] In addition, I'm playing ball a couple nights a week [and] teaching basketball several hours a day … Boredom is usually not a problem, and I enjoy the opportunity to keep busy …

The previous head of PE was a standout in the laziness department, even in this land of prime specimens of laziness … His replacement is a veritable ball of fire who seems eager to do a little better. I didn't talk with him until maybe 10 days after he had started on the job, but he had already started contacting schools about participating in a basketball competition. We haven't rounded up all the schools yet, but so far we have maybe 10 boys teams and half a dozen girls teams with quite a few more expected to participate eventually.

We are presently holding sessions, an hour per team, on the Ministry court (one of the ones I finished). A few of the kids have played before, but a lot of them have never even fondled a basketball. It's a fantastic opportunity to start the kids off learning things the correct way, and many of them are interested in hearing what I have to tell them. Most of them have seen me play at the Sports Center [Centro Sportivo] and are actually willing to concede that I may know a little more about the game than they do. In this country that is a tremendous concession to make—that someone might know as much about anything as an individual Somali does.

 ✍ *A week later I wrote:*

September 29 letter. So now we have 30 teams—half boys and half girls—that come to the Ministry 6 days a week for instruction in basketball.[183] [The kids were between about 14 and 20 years old.] ... It gets a little frustrating when a kid leaves the ground for a layup with the incorrect foot the hundredth time in a row, but I keep telling myself that I don't have any real stake in the thing. As far as I'm concerned, I'm there to teach if they're there to learn. Several of the teams have refused to have me as a coach—certainly due to skin color and religion more than anything else. I definitely know more about the game than anyone else in the country. No exaggeration. Isn't that scary?

But there are a few teams that are very enthusiastic. A couple may even turn out to have a few basketball players on them. The consummation of this crash effort at basketball training is going to be a tournament starting in about 3 weeks. Then we're going to go on to volleyball. As far as I'm concerned, it'd be damn nice if the people involved were more concerned with learning about the game and how to play it, rather than just thinking in terms of winning the tournament and then forgetting the whole deal.

At first it was pretty frustrating trying to teach kids [who had never played], but, after I realized that it couldn't be done in a day or two and after I did actually see some ability developing, it became pretty enjoyable.[184] This is saying something when one realizes that my job consists mainly of standing out in the tropical sun for 5 hours a day with my little hat, my shades, my black low-cut Converse, blowing my whistle—the use of which makes me official, you gotta understand. I alternate between bellowing at the kids and jumping up and down clapping my hands with glee watching little Mohamed slap 2 or 3 moves on someone and pop cotton [make a basket] from the head of the key.

There are a few guys helping me, some of whom are pretty fair players for some of the [adult] teams playing in the tournament.[185] The problem is that they've never analyzed what they do. They can make a layup, but they don't know how to teach someone else how to make one. Hopefully, when all the schools are rounded up, there will be a guy assigned to each who can take care of the immediate supervision of drills and stuff like that, while I provide the initial instruction and generally supervise the whole operation. It's a big order, but I've been getting good cooperation from the new head of PE so far.

October 1 journal entry. The basketball education program is turning out as must have been expected. Most of the kids have tired of being sent through drills to learn how to do layups, set shots and pass (none of which they can do). They feel they should be allowed to play all the time. As a result I've had one school come right out and say, and several others give very strong indications, that they don't need me as a teacher. They'd rather have a Somali who doesn't know enough to put them through their paces. Most of them are like Somalis you meet in other situations. They think they know it all, and they don't need a white guy telling them what to do. It is difficult being in a position where one has to rely on Somalis to get any job satisfaction.

Some of the schools seem OK; they've played more and maybe will learn more readily. But, of course, none of them are assigned to any of my 3 periods. It's generally a big hassle. Nobody is in it to learn about basketball; they're only preparing for the tournament that will take place during Ramadan. They see the guys play at Sportivo, but there is no real inspiration. They figure that in a week they'll be just like Ali Omar [one of the better players, who became a friend through basketball]. They have all seen me play, know that I'm really hot stuff, but still don't feel they should listen to me.

October 2 journal entry. The PE program might work out to a certain extent after all. If I can't always get satisfaction from working with the kids, I may get a little from working with the PE department. We had a meeting today at which we finalized the practice schedule and "elected" officials. Abdillahi is head; Ismail, Secretary; I'm adviser; and Abko and Ali Hamari [I think this was another name for Ali Omar] are something or another. Ismail and Abdillahi went to USIS and got *10* basketballs. I'd succeeded in milking them for all of 4. They're talking about uniforms, the whole bit. The tournament could work out all right after all.

I just got back from my PM session. I worked almost 2 hours with Disciplina. They are going to have 4 ballplayers who will be pretty damn good. We got to offense and defense both, and now all that is left is 100 hours of work. Right now, basketball is really turning me on.

October 2 letter. Some kids learn amazingly fast, and others seem incapable of learning anything.[186] I have from 9–10:00 AM (I finish that session with absolutely baked brains and scabs on my forehead from the sweet kiss of the tropical sun) and 4–6:00 PM.

… We get Fridays off from coaching (Muslim holy day), and the last week has just flown by. There's not much variety in the things I do, but the day is always full. In addition, although I don't always get a tremendous amount of satisfaction out of working with the kids themselves, it's been encouraging to see the enthusiasm of the new PE head and the other teachers [meaning adult Somalis acting as coaches], who are also volunteers. To get anyone to do anything in this country for nothing really says something.

Settled Into a Routine

In general, I was enjoying myself much more in Mogadishu than I had in the bush.

I'm enjoying working with sports because it's an area where there's a lot of interest among the people.[187] It doesn't make them any more willing to listen to anyone else's advice, but I've gotten pretty used to that.

August 19 letter. I kind of enjoy living in Mog, although I run through money like mad.[188] And I'm especially happy to finally have something to do that occupies more than a few hours a day. There's a lot less time to sit and think about the pointlessness of my situation when I have things to do, be they of earth-shaking importance or not. I don't kid myself about the overwhelming significance of what I'm doing, but I generally enjoy it. In addition, I'm learning to get along in Mog, learning the million and one ways to tell an arrogant jerk to go ream himself.

I would have gone back to the States if my proposed [move from the bush into Mog] hadn't been approved by PC staff.[189] I enjoy the relative anonymity of Mogadishu, where the people have seen a white guy before and, although maybe not falling instantly in love with the color of our skin, more or less let us go our own way. (There are exceptions, of course, when you appear in public with one of their women—when they always have a lot of snide remarks to make.)

My Somali is picking up, almost to the point of being conversational. Once they realize that you can more or less get along in their language, most of the people are either pretty nice to you or at least reasonably civil. I've also gotten used to going places where I have something to do, since the people don't dig white sightseers too much. I've learned a lot of the ins and outs of life in Mogadishu—how to get along with my position in this culture, where I can go without getting a lot of trouble, things like that that help make life a little easier. I'm staying busy. Not always productively, since it's frequently necessary to deal with a ridiculous bureaucratic structure.

August 31 letter. There are a few other things that keep time moving very fast.[190] I was eager to play some volleyball, having been away from it for more than a year. I went to the Russian Embassy, asked around, and have been playing with the dirty Reds twice a week ever since. (Please don't breathe a word about this to the State Department.) Many of them are damn good, and I'm rusty as hell, but it's still good to be back at it. The few who are teachers speak some English, and we've been invited over for vodka and Russian food on a couple occasions. We have gotten really blasted on a couple of occasions, as a matter of fact. The guys who play who work as advisers to the Army are none too friendly, but I imagine that they are not getting paid for being pro-American.

September 2 letter. Any real feeling of accomplishment is pretty well self-determined, and achievement is sort of a meaningless concept here anyway.[191] So I continue to work at it, working up a good sweat every day, studying the language, playing basketball with a team called Internazionale, ... getting drunk whenever finances permit (the cost of living is maybe 5 or 6 times as high in Mogadishu as in the bush), and trying to enjoy myself as best I'm able. One cannot expect to gain tremendous satisfaction from his relationship with the culture. It just doesn't work that way.

... The old routine has taken over. Get up at 6:00, work at the prison 7–9:00, hop in a taxi to get across town to the Ministry of Education for 9–10:00 basketball. Then to the PC office for anything from working on a motorcycle to hustling down funding by phone for a new set of lights at the Ministry court. Then it's an hour of language from 12:30–1:30 and a huge lunch. It's the only real meal of the day and consists of rice, meat, salad, vegetables, bananas, papaya, grapefruit, potatoes, lemonade. After that I take a nap and make another trip to the Ministry, 4–6:00. In the evening I play basketball, hit a movie (sometimes in English, usually in Italian at one of the local cinemas), get drunk if there's enough money, or just go to bed to get up the next morning at 6:00.

Sometimes it's pretty tiring, especially now, because the hot season is just beginning and from 9–10:00 it's really hot. Just to walk around is a completely enervating experience. I can always take consolation from the fact that it only lasts until April or May. I've just gotten used to the idea that I'm always greasy and have come to the conclusion that discomfort is principally a state of mind.

Playing Basketball

Basketball was growing in popularity in Mogadishu. A

team of Peace Corps Volunteers played a few games when we were first in the country. After I moved into Mog, in addition to coaching, I also played a lot. I was captain of my high school team, but my basketball career ended when I was cut from the freshman team in college. With this modest background, I was still the most experienced player in Mog, presumably in the country. Playing ball in Mog was a welcome outlet, but it was also a chance to associate with Somali players, many of whom were really pleasant to deal with. I told friends in a tape I recorded that I knew "hundreds" of people from teaching and playing basketball. I became quite visible, and lots of people knew me as Jama.

All the games I describe were played at Centro Sportivo, the best basketball facility in southern Somalia, probably in the entire country. It was an outdoor cement court, with six light bulbs to illuminate the games, all of which were played at night to try to escape the heat. And even though hundreds of people attended—more than a thousand for a big game—there were no bleachers. Everyone stood. We were struck by the fact that in pickup games, players frequently played in bare feet, either because they had no proper shoes or because they wanted to save them for real games.

August 17 letter. In just a few minutes I'm going to meet the captain of the Police basketball team (which we beat 3 times by a total of 5 points when we first got in the country).[192] We're going to talk about the possibility of my playing for them in an upcoming tournament. It is at their suggestion, so I'm game. Some of the guys are pretty decent (guys as well as basketball players), and I wouldn't have to play all the time, which is a good thing. I'm so out of shape. I've also been asked to play for an Italian team, but I'm not sure whether they're going to have a team or not. They're poor enough that they would expect me to be some sort of a star and that just ain't possible in my present condition. Besides, I think playing with the Police would give me the opportunity to get to know some young Somalis, something that is frequently very difficult to do. [For some reason that I don't remember now, the possibility of playing on the Police team did not pan out.]

> ✍ *On August 30 I wrote to a friend still in college with whom I had played intramural basketball.*

The local basketball season began last week with the opening round of a tournament.[193] Teams from the National Police, the National Army, a Soviet team, and a bunch of diddly little teams. Previously, the Peace Corps has always had a good team, but there just aren't enough jocks around anymore. (The relatively new group of teachers is an incredible bunch of non-jock, non-drinking people. All they do is sit around getting stoned and thinking they're cool ...)

So, I play for a team called Internazionale that has 2 Italians, 2 Somalis, a Czech, an Arab, a Frenchman, a *missione* (half Somali-half Italian) and me on it. The team name is appropriate. The language of communication is Italian, and, since it's not my team, I don't try to help out in the coaching department. The frustrating thing is that nobody knows even the slightest thing about the game. In our first game, we got ahead by about 10 points, the other team went into a man-to-man, and we had no idea what to do. I set a couple screens for guys, and then just gave up. I'd gotten no reaction other than a few funny looks. We're having a team meeting tonight, so maybe I can approach a few of the subtleties.

Our first game was against, get this, the Somali-American Friendship Organization (SAFO, what an anomaly), a team that I should have been on, since it has 3 or 4 PCVs, a couple of the Marines who guard the embassy, and 4 or 5 educated Somalis. I was never asked, though, and Internazionale asked me first. Since the Czech is our tallest man at maybe 6' 1", I figured we were going to be in for a pretty tough evening in front of maybe 400 - 500 people at Centro Sportivo. We played quite poorly, which was about par for the course since we only have 3 guys that are worth anything (and I have the gall to include myself in the 3, with my 8-month layoff and smoke-filled lungs). But the other team was really bad. We hung on and won by about 3. What a joke. Seriously, at no time did either team know what it was doing. I was awarded the MVP, having hit 1 out of about 8 or 9 20-foot slingshots, and a crucial free throw—for a total of 3 points!

September 10 letter. The Internazionale hoopsters are just going nuts.[194] After beating SAFO, we whipped some bunch of stumble-bums while SAFO lost again. I saw a few minutes of their game, and it was something. Never have I seen more incredible officiating. We had played the preceding game, and, when the whistle blew in their game, all too frequently you'd have absolutely no idea what the call was going to be—just that it was going to be against the *gaals*. During SAFO's game, Sherwood [I think he was a Marine guard at the US Embassy] was so pissed that he left at half-time. The nice, mild-mannered Somali coach of SAFO came within a hair of hauling off and taking a swing at the referee. It was really bad. Our team, though, somehow is getting pretty good. Nobody shoots well at all, but our defensive front guys just run their asses off, make some good passes, and we get about ²/₃ of our baskets on layups.

September 14 letter. [We are] rounding into shape.[195] I thought I'd never see the day. We play tonight, and, win or lose we'll be among the 6 finalists who'll play off. The only team that I think will make real trouble is the Police, who've been working together since before I got into the country. We've been playing quite a bit, and I'm actually sort of getting back into shape and sort of getting my outstanding, generally amazing, and fantastic ability back.

If it weren't for the fact that the referees don't have even the vaguest idea what they're doing (especially when one team is white and non-Muslim and the other is dark and devout), things would be fine.[196] I get so damn mad at the refs, though, that sometimes it's not too good. I've got to take it a little easier.

September 21 journal entry. I'm still playing for Internazionale. We finished first in our division and will be in the finals with Police, Hoga [the Army], Sovietici [a Russian team], Danta, and CSGL. We had a game with the latter that was really a joke. Of course, I got pissed at the refs. Ferrias [who must have been the Internazionale coach] had to take me out (or so he thought) to keep things calm. We played a practice game with the Police and won, to my complete amazement. We played so poorly I was beside myself. I didn't even believe the outcome when I was told. I thought we'd been slaughtered.

It's very frustrating to be playing with guys that do not try to learn. For the next tournament, we figure we'll be able to have an American team. Rich Gallagher is back [in Somalia] and he'll play, along with me, Leo, Jimison, Bill, Stephenson, Abbott, and a couple Marines. We'll be in good shape once we get in condition and get to know each other.

September 22 letter. Our big rebounder, who works for the Czech embassy, is leaving very soon, so we'll have a little compensating to do. [197] We're finally learning, I think, but I damn near have an attack before the end of each game, because of the incredible inability of my teammates to listen to even a small portion of my advice. A well-disciplined, steady ball club would be one of the best things as far as developing basketball in this country. It would provide an example that the beginning school kids as well as the professionals could learn from. After this tournament is over we're going to form an American team, with 5 or 6 PC and a couple of the Marines who work at the Embassy. We'll be able to play together quite a while, so maybe we can become that well-disciplined example I am talking about. It'll be nice to work with guys who will listen and work with each other instead of feeling that everyone's got the appropriate answer.

October 1 journal entry. Before Sochek and Khalif left for Czechoslovakia, there was one last ball game at Sportivo between us and Police. In amazing contrast to earlier games, the refs were OK and the fans were good. Because of the fact that the players on both teams are becoming friends, there was no trouble at all. We lost 41 - 36, but it was a really enjoyable experience.

✎ *I shared this reaction in a letter I wrote to the local English-language paper:*

Dear Editor, *Somali News*—September 27, 1969

It was my pleasure to participate in an exhibition basketball game at Centro Sportivo on Wednesday, September 25, between Internazionale and Polizia. Games played in the past at Sportivo (involving all teams) have been marred by incompetent refereeing, discourtesy on the part of the spectators, and open antagonism between the players of opposing teams.

The night of the 25th, however, was an entirely different and extremely pleasurable experience. The referees did an excellent job of officiating and controlling the game. The spectators, easily numbering several hundred, are also deserving of praise for enthusiastically supporting their own team and being courteous to the players on ours. The players of both teams played very well, and there was not a single incident of friction between members of the two teams. The game ended with the players on both teams (as well as the spectators and referees, I'm sure) satisfied with the game they had been part of.

Basketball is becoming more and more popular here in Mogadishu, and good sportsmanship, competent refereeing, and constantly developing ability on the part of the players are three elements that must be present if the caliber of basketball in this country is to continue to improve. The game last Wednesday served as a fine example of how far Somalia has advanced in all three areas over recent months. We can only hope that the example may be followed during the upcoming tournament that will take place at Centro Sportivo after the Fiera and during the following months.

Sincerely yours,
Jim Douglas
Mogadishu

October 1 journal entry. I am, though, getting tired of playing with guys who are basically not basketball players despite the fact they have a few of the skills. Rich [Gallagher] is going to play for Internazionale and played for us against Wil Wal on Monday. He was rusty, but what a treat to be back on the court with a guy who knows what he's doing. I can't wait to get USA back into action. Ferrias asked what our plans were for after the tournament and wasn't at all pleased when we told him "there'll probably be a PC team." He was kind of a jerk about it, as a matter of fact. I can hardly wait to quit.

October 2 letter. The Police are far and away the best team.[198] We had a practice game with them at the local Sports Center, were edged 41 - 36 and were lucky to have been within a hundred points. The police have learned a lot since I arrived in the country, and they used it all on us that night. My team is the second best in the country, but the Davis High School Blue Devils of old would have beaten us by a thousand points or more.

... The Somali athletes have fantastic potential as far as their ability goes, but the pervasive attitude is that they already know everything. (This is also true for the average man on the street about any subject that you'd care to name.) When this attitude changes and they get some capable instruction, they're going to take off. The African Games are in March, and I'm going to see if I can get in on the training and preparation. I would dig that, needless to say.

Our Decision to Move

> ✎ *The rustic nature of our living situation was starting to wear on Randy and me, and we set out to locate an upgrade.*

August 30 letter. My place in Mog is half-way between a dive and an all right place, with attributes of both.[199] [Actually, it] is basically a dump; the neighborhood reeks of goat shit and other garbage (sure it's ethnic, but, in this case, ethnic-ness doesn't count for much).[200]

We have the benefit of [a good] view [of the ocean], [a nice breeze], good privacy, and an adequate cook, but we've now gone the last 10 days or so without water.[201] But that makes life sort of interesting—trying to figure out where the next shower is going to come from.

… We've received absolutely no sympathy from the landlady (who is a 101% Muslim and just doesn't regard *gaals* as even being closely related to the human species) when we've complained about the fact we're paying full rent when we have water only about half the time.[202]

> *We found a new place under construction that was going to be very nice: three bedrooms, a balcony, tile floors. That place never materialized, but a much better place did.*

We got an incredible run-around on the house under construction near the office, and the guy finally confessed to John [Jimison] that he'd run out of money and that it would be months, if ever, before we could move in.[203] So, one Friday morning John, Rich, and I took off to look at a house John had found [a magnificent place right across the street that goes up the hill to Wardiglei from the National Theater]. It was nice, but the rent, we felt was too high … We talked the landlord down from either 1600 or 1400 to 1000, which split 4 ways [including Randy] ain't bad at all. We had a contract written up, attested, stamps at the Municipia—all after having wheeled and dealed our way to 6 months living allowance in advance.

The landlord of the old place was a bit upset when we informed him—on the day that we were moving out. He must have known that nobody but a *gaal* would be foolish enough to pay 300 for that rank joint … We found the new place just in the nick of time to get out of the old one without having to pay another month's rent. We were luckier than hell to find a nice empty place in the first place, because they've been very difficult to find ...

[We moved in on October 12, and] since then, we've painted furniture, had the Knauths' [the departing PC director's] furniture recovered, re-arranged, arranged, and now things look pretty good. The landlord built doors for Randy's and Rich's rooms and everybody's pretty happy ... About the only improvement still to make is for the landlord to follow up on his promise to put in new windows. The only small problem is that we have gone without water for a few weeks, but we've adapted pretty well, using the small tank on the roof filled with donkey water [that is, water delivered on donkey back]. We take baths in a bucket, but we've all done that more than a time or two before.

Gallagher, Randy, Jimison and I are the tenants, and the house is plenty big enough for all of us and our various partners.[204] We have a roof and are already plotting our first party.

... We lucked onto a fantastic place ...[205] We each have our own room, and we have an enclosed porch area, a dining room, adequate bathroom and kitchen ... We had to pay 6 month's rent in advance and sign a year's contract, so it looks like we'll be here a while.

Unlike at home, the weather here is starting to get hot again, but by now everyone's pretty used to it. The rains are due soon and they cool things off a little bit and so are very welcome. It gets steadily hotter, though, until next March or April. It's nice that our new house is always blessed with a good breeze.

A Rant

Despite the fact that things were going relatively well, I did send a rant to a friend from college.

I've been over here letting my mind rest for long enough that the thought of such a grind [he was attending medical school] is soul-wrenching to say the least.[206] I still have thoughts in the back of my mind of possibly showing up in my volleyball shorts and teeny bopper t-shirts (colored and with a pocket for my Marlboros) at Yale Law School, that haven for rebellious but promising law students. [I did go a year later, without the shorts, t-shirts or cigarettes.] I guess God only knows what I'll end up doing ...

Here, because of the language as much as anything else I guess, most of the time I'm in the dark. Some situations occur frequently enough that we can handle them easily. Examples are dialogues in taxis or teashops where some idiot has to see just how much Somali you know by discussing whether you are going to heaven, where you learned the language, whether you're Russian or American, etc. But this isn't being in tune with anything. And it is nice to be in a situation at home where it is possible to have things wired in a social context.

So, in a country where it's not the most rewarding experience to go down into the market place and get surrounded and laughed at, it's nice to have other things to do. There seems to be very little. There's one night club that has a band once a week, but it's pretty expensive. There's a beach club for the Americans that has the cheapest beer in town, so we go there pretty frequently. (The business of cultural exchange just doesn't work out to anyone's satisfaction here.) There's a theater that occasionally shows movies in English, and twice a week there are movies at a UN compound. There are a couple pretty nice restaurants where you can take your girl for dinner without getting remarks about her being a whore and a lot of jerks staring at you from the first bite of dinner to the last.

And that's it. Without a girlfriend you can imagine how bored you could get. It would be truly fantastic if the cross-cultural exchange would work out, but the tremendous majority of Somalis are so unreceptive to our trying to deal with their culture like they deal with it. As an example, it would be great if we could go to the market and bargain for stuff like they do. But, the first thing that happens is a huge crowd gathers around. Then some jerk quotes you a price that is at least 50% more than one he would quote anyone else. Then, when you try to bargain like the Somalis do (which is a hard thing for me personally to do because of the whole scene), everyone just laughs at you and fails to understand why these white guys with limitless wealth don't just cough up the money without trying to be assholes about it.

Enough of that stuff. In general, my reaction to the city has been different from the one I had to living in the bush in that I'm very seldom wound up about the fact that it's impossible to fit in. I've sort of accepted my place and am trying to get along with it as well as I can until my time is up—then I'm going to split.

Anti-Peace Corps Propaganda Starts

✎ *Even when the situation in Somali was relatively calm politically, the Peace Corps was the target of negative propaganda.*

August 19 letter. [Here's] what the rest of the PC and I have been doing since you took off, quoted from a mimeographed newsletter published by some Hoga [the army] asshole.[207] [The Army was a client of the Soviet Union and the Cold War was still in full swing.]

CIA PEACE CORPS [sic] INVADE SOMALIA: One of the Central Intelligence Agency's most notorious of spies, Peace Corps, have now completed the peaceful invasion of the Somali Republic. The number of the 'teachers,' who have arrived of late, are estimated to exceed a hundred and forty. [There were more like 29 in the recent group of teachers.] They are attached to the CIA's Peace Corps. Unlike the previous groups, their main mission is to corrupt. The target is the youth of the nation. Ferreting out intelligence secrets is their secondary task.

How do they come and corrupt the teenagers? As usual they enter the country under false pretenses. They are teachers, so claim the CIA. Most emphatically they are not teachers. The facts categorically refute their claim. The name of the profession is given to them as the best cover. It enables them to cross the road unmolested and come in direct contact with innocent children. They are assigned to various schools to teach English. Under the guise of education they have made a headway. They have taught and still teach a vast program of political ideology and propaganda. The most shocking part of the story is that they are not only teaching alien to the Somalis but also contrary to the Holy Koran: debauchery, alcoholism and homosexuality. (Let's hear it for the big three.) This is the real subject they teach. And at night the bastards look for our girls to entice them away.

If the government fails to kick them out of the country forthwith, the parents have the right to take the law in their own hands to protect their children.

✎ *There were a lot of changes among the 8s.* Zak was the first to leave Somalia, followed by Fritz and Duane. Baker had a terrible car accident and went home. Bill Shirrar, one of the PC doctors, finished his term and left. He was replaced by Dr. Sampson, an African-American who was career military and had his "head too high up in the clouds." Bill Thompson, the associate director who was in charge of our program, was on-again, off-again ready to leave. Jimison had moved into Mog to work at the national library and museum. John Marks had some quick training and was teaching in Beled Uen. Rich Gallagher, who was a member of the legendary 5s (the school construction team), returned to Somalia.*

September 10 letter. There's a pretty well-substantiated rumor being passed around that we're going to get a raise of 140, 150 or 200

---

* In addition to the newsletter describing these comings and goings (Appendix D), I also sent several letters on the subject. Primarily for the curiosity of those described, I'm also including the letters in Appendix E.

shillings.[208] That would be nice, to say the least. It's supposed to go into effect in a few months.

September 14 letter. We had a good party at Sam's last night.[209] It was unusual in that there were a lot of Somalis there who were good guys. There were several who had worked on the 9's program, and one really interesting guy [Abby Gedi] who had returned 4 days earlier after spending 4 years at Northern Illinois U. He has a goatee and a natural. [The only people in Somalia with natural hairdos were the Rahan Weyn. Other men kept their hair short.] We went out to the Lido after the party, and it was interesting to watch people's reactions to him. He was pretty drunk and outgoing as hell. I dug the guy. All the Somalis thought he was crazy. I'm afraid he's going to have a difficult time readjusting to his country. People just won't know what to make of him. Just like Suliman.

September 16 letter. Leo is at a meeting in Washington of all the country directors that is supposed to be extremely pregnant in content, with topics such as firing directors, complete re-orientation of PC, and other things that are not that easily sloughed off if you're a super-duper administrator.[210] Leo has turned out to be a pretty reasonable guy and may someday come close to being another Thompson. I would have never believed it, but I'm seeing it. He's sure no Felix [Knauth, the PC/Somalia director when we arrived]. Doggone it. Felix was such a good guy.

Assassination and Revolution

> ✒ *On October 15, 1969, the president of Somalia was assassinated by a member of his security force. The political changes that followed affected everyone, including the Peace Corps.*

Assassination

October 16 letter. We would have had [our house warming party] last night, but someone had to go and assassinate Abdirashid Ali Shermarke and send the country into a 6-day period of mourning.[211] The president was in Los Anod and was machine-gunned by one of the policemen who were assigned to protect him against just that sort of occurrence. The period of mourning is very interesting. The schools are closed, as are banks, a few offices, and "places of entertainment" (e.g., Lido, Gezira, theaters). But other than that, things are going completely normally. What this means is that the only people affected by the period of mourning are the PC. We're all out of work because of the fact schools are closed.

As would be expected, very few people are broken up about it at all, figuring that things may get a little better now that the old *mataha wenni* [literally "the big head," the nickname for the president] is dead. To a hell of a lot of people he represented the corruption of the way democracy is practiced here. As a matter of fact, it looked like there would be a small-scale celebration the night that it happened, but the government slapped a dusk-to-dawn curfew on the city and that eliminated those plans. It'll be very interesting to get the reaction of the world press, whom I expect will be more shaken by the turn of events than the people here are.

[When the president was assassinated], the Premier [I think this should have been the Prime Minister] was in New York to address the UN, so the President of the Assembly had to take over.[212] It seems that serving as leader of this country can be a pretty fatal proposition, so I'm not sure who's going to be eager to be named successor. Such a system makes progress difficult. Unlike in the US, where politicians get killed in individual incidents, violence and politics are always closely connected here. Things can get pretty rough, because the many different tribes have always had a history of violent solutions to their problems. Politics now are just an extension of tribalism.

The October 21 Revolution

November 5 journal entry. During the few days between the assassination and the burial, about the only noticeable changes in daily life were that the schools were closed and there was a nightly curfew.[213] People were talking about the constitutional process for electing his replacement, etc, and I think that a lot of people pretty much expected that the tide of corruption and greed would continue to flow unimpeded.

But—at 3:00 in the morning on October 21, the day after the burial, the Army took over in a coup that had obviously been very well planned and executed. We were awakened about 5:00 by several tanks crawling by outside—some going to the executive palace where [the former president's] widow was and some going to parliament, the two places that best symbolized the previous government.

It was a military coup, pulled off at first by the Army (almost certainly guided by the Russians who support the army), but then joined about noon by the National Police (supported by the US).[214] There was some shooting before dawn, and the tanks were rumbling around. But other than the fact that a few people got shot it's been completely without bloodshed.

There was a curfew last night from 4:00 PM, which makes life pretty goddamn boring for us, but the Somalis don't seem to mind at all what's gone on … Yesterday everything was closed except for the market, but today small stores and restaurants are supposed to be open. There will still be a curfew on tonight; it will probably go on indefinitely.

With both the Army and the Police in on it, I don't see where any resistance on any grand scale is going to come from. Like I say, most of the people are either in favor of the coup or indifferent to it. The members of the national assembly are in the clink, as are the heads of the ministries (e.g., education, for whom almost every PCV in the country works). The new government has promised to get things under way as soon as possible, but who knows what that means.

A Supreme Revolutionary Council was set up to take things over, to get rid of corruption, nepotism, tribalism, and all of those bad things …[215] The SRC is an anonymous body who clamped a curfew on the city just about as tightly as one could on a large city of Somalis. It gradually relaxed from 4:30 to 6 to 9. It is now midnight, about two weeks after the SRC took over. Gradually, the name of the head of the SRC was revealed, and a few days ago all the names were released. Because of the very mysterious nature of the SRC, the first days of the revolution were filled with speculation. Nobody knew what it stood for and nobody knew who was on the SRC—just that it was probably almost entirely Hoga [Somali for Army] and that the Russians must have had a little to do with the actual planning of the overthrow.

The day after the revolution, people sort of hopped on the band-wagon, running through the streets, hollering "Viva Hoga," etc, but it was more a matter of being excited for a party and for something different rather than out of any grand expectation that the new government was going to really improve things. People's best guesses were that the government would become a Russian-leaning total dictatorship that would continue to run things the way the previous government did, but with the graft sliding into a different set of pockets.

The day after the revolution, 13 Americans, including Leo, were kept cooped up in the [American] Embassy, having wandered in to see just what the hell was going on. At the Russian Embassy, on the other hand, carloads of Hoga and Russian personnel were hustling in and out like the place was a McDonald's restaurant. [A day or 2 after the coup, Jimson walked by the Soviet Embassy as a Russian was walking out the gate. John said, "Well done (implying they had helped organize the coup)." "Thank you," the man replied.]

The reaction of the people has been very interesting.[216] They have no conception of, call it, "morality of government." An outsider's reaction at hearing that there had been a military takeover would probably be one of "Oh, how immoral. Imposing a military dictatorship." There's none of that. Not even among the PCVs. For the most part, we were pretty disgusted with the previous government and saw absolutely no changes in sight. Something had to be done.

Although the military will almost certainly to be more conservative in the area of foreign affairs (i.e., start more border trouble with Kenya and Ethiopia), it will probably be a hell of a lot more efficient. The people regard the whole deal as sort of a party, something exciting, something they can talk about. As an example, our girlfriends, for the most part, are excited about the change in government, because they think that they'll be able to wear western style skirts in public without being thrown in jail. (A reaction based on nothing short of the highest imaginable political ideals.)

✍ *Rumors abounded in the first weeks after the coup.*

At least the guys I live with are excited for the takeover because Hoga dislikes the US, and the PC is taken as the number one symbol of the debauched imperialism of the white world. We figure that the chances are fairly good that we'll be given the boot. The fact that we certainly hope so must be some indication of just how much we enjoy being here.

It's begun to look as if the government will become more conservative, with rumors being bandied about that all liquor sales will be banned, no more Lido or Gezira, one year in the clink for girls in short dresses.[217] Other good rumors during the 3 or 4 days after the takeover were that the Coca Cola factory had been burned down as a symbol of neo-colonialism and that a group of wild men broke into the US Embassy and smashed the radio.

The government moved very slowly, furthering the mysterious air that surrounded the takeover. Early on, there were general statements concerning what the SRC stood for, but nothing specific. There was contradictory information concerning the future of foreigners: one statement would say that foreigners whose presence was detrimental would be expelled, and another would say that the government planned to honor the obligations made to foreigners whose presence was beneficial. So, by reading between the lines, one could reach any conclusion one wanted about the future of PC/Somalia—needless to say, we were sure that we would be leaving any day. Jimison even went so far as to get his stuff arranged so that he could split quick if a soldier came to the door with our walking papers in hand.

We were back to normal rapidly, however—surprisingly so. The schools were back in full swing only 4 or 5 days after the takeover, and offices, stores, etc were only closed a day or 2. It was amazingly efficient as far as we were concerned. The only thing abnormal was tanks and soldiers all over town, but they never did anything to make their presence felt. They were just there, but they never had to do anything. They're still all over the place. Ali Omar [the friend and basketball player for the Police who was also a cop], for example, has been working days and nights guarding the streets ever since the 21st. Needless to say, when I run into him he gets a little bit of ribbing about there being order in the streets when he's on the job.

🐚 *The SRC started to implement new policies.*

Although they have moved very slowly, so far the government

has done a lot of good things, although few are of monumental proportion. They've banned the export of charcoal, they've ordered the confiscation of all privately owned guns, they've named the new ministers (almost all of whom have degrees from the US or Italy), they've reclaimed a bunch of cars that the previous government had passed out to its friends, and they have begun to collect taxes in the bush. To a lot of people, they've definitely symbolized a shift from the previous corruption. They're ruling indefinitely, assuming all powers of all branches of the previous government, but promise free elections when things straighten out. Other countries took their time recognizing the new government, but a lot of countries have done it now. Every day there are 2 or 3 pictures in the Somali News—renamed the *October Star*—of General Mohamed Siad Barre [head of the SRC] being *salaam*ed by an ambassador from somewhere or another.

The government has established a public relations office, where people are urged to complain about people or practices of the previous regime or of this new one that are contrary to the national interest. [Mohamed Ibrahim Egal, the Prime Minister in the previous government,] has been under house arrest since the coup, and there have been rumors that he has committed suicide or been killed by the Hoga guarding him. [He did not commit suicide and in the '90s served as the president of Somaliland, which was the northern part of Somalia until the country dissolved in 1991.] Joe Candiotti, whose house is behind Egal's, said that he heard a single shot at 3:00 AM one morning right before the rumors started circulating. [Joe was the Director of English at the Training School for Animal Health Assistance.] Nobody knows, of course, and the *October Star* printed an article discrediting such rumors. It would make sense to have a big show trial to show just what should happen to corrupt people.

John Bainbridge was thrown out of the country, but was then rearrested just hours before he was to leave. [Sounds interesting, but no one in our group remembers who he was.] Apparently, Egal had been slipping him a little capital out of what the Prime Minister had been able to suck in through various devious means. The guys in the Gezira Club band left, but nobody knows whether they were thrown out or just felt that they should take off considering the hot water their benefactor was in.

My Ongoing Relationship with Fadumo

November 5 journal entry. The girls are still here.[218] Sahara is getting easier to live with, and Fadumo is usually pretty well behaved. [Fadumo can get erratic] when she gets drunk, but that hasn't been too frequently lately, with my financial situation like it is and the curfew on at midnight every night and no bands in town. Her teaching me language just didn't work out. It was just too big a hassle for me, and it was too much pressure to do it every single day or else lose that much money. Besides, my interest in the language has more or less waned. I can get along in the normal day-to-day existence [in Somali], can talk to most of the [adult] basketball players in Italian or English and could generally give a big rat's ass about most of the rest of the people.

Fadumo is now learning English, mostly from me, but with help from the other people in our house. [She had no formal education but was very smart.] She's a good student and I'm planning to finance a 400 shilling intensive course at the US Information Service school starting in January. Her progress has been amazing; within a month she has gone from learning the alphabet to reading and writing such ethereal sentences from the New Oxford English Course for East Africa—Book One as "The boy is looking at the fly," and "This goat is standing on two legs."[219]

We've had several conversations about what she's going to do when I take off, and her conclusion that she'll have to become a hooker doesn't fill me with any great joy.[220] (Her family—or at least her neurotic brother—is no more excited about me than they were a couple months ago.) I've toyed with the idea of trying to help her get set up in business, but that would be a hell of a hassle. Discovering that USIS had English classes (PC only teaches government employees) was a godsend, since, if she can read and write when I take off, she can learn to type and get a nice spot like Sahara has for 800/month.

Working as Normal—Sort Of

🖎 *It was uncertain how the coup would affect our work as Peace Corps Volunteers.*

November 17 journal entry. I haven't been to the prison since the death of the President, and I'm not sure if I'm ever going to go back.[221] They wouldn't permit it for a couple weeks, because of overcrowding, and now I have the opportunity to work with a couple of the intermediate schools in the mornings. I certainly prefer working with the school kids than with the jailbirds. They're a hell of a lot smarter and most are reasonably motivated to pick up what the teacher has to say. [This is my last reference to working at the prison.]

Now there is a 2 week vacation between terms, and attendance in the case of some schools has been sort of bad, but a lot of kids are learning about ball. Right now, I have Villagio [a school] in the morning at 8:30, which is another good thing about not going to the prison: I get some more sleep and get to indulge in a little breakfast. Considering the fact that I'm down to 141 pounds, I'd better work on getting as much food in my stomach as possible.

The kids from Villagio may be the best team in the entire bunch, which isn't bad considering the fact that they'd never even seen a basketball 2 months ago. Industriale has gone the way of Hodan— they know it all and can't be bothered with showing up every day. PC [this must mean something different from Peace Corps] doesn't have enough players who can show up at the same time. In the afternoon, Disciplina is sort of at a plateau and Marittimo has attendance problems. Both would be pretty good if they reached their potential, but they could never match Villagio Arab, who I more or less expect to win the tournament after Ramadan. Those kids are smooth and frequently they listen to advice. Whenever the Peace Corps team plays anyone, I urge the kids to come to Sportivo and see how we work things, because the offense and defense are the same as what I'm teaching them. A lot of them do come and it's interesting to hear all the kids yelling "Jeeem."

The plans for the Ramadan tournament [for schools] were scrapped for several reasons. We had several lengthy meetings to discuss it, which were mostly chaos and stubbornness. I'd make a suggestion and people would dump on it. I'd worked pretty hard, I felt, preparing the kids for the tournament and had worked out schedules, sample regulations, other suggestions. As could have been expected, at one of the meetings people jumped to the conclusion that I was telling them what to do, which, in this new era of anti-neocolonialism, just doesn't go.

In several cases, I got pissed off because I thought that they had their priorities all screwed up. In the end, the [school] tournament was postponed because 1) there were no uniforms. As far as I was concerned, this was easily overcome, but no one else thought so. 2) There were too many teams (intermediate school boys, secondary school boys and girls, and Seria A [the best adult league]) to get all the games in playing 2 games a night, which seemed necessary because the games will not start until 9:00 (because of the fast) and the kids will still have to get to bed in time to make school in the morning.

So, there will be a tournament of 12 teams from Seria A (double elimination, which I introduced) and round-robin for 8 girls teams selected from the girls who have been working out at the Ministry. The proceeds will go to buy uniforms for the school kids whose tournament will come after Ramadan (hopefully in January so I can go to Kampala for Christmas). I think that the proceeds of their tournament will probably go to finance the national team's trip to Cairo. (I would sure welcome the idea of working with the national team. I'll just have to bide my time and see how things work out. For the most part, the guys have gotten just about as good as they're going to get without some coaching.)

Last night I went to a meeting of the Basketball Federation as PC representative, having severed my relationship with the bald-headed fascist's Internazionale squad a few days earlier. [I guess I didn't think much of the Internazionale coach.] The meeting was interesting. Everybody shouted and hollered for a little over an hour concerning the necessity of having new elections for officers, considering the spirit of the revolution and all that jazz. Then that subject was miraculously dropped (in time for breakfast!) and they got all wound up about something else. Finally, the tournament was arranged. The head of SAFO's team and I drew up the brackets—everything above board, of course, seeding October 21 and Indipendenza (both comprised of ex-Hoga and ex-Police), and then Orfano and CGSL instead of PC (who are certainly stronger than anyone), and SAFO [Somali-American Friendship Organization] (who if they get organized, won't be too bad either).

🖎 *A short while later, I wrote:*

I was serving as adviser to the Interscholastic Sports Commission [ISC] as well as to the Basketball Federation.[222] Needless to say, neither group was listening too well. Things seemed more or less ready to go. It seemed to have been decided that the ISC would get almost all of the money [from the tournament]. Well, the Basketball Federation did not find out about this until the night before the tournament was to start. It seems that Abdulkadir had made their decision for them. Boy, the shit hit the fan. We had to have another meeting, of course, which accomplished nothing in maybe 1 1/2 hours of screaming. So, as of the first night of the tournament, nobody knew who was in charge of the money and no one knew who was to get the proceeds. I was told that Hoga was collecting the opening night, and a Hoga officer made a speech before the game saying that they would administer the money to the school kids and to the Federation.

The next night, the ISC had decided that, if they weren't going to be put in charge of the money, then they would just pull the girls out of the competition. The Federation had a meeting to discuss what was to be done about this turn of events. I didn't have the strength to sit through another one of their meetings, but the next day (yesterday), it had been decided that the proceeds would be split 50-50—the only solution, and a very obvious one at that from the very beginning. People from each group would collect the money. Now, if we can just manage to get the money to the bank where it might eventually be put to good use.

This example of just letting things work themselves out was not the only one. This had a way of working out fairly well, but I had nothing to do with events as they ultimately turned out. I'm serving as an advisor whose advice is not being listened to. I think that I'd probably consider myself more of a PE teacher than an advisor.

Hadi and I were supposed to get together and make a big chart for public display and something to stick outside telling the public who was playing that evening. He stood me up twice, and I sort of wondered how the thing was ever going to get done. Last night he informed me that he'd finished both things. I didn't see it, so it might be a lousy job, but the point is that, when it came right down to it, he seems to have wanted to do it by himself. Like I say, I think I'll stick to teaching the kids.

🖎 *Later, I summarized where my work had ended up.*

I had helped organize the basketball tournament and was working pretty conscientiously the first week or so, serving as general honcho and adviser.[223] But it was like so many other things. They have an incredible string of meetings, at which each of the 30 guys present is sure that he has the answers. The chief light-skinned adviser is, of course, never asked what he thinks about anything. After maybe 4 hours, things are still completely unsettled—mainly because no one ever shuts up long enough to listen to any of the suggestions. And the meetings keep right on coming. I was just going nuts watching them completely ignore the obvious solutions. Then—after all of this—they come up with the answer. I've about given up on trying to affect anything concerning administration of athletic programs. The people in power just aren't interested in listening. So, now I save myself a lot of grief by staying away from the meetings. I just make casual suggestions to the right people, not actually caring whether anyone listens or not. As an instructor, though, there are a few people who do listen. I'll continue to work with the kids.

Also, although I'm not sure how things are going to work out, I think that I'm going to be working with the national team when it starts preparing for the Pan-African games in Cairo in March. The players here have such fantastic potential, but they've never been coached at all. For example, they have no idea how to play a man-to-man defense. They have no set offense. They just play. With a little coaching, there would be some truly amazing ballplayers here. Maybe this is one of the reasons I keep trying to the minimal extent that I do.

Initial Impact of the Coup on Peace Corps

Two and a half weeks after the coup, I wrote:

All of the PC teachers came into Mog for a conference but then it was cancelled, because the Ministry of Education was not excited about the idea of cooperating with Peace Corps because of "the growing suspicion of PC in Mog."[224] As Thompson said, "Why don't they decide what they're going to do about us and cooperate or ship us out?" I, myself, for the most part have sensed almost the opposite. The revolution has kind of cleared the air as far as the people are concerned, and a vague spirit of optimism even seems to include friendliness toward us.

🐦 *But the government paid us increasing attention.*

Even after the revolution, the people have certainly been no worse off than before.[225] And if anything the average guy on the street actually seems friendlier to us. The forces of the state, however, have turned into Big Brother himself, and it's not too cool. And it seems as if the PC is getting a hell of a lot more than its fair share of harassment. Enough that the old song "I'll be Home for Christmas" seems to apply. Examples: Guys are being followed. People's houses are being watched. People who know individuals in the PC are being asked to spy on us and report concerning where we buy our marijuana and heroin and how we get our secrets out of the country. [There was some marijuana, absolutely no heroin, and no PCVs that I knew had access to government secrets.]

November 13 journal entry. It's been interesting to compare notes with the other volunteers here in Mog.[226] Dennis Viri sees the same guy sitting outside his house every morning. Dunne sees the same guy no matter where he goes. We've had a car parked outside our house, with two guys in it from 10–12:00 at night. When we took Jimison over to Bob Siegel's, there was a Mercedes parked in front with two guys just passing the time of day inside. The cops took Lul [Thompson's girlfriend] in to see what she knew about the PC spy ring.

Leo told us at a meeting of all the volunteers who happened to be in town that there are a lot of indications of our imminent departure, but that "the dust just hasn't settled." When Ambassador Hadsel went to talk to the new Minister of Education about the Libya transfers, he was told that the Minister was not prepared to make a definite statement at that time. [These were presumably PCVs expelled from Libya earlier in 1969, after the coup led by Muammar Gadhafi.] Since then the rumor is that they have been definitely refused. There is also a rumor that the huge group of volunteers that was scheduled to come in the spring will be up for the big decision within the next two weeks. Then we'll actually know where we stand—although we have a pretty good idea right now. Leo said that, if any of us feel that we are unable to work within the repressive system that seems to be developing, he would urge us to leave and promised to do all he could to see to it that our way would be paid home,

I, for one, expect that we'll be gone quite soon. If we stay that long, I'll stay to finish the basketball tournament. Somehow, the idea of beating a team named October 21 [after the date of the coup] is pretty appealing right now.

A few nights ago, the Russians were [at our apartment] for some solid drinking. When it came time to say goodbye (I wasn't there), apparently Ruben [one of the Russians] got kind of emotional about the goodbye. When Randy wondered just what was going on ("After all, we'll see you again."), Ruben said "Don't be too sure." Maybe he knows something.

November 15 journal entry. The PCVs have a hunch that the staff knows more than they're telling us, judging from the way they laugh off certain questions and then have one meeting after another.[227]

A very interesting order has come down. Employees of government ministries are not to extend invitations to or receive social invitations from non-Somalis. Gee whiz. You'd think they didn't like us or something.

Radio Mogadishu said that Egal spent 23 million shillings from the end of April to the time of his arrest in October. Might have been corrupt.

Local people have been thrown in jail for drinking.

A friend of John's, who has an uncle on the SRC, has been having very interesting conversations with the old boy concerning the future of our organization here in the Somali Democratic Republic. The word is that there is a group of 10 Russians (call them spies, if you like) who have been doing a little checking on the activity of various foreigners. There is to be a meeting today of these men with the 4 top guys on the Council to discuss just what's been happening. It'll be very interesting to learn what comes out of the meeting.

Randy's speculation is that we'll be allowed to stay until the end of the school term. If that's the case, we can take our full leave starting in December, and get back just in time to be thrown out. However, with all the harassment recently, I wonder if some goon in a uniform just might show up one day inviting us to leave immediately. That would also make sense.

Just for the hell of it, Gray and Love strung a toy phone between their two houses. Kind of stupid, actually, with the present set of idiots in power. Some of the neighbors must have been interested in trying to score some points with the new administration, because the cops hit both houses about midnight and had to have everything very carefully explained. It was about a three-hour scene (and even involved Gray having to explain how his tape-recorder wasn't a radio) that could have been chock full of laughs but wasn't, apparently.

Dan Krall's Departure(s)

    The way the new government treated Somalia 8 Dan Krall when he tried to leave the country was a memorable harbinger of a new stage in our relationship with the Supreme Revolutionary Council.

November 15 journal entry. The Saga of Dan Krall, though, is what's made my mind up for me.[228] It's the thing that has convinced me that I'm tired of the way things are going, the thing that has me wondering why I'm putting up with the BS they've been dishing out. Kraw [our nickname for Dan] decided last Saturday, on the spur of the moment, that he'd rather be in Cerro Gordo, IL than in sunny downtown Mogadishu. Since the new government took over, there has been a considerable increase in the amount of paper work required to get out of this toilet. But, determined as he was, Kraw hurried around to get tax forms filled out, releases signed, etc, and it looked like he'd get on the plane OK. We had lunch at Capo's, a few beers at Thompson's, and headed for the airport, getting there at least 45 minutes early. [This was in the pre-security era when 45 minutes ahead of time was plenty.] We didn't realize the extent to which they were going to be after him. It took him a little while to get his stuff weighed, of course, and there was some trouble with his money or something, but it finally came time to check his stuff.

The SRC must have read about custom checks somewhere, but what they didn't realize was that most countries have them for incoming passengers. Well, Kraw's stuff sat around for quite a while, along with that of a Mennonite Mission family who were going to Nairobi on leave. They finally got around to it, and, of course, had to check everything—even the inside of an ostrich egg. Then there were minor problems with his passport, etc. And it was unfortunate, but they just didn't manage to get his stuff cleared in time for him to make it onto the plane.

It seemed a little like harassment then, but the best was yet to come. Krall was a little upset, but took things in pretty good stride. He was pretty quiet for the next few days, which he spent making certain that things were going to be exactly in order. (He'd been told that the hang-up the first time was because of a problem with a tax form.) The flight was to be Wednesday, and the guys gave him a sendoff at the Lido Tuesday night.

The plane was to leave at 1:45, and we got to the airport at 12:15. In plenty of time, but they did it again—in even grander style. They checked his baggage, looked at his passport, but decided that he was in big trouble because he didn't have a boarding pass!! He and Bill had to speed back into town, get permission from the Ministry of Foreign Affairs, and get back to the airport just in time to have the civilians do a pretty understanding check of his stuff and hustle him on the plane just in the nick of time. He'd been hassled and harassed enough for any 12 departees, but at least he was finally on the plane.

Sherwood, the MSG [likely Marine Security Guard, whose assignment was to guard the embassy], was also on the plane, after an initial run-in over the $200 cash he had on him. Two military honchos took him aside and demanded that he hand the money over to them. He said, "Sure, boys, but let me phone the embassy first, OK?" They said, "Oh, sorry, sir. Get right on the plane." We could never guess into whose pockets the money was going to go if he handed it over. No corruption in the new government, huh, guys? But Krall was finally on the plane and off to Roma and Cerro Gordo, having been the last guy on the plane by 10 or 15 minutes.

So, we piled into the PC truck and headed back into town. However—just as we were leaving the airport, a Jeep-like vehicle with government plates screeched to a halt and a little shit with a swagger stick and shiny khakis sprinted into the terminal. Uh-oh, we said. We drove down the road back into town and stopped where we had a good view of the runway. Maybe he'll make it. The big bird taxied down to one end of the runway, turned around and pointed to Roma and freedom. And then it slowly taxied back to the terminal.

Well, we thought that we should hustle back to the terminal and see just what was going on. Tom Fitzpatrick, chief advisor to the National Police, was at the airport to see that people got on the plane. He had kind of a tough job ahead. The plane taxied back to the terminal, they wheeled up the stairs, and several officers and a whole bunch of self-important fools in khakis [I estimated 50 at one point] hustled out to the plane, accompanied by Thompson and Tom Fitzpatrick. The Italian crew, apparently, was baffled by what was going on. They must have been thinking, "All this trouble to take one PCV off the plane?" Dan said later that, when the plane started back to the terminal, he had a damn good idea what was happening.

He was escorted into a little room by 4 jerks with bayonets protecting him from any attempted seizure by enemy forces. Tom F. had asked at the plane whether he was being held under arrest and received no answer. He then asked whether he was being held without representation and still got no answer. Finally the big shot sergeant asked "Who are you anyway?" His answer—"Representative of the US Embassy"—obviously didn't make too great an impression.

Anyway, Kraw was held in this room while the idiots in residence checked through his old correspondence. We all took off, having had our minds pretty well made up concerning our future relationship with the new government.

Next, they had Kraw, Bill [Thompson], and Dr. Sampson follow the guy in charge to military headquarters where they were told "Sorry for the inconvenience. You are free to travel as you please." Since they didn't arrest him for anything, it seems like it was strictly harassment.

We figure the government feels they probably made a lot of political hay by pulling him off the plane like that—the idea being that everybody will say "Boy, the Peace Corps really must be doing horrible things if the new government won't even let them stay on the plane." The last minute deal also might have been the result of a [division in the thinking within] the regime. One group of officers said, sure he can get out of here, while another group wasn't notified until the very last minute. The first time he didn't get on the plane, he was told that the SRC had phoned an hour earlier and said that he was not to get on the plane. It seemed that the people in power had not decided just what to do with him.

PC staff suggested, and Krall agreed, that the Marine house [where the US Marine embassy guards lived] might be a good place for him. The place has diplomatic immunity, and the local idiots wouldn't know where to find him to dish out any more of their trivial little harassment. So Kraw spent the next two days drinking beer, doing physical training with the MSGs, and sitting by the pool. When Friday came, he was driven to the airport in the Ambassador's car, and got very little BS at all. He finally got off.

There are other things that made us wonder just what the hell we're doing trying to work under such a small-minded regime.

While Krall was staying with the Marines, a pair of guys (not in uniform) came to Thompson's asking for Mr. Daniel. They said they were students of his at the PC school here in Mog. Right [since there was no "Peace Corps school" in Mog]. Later in the day another pack of dogs, this time in uniform, showed up wondering where Mr. Daniel Wayne Krall was. Bill wasn't sure but thought that he was at the Beach Club. The group returned shortly and—funny thing—they hadn't been able to find him. The SRC still couldn't agree what to do with him. One faction said that he was free to go, and another wanted to check him out some more.

... The latest report from John's source whose uncle is on the SRC: They had their meeting with the 10 Russian informants.[229] Unfortunately, one of the generals stuck up for us and a couple others felt that more investigation should be made. The Russian experts had informed the group that we were involved in espionage and other information-gathering activity. Unfortunately, the Somalis didn't buy this info. Instead, they are to have another meeting in 5 days to go over things again. In the meantime, according to John's friend, there are 5 "spies" assigned to investigate the activities of the Peace Corps, specifically observation of houses and the office. I'm going to keep my eyes open in the next week. I imagine that a Somali acting as a spy would be a fairly comical sight.

> ✎ *In the middle of this craziness, John Marks' parents came to visit him.*

Marks' parents got here yesterday morning, about 3 hours after Dan took off.[230] Their first night, we went to Azan's for dinner and ended up paying one of the most incredible bills I've ever run into—something like 240 shillings [$35] for 6 people. We had a couple bottles of wine and several plates of antipasto, but we weren't sure that the prices had been on the menu. And, to boot, Fantas were 1.50 shillings. Scale that up proportionately and you're paying something like a million shillings for a steak. Lulu was with us and, boy, did she snow Marks's folks. ("She's so alive, so dignified, so beautiful.") John and I just about gagged.

The next day we drove out to Afgoi for a quick look at the bush. Driving through the backstreets didn't exactly thrill me out of my mind, but Mrs. Marks dug it, to the tune of "Watch those chickens" and "Don't stop too quickly, because a bunch of kids are chasing after the car." She also was pretty sure that one of the reasons we often get a bad time is because of the colonial oppression that the people experienced for so long! The world needs idealists, though, and thank god there are a still few left. Somalia cured one guy of his idealism. John put it very well: It's one thing to know why the shit's there, but another to have to walk through it every day.

Coaching Continues

> Ramadan affected my coaching more than the political situation did.

December 16 letter. Recently there has been a series of interruptions in our otherwise flawless [sports] program.[231] Once a year, during the lunar month of Ramadan, all devout Muslims are expected to fast from sunrise to sunset. They're not allowed to eat, drink, or even swallow their own saliva. Nowhere near everyone fasts, but they all say that they do. As a result, we had to discontinue our PE program, because it's kind of tough to expect kids who aren't going to eat or drink anything until dark to sweat their butts off from 8 to 9:00 in the morning, running in their bare feet up and down a basketball court.

Things had been going well, kids were learning fast, and I'd gotten things figured out pretty well.[232] After the break, it'll be like starting all over again.

I have had a bunch of kids ask me when we can start playing again.[233] My opinion is that, if they want to go out there and bust their asses and then go without food or water until dark, then I should certainly be willing to give them whatever I have to offer. Abdillahi Said [he must have been the Education Ministry's head of PE] is not hot for the idea.

As a result of this unrequested vacation, my activity during the last month has been pretty much restricted to seeing how much sleep I can get as I attempt to gain back some of the weight I've lost.[234] I'm down to a husky 138, in fantastic shape, but not exactly bulging all over with enormous muscles like I used to be. The tropical sun has a distinct slenderizing effect on every guy who comes over here.

… Ramadan, though, has just ended. The city is all lit up. All the beautiful girls are parading around in their holiday best. People are dancing in the streets. After the 3-day Eid celebration, things should start to slide back to normal.

✍ *Although things were heading back to normal, a month after the coup, I recorded one of my few rants during my time in Mogadishu.*

I'm tired—[235]

- I'm tired, basically, of having to get job satisfaction from working with people who either dislike me or feel that I have nothing to offer. It's ridiculous, it would seem, to bend over backwards to offer advice to people who not only ignore your advice but treat me as if I was an insignificant little piece of crap.

- I'm tired of living with a salary that is not enough for me to do what I want. When I go without dinner or wonder whether someone is going to offer me something—that is no way to live when there are other possibilities.

- I'm tired of being treated like a goon, a freak, a piece of shit by people in general. At home, if there were no draft, I could be studying for a law degree at one of the country's leading law schools. I would be ignored by the masses and, presumably, be happy within a certain group of peers. Why should I be called a spy by some fool who doesn't know a thing, whose little uniform makes him so important? Why should Dan Krall have to put up with all that trouble at the airport?

- I'm tired of dealing with people whose way of approaching problems is so different from the way my culture does it that I am unable to understand how conclusions are ever reached or decisions ever made.

- I'm tired of not being able to use my potential usefulness to its full extent. If it weren't for the fact that a few of the kids listen, watch, and learn, I would be completely wasting my time. And then I have to wonder just how significant my working with basketball actually is. The good basketball players seem to refuse to learn anything from me. Knowledgeable basketball players cannot be produced from scratch in a year, and there will be nothing left when I leave other than a bunch of kids who know a little—probably only enough to lead them to believe that they know it all. Nobody will continue the program when I leave, because the better players—who could become the teachers the country could really use—feel that they've already got things wired.

The Tournament Continues

In the short run, basketball continued as it had, and Peace Corps Volunteers had formed our own team. One of my principal motivations for leaving Internazionale was to create a team that would play a more fundamental and disciplined game as a model for the students we were coaching and for the other adult teams. I had hoped to show them how people who had grown up with the game played it.

November 7 journal entry. The PC team is looking pretty good.[236]

We've had a couple practice games with Orfano and the Police, winning both of them. The Police were way ahead of us, but our starters went back in and it was all over. The tournament is going to be interesting, I think. When we played Orfano, we had something like 11 guys (including 3 Marines and Jack Swank from NTEC [National Teachers Education Center, in Afgoi, partly funded by USAID]), which is really more than we need. I talked with the head of the SAFO team and suggested he talk with the guys who had played for his team in the last tournament and leave it up to individuals to decide for whom they were going to play. The way things sounded I think that we'll end up with all the PC, and SAFO will get the other Americans. That gives them Gipson, Sherwood, and maybe Swank, but we've got Leo, Rich, me, Bonnewell (who's blown off Huddor for working with oxen at the Afgoi farm), Thompson, Jimison, Abbot and Bob Siegel.

It's going to be fun playing with a team with a modicum of organization and more than a pinch of basketball sense. After our game with Orfano, a lot of people were saying that we had the cup wrapped up. It was interesting, though, because the people who said it weren't too pissed when they said it, just being sort of rueful. It could be a different situation when hundreds of people, the police band, and a dozen guys with drums pack the Sportivo for the final game. Like I say, it'll be interesting. I think one thing that will help things immensely (perhaps over-estimating my influence) is that I've gotten to know a lot of the players more or less personally, which I've found makes a big difference eliminating friction between the two teams. Now if the refs would only know the rules—it doesn't matter if they're partial (that's expected), just act as if they know the rules.

November 16 journal entry. The people are pretty darn worried about the strength of the PC team.[237] I expect quite a bit of psychological challenge when it comes to winning the tournament. They've taken the best players from both Hoga and the Police and made a new team, October 21, that is stronger still. The leftover guys are on Indipendenza. There would seem to be no reason for having done what they did other than trying to get a team strong enough to beat us. October 21 has Adamo, Yusuf, Issa Der, Abdi Salaan, Malanie, Farah, maybe Ali Omar. They could be tough.

We played last Thursday against WilWall and didn't have too much trouble. The crowd was OK, and, I'm not sure but I think that, if we can somehow manage to keep from getting pissed at the refs and the other team, the crowd will stay reasonably neutral. There could be an interesting couple of ball games near the end of the tournament.

> ✍ *But eventually the frustrations in trying to work with the Basketball Federation spilled over to the game on the court.*

November 30 journal entry. The last straw was a ball game against Orfano, a team that has several of my students on it.[238] It was a real dandy, and it discouraged me to the extent that I'm not going to have any more to do with the organization here. I'll just teach the kids and let the Somalis do the organizing. I tried, God knows, but my advice just didn't seem to be regarded as something worth listening to. Anyway, about the game with Orfano: They've always had the reputation of being closer to kamikaze pilots than basketball players, of delighting more in a blocked layup that results in the removal of the offensive player's shooting arm than in anything legal.

Thompson and Bone were in the Upper Juba cleaning out people's stuff. (Bone left Huddor and Tim blew off Gorisane.) So we figured that we would be in for a pretty tight game. Little did we know what was in store. To start with, no one would let us in the door, because we didn't have our passes. I had been assured that we didn't need passes, because any fool can tell by the color of our skin whether we're playing on a particular evening. The idiots at the gate just didn't buy this line of reasoning, however, and gave us a whole bunch of trouble. I wonder what we were doing carrying a basketball and wearing jerseys and tennis shoes if we weren't supposed to play that evening. You know about those non-Muslims, though: they pull some sneaky stuff. I was higher than a kite for the game and definitely got out of hand—poking guys in the chest, insulting the cops and Hoga who were standing around like a bunch of idiots. Finally they let us in, but I was still pretty wound up.

When we walked on the court, the crowd just booed its ass off, which got the old adrenalin going. While we were doing layups, Abbott got hit in the head with a rock, blood trickling down his neck. We told the officials at the scorer's table that we weren't too excited about this turn of events and what did they suppose could be done about it. We were expecting a few more police, an announcement over the loudspeaker, or something. "Oh, we'll try to find a rag to clean him up with," is what we got. [We didn't think that was a very sympathetic response.]

We got started, in front of a completely packed house—just about completely hostile—and knowing that the team we were playing was just plain dirty. They were, and we didn't do too perfect a job of keeping our cool. Thank god the refs weren't too bad. Score at half, 11 - 8 and final, 38 - 26, as we finally pulled our game together. I was ashamed of some of the guys on their team, who were kids I'd worked with. The way those guys played ball (ball?) it was actually impossible to shoot a layup, because they had such a firm hold on various parts of one's body. We had been through the most incredible test of self-control. I only hit one guy, and then not very hard, so I was reasonably pleased with my restraint. The PC is never so obvious as a group as when we play ball, and we realize that we should attempt to restrain ourselves, but it's just not always that easy.

We got a lot of trouble after the game, maybe deservedly so, about being too rough and getting mad. I guess it doesn't matter about guys getting hit in the head with rocks, boos, and an opposition that practically necessitates the wearing of crash helmets. I was so ticked off at the way things went that I then and there washed my hands of the entire tournament.

Then we started to get psyched up for our game on November 29 with October 21—anticipating the crowd's reaction, the number of boos, the squadron of military brass present, how things would necessarily get out of hand. Things seemed to take on all the aspects of a religious, racial, and cultural war as the forces of the revolution were taking on those of the white, neo-colonialist imperialists.

We had a practice game with some guys at WTSC to prepare for the big clash. What a farce. Rich and all the staff were absent, so we had a skeleton crew. They played their usual game, which usually doesn't even vaguely resemble basketball, and, about midway through the second period, the white guys started to get a little pissed. We showed the boys from NTEC how subtle and dirty the boys who've been playing ball all their lives can get. And, boy, did they cry their eyes out. When the whole thing was over, we just walked out of the gym, saying "Bye, probably won't see you again." Then there was some idiot demanding that somebody pay for the watch that he said Abbot had broken. How that happened—considering the fact that the guy wasn't even in the game—never did get cleared up as we just drove over the guy [not literally] and headed for town.

We Take on October 21

The big night came, and we had to play October 21 without Leo, who was in the States because of his father's illness. We could have used him. As I've stated, we had anticipated the worst, but things went well—except for the fact that we lost, 30 - 28. It was the first time I've played on a losing PC team. The place was incredibly packed—there must have been 1,000 people at the very least [all standing, since there were no bleachers]. We tried to get in the back door, but couldn't fight our way through the crowd that was trying to fight for the last spots inside. Finally, we were told to go around to the "players' entrance." We got in.

When we walked on the court there was a lot of booing, but there were also a lot of people cheering. There was one whole section, in fact, that was cheering for us the whole game. People were betting on the games, the whole bit. When October 21st came on the court, we thought that they caught more boos than we did, although, needless to say, they also got more cheers. Rocks were flying all over the place while we were warming up, but it seemed like they were coming from outside, because the other team got its share, too. There were cops all over the place, and a nice little section blocked off for the various dignitaries. Someone said that they spotted General Mohamed Siad Barre, head of the SRC. There were people standing or sitting on every available square foot, and people sitting on all the walls. There was even a crowd standing on the roof of the tea-shop. The amount paid by the crowd was 1400 shillings, an all-time high. [I also remember that there were supposedly a thousand people there and that the price of admission was a third of an average person's daily earnings. How all these recollections fit together, I can't say.]

The refs weren't great, but they shouldn't have made any difference. We just didn't handle the ball well enough. October 21st had a tight defense, and the only way we could have expected to win would have been to make really snappy passes. Our side guys just couldn't get untracked. It's the best defense I've ever seen from any team of Somalis. Damn good. Like I say, though, we would have won if we would've handled the ball adequately. It was 15 - 13 at the half; then we had them 22 - 15, but they came storming back to 24 - 24, as we kept giving them the ball.

Then, with 5 minutes left, while we were standing for a time out, the roof on the tea-shop collapsed, taking maybe 8 people with it. An incredible crash. The Grays, Dunne, and maybe a couple other PCVs, missed going down with it by only a couple feet. The word is that somebody broke his leg, and another got shocked by an electric wire.

We got 2 quick baskets to make it 28 - 24, and I thought we had it. Then we made a bunch of mistakes, and they finished the game when Ali Omar stole the ball and drove the length of the court for a layup. We brought the ball down, lost it, and they stalled the clock out—and who's to know whether the last 5 minutes were only 3 or 4.

… There was absolutely no friction between the players and very little real complaint with the referees. Like, I say, we didn't deserve to win. Now, we have to win 5 games in 5 days to win the whole thing. Without Leo we have our work cut out for us. I would really like to win it, but losing last night didn't leave too bad a taste in my mouth. Even the fans were decent about it, with very few wise cracks after the game. The whole evening was a surprise. I had expected to win and catch a lot of shit, and just the opposite happened.

The Grand Finale—a Game to Remember

We went to the losers' bracket, where after 2 victories we met October 21 again.[239] (They'd lost to Indipendenza, another one of the "political representative" teams.) As relatively trouble-free as the first game with them had been, we expected the best. But, my friends and neighbors, it wasn't that simple.

> ✎ *The game was to be one of the most enduring memories from my time in Somalia.*

When we walked onto the playing surface, we knew that something had changed. We got many more huzzahs than boos and a much more favorable welcome from the crowd than the other team—which actually got more boos than applause. It seemed pretty obvious that we had been picked out as the team that could act out the people's growing disappointment with the pretty oppressive new government. There were people chanting "Peeskah" from the second we walked on the court. (I guess this was a hurried version of "Peace Corps," since the usual pronunciation is "Bees Korpis.")

We were fantastic the first half and were well out in front. Then, certain political forces obviously went to work. The referees were seen having a short briefing at half-time with the military brass, who occupied a special section, roped off right behind the scorer's table. [They were the only ones with places to sit.] One can only guess at the substance of the little confab, but the officiating in the second half became truly amazing. The refs fouled out two of our best players in the first few minutes of the second half, on calls that manifested an extremely fertile imagination on the part of the guys with the whistles. And the other team might as well have been issued small arms at the break for all the protection we got from the refs.

Needless to say, the other team caught up in fairly short order. But then, despite all the efforts of the whistle-blowers, we stayed with the bad guys. And with 5 minutes left the fun started. The refs became even worse in their obvious efforts to see to it that the forces of the revolution would emerge victorious. A few guys on our team were getting pissed, but most everyone reacted just like I did: all we can do is keep trying and wait for the whistle to blow. We went ahead of them; we were told there were 2 minutes left; we were told there was 1 minute left; then we were told 2 minutes. (There is no visible clock at these games.) Finally, with the score tied, one of their guys got loose for a layup. And—would you believe it—just as time ran out, too. After a final 5 minutes that must have been closer to 15. And, of course, the basket was good. We just left, sort of glad that the game was over.

As we were leaving, we got a lot of genuine sympathy from spectators who were upset with the farce, and a significant number of people advised us to never play there again. Near the other team's dressing room, a bunch of people started to clap in unison, applauding their team's fine victory. They were drowned out by boos from the people rooting for us. At least the people were with us.

It was after the game when everyone compared notes and observations that things really got interesting. One of the guys' girlfriends had been in the audience and had heard cops with nightsticks going around during the last 5 minutes, saying that anyone who yelled for us would spend a night in jail. Later, we talked to a group of guys who had one of their buddies thrown in the pokey for trying to keep an eye on the timekeeper during the last little stretch. One of our players on the bench said that, from the way the timekeeper kept looking from score to stop watch in the last minutes, it was hard to believe that the game was ever intended to end on anything as neocolonialist as the predetermined time.

But the best rumor—and to be honest it was only a rumor— was that the referees had been threatened with imprisonment if the enemies of the new government won. As for us—we learned our lesson. When the new people's government of this the Democratic Republic of Somalia is so set against the evils of tribalism, neocolonialism, imperialism, nepotism, and, above all, corruption, who are we to fight it?

We're the New Government's Target

November 30 journal entry. About the only other news is the effect that the SRC is having on our day-to-day lives.[240] There are lots of rumors, as well as a lot of things that are for sure happening. What are some of them? Ardo told Gallagher that the Hoga has decided to throw us out because we dress sloppily and don't ever bathe. Also, the Lido girls have been forbidden from going with PC. (Apparently this one hasn't gone into effect yet.) There was a dandy rumor: Halimo, Rich's old sweetie, told Sweet Pea that the police had come here one morning to arrest the girls, but there was no one here. The only thing wrong with that rumor was that Jimison was here all morning.

Another time, Jimison was tape recording music over at Sam's, and Sahara and Fadumo came over. They were there only long enough to catch their breath and have a Fanta. When Sam's houseboy left, 3 plainclothes cops asked him just what the hell was going on in there. They asked how many other girls John had in the house. They also told him that John had committed a horrible crime against the Somali people. And, of course, they weren't at liberty to say what it was! Such things would make one think the place is being watched.

Because of all the recent trouble, Bob and Leo asked our household to kind of cool it. We just stand out too much. I could see their point, but I had definitely gotten used to having all the girls around. So, we decided to cool things around here for a while. Fadumo and Sahara have a room nearby, for which the landlady collects a tidy 200 shillings or so a month. As attached as I've become to Fadumo, 3 nights of sleeping by myself weren't too cool. Soon, they'll be welcome as soon as it gets dark. What we want to get away from is the constant traffic of PC and Somali girls that has been making the place so noticeable. We're just going to be a little more discreet and see how things go.

Something interesting went on outside our place the first night that the girls were gone. John was watching as a Land Rover of cops pulled up to our gate and the guard opened it for them. A VW of officers parked in front and went across the street to check with the PRO [I don't know what this means]. There were gestures in the direction of our apartment. Interestingly enough, not too much earlier, a group of young lovelies in short skirts pulled into the apartment downstairs, which is rented by a ranking Hoga honcho. Then the officer came over to this guy's apartment, and they stood outside talking quietly. Then they both looked up at our place and saw John checking them out. If only there had been a cute line to use on those guys.

Zwink was in Dinsoor when a telegram came from Mog regarding a volunteer in the bush, not a member of the 8s. It said that he had raped a young girl while under the influence of marijuana and that the authorities were looking for him.

When Bonnewell and Love went to the Upper Juba to pick up Bone's and Krall's stuff, they had an interesting time. In Lugh, they saw a telegram sent the day Kraw was pulled off the plane. It said that he had assaulted a young boy homosexually and was presumed to have stolen a PC Land Rover and headed for the border overland. Leo let it slip one afternoon at the Beach Club that the rumor about Kraw having assaulted a young kid was the final straw as far as his making the decision to leave was concerned. He figured that it would be easier to just get the hell out rather than to stay here and listen to the government's bullshit for the next year.

While Bone and Love were in Baidoa, they got permission from the head of Upper Juba police to travel around, clearing their use of a car with government plates. Things were OK in Lugh, but they were detained overnight in Wegit while the cops sent telegrams to Baidoa and Mog. Apparently the chief of police was willing to let them go, but some little bureaucrat was jumping up and down about things—probably threatening to report the cop for not doing his job properly if he let them go. We heard about this from Iman, who saw the telegram sent to the Minister of Education. As it turned out, Bone and Love were only detained overnight and stayed at the DC's house. We thought that might happen, but had also considered the chances of their being tossed in the jug for 3 or 4 nights. We can never predict.

The boys from Beled Uen gave up the ghost, after Dunne and Quinn were held at gun-point for several hours. It was a pretty involved story, but the guys meant business and it was just the first of a string of similar incidents. The Hoga would accost them (in an area where they had previously been given permission to go), hold them at rigid attention at the open end of a rifle barrel for a half-hour or so, and then take them to headquarters. There they would receive the profoundest of apologies and be assured that it would certainly not happen again. Then the Hoga would give the towns-people another story, and it would happen again. The Ministry of Education even had the audacity to get pissed off at [the PCVs because they left] their posts without authorization, although it looks now as though they'll be given new posts.

Charley's Bar has been closed indefinitely. Pure harassment. The Police had complained to the Municipia about Charley's license (a supposed impropriety when he switched from a bar to a bar-restaurant). And about his staying open so late (just like the Lido, no Abdi?). And about his not allowing Somalis in (not if they haven't paid their membership fees, air-head). He may open up again soon or he may never open up. Nobody knows.

The PC still has heard nothing from the Ministry about the group scheduled to come in the spring. Supposedly, PC/Washington had to know by December 1.

Fadumo has some good stories about conversations she's had with police officers. The ones who know that she's a PC girlfriend, greet her as such, and then ask her for the inside information. They ask her if she'd like to be a spy, ask her what she's observed. One guy said that they want to throw us out, but don't have a good enough reason—although we are suspected of using marijuana and heroin! One guy asked her if she would help them find out where we got our heroin. Officers who didn't know that she had anything to do with PC asked her what she knew about us. She said, "Nothing! Why should I hang around those unwashed savages?" Good line, girl ...

New policy: Girls without visas are not to be allowed to leave the country. Shukri Jack, for example, was to fly to Italia to meet her prospective husband. She has a ticket, but he has not sent her a visa. They won't let her go, as of now. Fadumo also said that the government wants to recall all passports issued to girls, saying that the only reason a person should be allowed to leave the country is to study abroad. It makes people very unhappy, to say the least.

Another rumor is that there are 33 lower-ranking officers under arrest for plotting to overthrow the government. This could certainly have been expected, as various groups get a little ticked off at how the power is split up.

Thompson's houseboy is still on his ass. The jerk fell off a chair and broke his arm while washing windows maybe 7 or 8 months ago. Thompson paid his salary for the 3 months he didn't work, paid for x-rays, doctor, etc. So the guy sued him for 18,000 shillings. (The rumor is that the fine for killing someone is only 10,000. Needless to say, Bill had another alternative as far as settling the case was concerned.) CAMD said that they would take care of everything and that Bill didn't have to appear in court. [I don't remember more specifically, but CAMD was an office of the US government.] So, in his absence, the court decided in favor of the guy to the tune of 20,000 shillings. The next day, 2 cops, 2 other idiots (God only knows who they were), and the guy came to the office. Thompson was to give them the cash on the spot or they were going to go to his house and take all of his furniture—which belongs to the USA, incidentally. (There was a Land Rover full of flat-feet outside the office ready to head over there.)

Thompson talked them out of that somehow and immediately enlisted the services of an Italian lawyer. The boys were back the next day, however, with the same orders. Get the cash or the sofa and chairs. Fortunately the lawyer was at the office at the time and somehow stalled them. The normal procedure is to give the convicted person 30 days to appeal the case, but Bill had never been informed of his rights. The lawyer said that he had never seen a decision implemented so quickly. (No harassment intended, of course). Again, Thompson somehow got out of it. The latest is that he's due in court tomorrow. The case will be reviewed by an Italian judge and is expected to be thrown out on the grounds that the job as a houseboy is not considered a dangerous one and that there is no precedent for an employer having to pay such compensation. We'll have to wait and see.

A Police Raid—My Friends Go To Jail and We All Go to Court

> *A decree was issued prohibiting Somalis (perhaps only those employed by the government) from socializing with foreigners. The Big Raid and my arrest for throwing an international party showed us that the Supreme Revolutionary Council was not messing around.*

November 30 journal entry. I've saved the best until last: THE BIG RAID.[241] A week ago last Saturday we decided to have our first party at the new house. The word got out, and we invited Somalis, several of whom, including Iman, were affected by the government order prohibiting Somalis from seeing *gaals* socially. [Iman may have been the guy in charge of PE at the Ministry of Education.] The girls were excited, we bought the beer, and everyone was ready to go.

Initially there was quite a bit of trouble with the girls. Sahara Sexy, who had been specifically warned against ever coming back because of all her wily falsehoods, showed up. Fadumo told me that Gilles and Zenab had invited her and that Rich and Randy didn't mind. As the evening wore on, it was discovered in conversation that Rich and Randy did mind and Gilles had had nothing to do with the invitation. Rich and I, being in a completely blissful state of semi-drunken euphoria, went into our OUT!! routine (not in the presence of the accused), which stopped the party cold for some seconds. [As I recall, this was a loud rendition resembling a baseball umpire ejecting an unruly manager.] We really didn't give a damn, as long as she didn't give us any trouble, but our actions were misinterpreted.

The next thing I knew, Fadumo was so furious that she was packing her clothes, making ready to go who knows where. She put on her usual show after 4 or 5 beers, saying "I'm not drunk. I know when I'm drunk." But she was being completely unreasonable. Next came Zenab, leading Sahara Sexy down the stairs, making ready to throw her out. She asked me, "You want to throw her out, right?" Hell. Let her stay. Everybody was placated except for Crazy Fadumo, who was completely out of her head. She informed me that the entire affair had been none of my business. After all, she had never lied to me. The fact that the entire household had been in agreement against Sahara ever returning didn't seem to make any difference. Anyway, with Abby Gedi's help, things finally cooled down. Normalcy had returned.

And then the word was passed … Hmmm, the cops are here.

My first reaction—which was definitely the wrong one—was, well, we'll just handle it like in the States. Turn the music down, take a couple fairly sober people to the door and promise it won't happen again. I had started down the stairs, when the goon squad started the march up, a 5-foot tall inspector and 3 or 4 ordinary flat-feet. They just pointed at the Somalis and said, "You, you, and you, come with us," and everybody went with no ifs, ands, or buts. Thank goodness the girls [the PC girlfriends] had been warned by somebody and had locked themselves in one of the back rooms. Arrested were 5 guys, 3 hookers, and 2 very proper girls who had come with Somali guys and probably had absolutely no desire to come to a *gaals'* party in the first place.

Needless to say, a few of us were a little ticked off, and, after the paddy wagon rolled away, we insulted the small group of idiots left "on guard" as best we knew how. We started with the traditional rank insults and then went to the subtle: "How do you guys like working for the new government?" "You'd better not leave yet, there are 250 Somalis hidden in the bathroom." (The girls had, in fact, hidden up near the water tank, pulling the ladder up behind them.) "You guys are our guests. You look thirsty. Would you like to come in and have a beer?" We got pretty good at the ultimate in sarcasm as the night went on.

The next morning, I was awakened by Jimison, who had a note delivered by a cop that he wanted me to sign. Now, the truly ludicrous was to begin. By signing, I was agreeing to appear at the police station at 10:00. I signed, anticipating a bawling out, which I planned to receive at my most humble sarcastic best. I went to one police station, was directed to another one, walked in the door and asked to speak to the man who had signed the note. A real yoyo appeared and said that that guy wasn't here, but that he had written the note and signed his name. (As a potential lawyer, I didn't think that was legal.)

He asked me if I had invited a bunch of Somalis to my place the night before and I said "Yep". He wanted to speak to me in

Somali, but I said "Gee, sir, I don't know any Somali." He said, "Oh, but you do. You don't know me, but I know you. I know all the PC in Somalia." Randy was there with me, and I said, "Oh, really, who's this?" "Well, uh...I don't know, but I can sure find out." He had gotten my name from several of the guys who were arrested, when they had been asked who invited them to the party. And that's how I came to be invited to come to the clink. He said that I was to be arrested, and I asked, just for the record, of course, on what charges.

On the phone and to other cops, he had explained the charges in Somali and Italian, but he never explained to me what they were in English. I asked to see a copy of the statute that I had broken, and he showed me one that, in essence, said that it was against the law to break any ordinance or decree passed by the government. I took that as meaning that it was against the law to break the law, and I had to go along with that. As an individual, however, in my case I was more than curious to have things explained just a bit further. I kind of wanted to know what decree or ordinance I had broken.

Over the phone in Somali and Italian, the jerk had said that we had "been violating some ordinance concerning *sicurezza pubblica* [public security] by having a "public meeting"—in a private house. (The public-ness of the entire affair was later to be justified by the police's statement that the front door was unlocked and that they marched up the stairs without any trouble.) Arlo Guthrie would have had a field day as I was booked (not knowing what for) and fingerprinted. I was pleased with myself, because I definitely pissed the guy off, by refusing—very politely, mind you—to sign the statement he had written in Italian, saying that I couldn't read it—which was completely true, since no one can read Italian longhand but an Italian.

Then Abdi Hot Shit called the other 10 people before him (they'd been held in jail overnight) and read them the riot act. He was so damned important for being such an ignorant little turd. As we were being hustled outside to climb into the big blue police truck, it dawned on me that we were going to court for some ungodly reason. I requested permission to telephone the Embassy, but it was denied on the grounds that the head guy's working day was over.

We climbed into the truck, and phase three of the farce was about to begin. We got to the court and were herded into the smallest room in the building, I'm sure. We were sort of an incongruous sight, to say the least: girls in pants suits or long dresses, guys in their good clothes, and me in Levis and *da'as* [flip-flops]—and, of course, the usual collection of gawking assholes collected outside the window. There must have been 20 people in the room, something like 3 cops, the judge ("here come da judge"), the prosecutor (a real jerk), the defendants, 2 or 3 guys whose functions weren't exactly clear, and the chief butt whose job was to guard the door.

The Somalis were charged with having a public meeting, presumably a security violation, dancing (apparently against the law during Ramadan), and going to a white person's house. There was not the slightest indication of justice anywhere, needless to say. I was charged separately with holding the debauched session at which all of this damnable behavior went on. After grumbling a bit too long, Abby Gedi was charged with contempt of court and had to spend from Sunday morning to Thursday in jail—where he didn't get the best of treatment, for example, being served food that he said a human being could not have eaten. The self-righteousness and the overpowering attitudes of self-importance were the sickening things about this, call it a preliminary hearing. Here are some of the people who are the hope for the future of this goddamned country being dressed down by a bunch of no-minds for having a "public gathering in violation of public security."

We were told to come back on Thursday, presumably to hear the verdict. In the meantime, the PC got me a lawyer, the same Italian who was working on the deal with Thompson's houseboy. A couple good rumors went around. The fine was supposedly to be set at 300 shillings. Double O Madow was supposed to be looking for Marks for her 300, then she was supposedly going to get it from some Italian. Zwinko supposedly had had to go to the court and pay 300 to free Ibadu. These were great stories—considering the fact that the fine hadn't even been set yet. It did, however, look as though we were definitely [going to be found] guilty.

We went back on the appointed day and were told to come back an hour later. A Somali colleague of the Italian lawyer represented us in court, and things from the start began to look better. Mysteriously, the charges had been changed to the single charge of causing a public disturbance, which made much more sense. We were still under the jurisdiction of the law that said "it's against the law to break the law," which carries with it up to 3 months in the jug and a fine of 3000 shillings. The arresting officer was examined and cross-examined concerning the night in question and testified (rather falsely, in our estimation) that he had heard the music from the police station. It would have taken Gemini on a very still night for that to have been true.

Next, one of the average Joe Flatfeet was examined. He said that he heard the music when they had arrived at the house. This statement was definitely in conflict with the one given by the inspector—who had seemed very eager to set everybody straight concerning what had happened. (He told Randy when we were at the station that he had been ordered to arrest everybody, but had ignored the PC because he likes the teachers.) The whole trial was run in an amazingly legitimate fashion, with the prosecutor and the defense lawyer taking turns on the witnesses. At one point, however, there were 25 people in the room—a small one at that— including all the people who had been present at the first hearing (or whatever it was). The last witness was one of the guys at the party, the one guy I didn't know. He did a fine job making sure that everyone knew that the tape-recorder was not turned up full-blast and making such shaky statements as "Yes, he was positive that it was my house."

The 2 lawyers wrapped up their arguments. The prosecutor did a pretty poor job, bringing in irrelevant facts such as the girls in short dresses and drinking and dancing during Ramadan, when the issue under scrutiny was whether or not we had disturbed the public. Our lawyer stuck to the point, saying that we hadn't been making that much noise and that there had been a government decree saying that it was permissible to keep teashop radios going later because of the way that Ramadan was traditionally celebrated. (We were raided at midnight, when the teashops keep going until 3 or 4:00 AM.)

After what was a very interesting and amusing experience in court … eventually all 11 of us were fined 101 shillings apiece ($14.50).[242] The Italian lawyer who was hired to defend us said that, when the official complaint comes from the police, conviction is automatic. In addition to the fine, I was told to stop messing around with Somalis and that everything would be peachy—not exactly in line with the traditional PC ethic. Needless to say, harassment like this hardly endears one to the system and the people who run it.

It was interesting to listen to the rumors concerning who had originally made the complaint.[243] We sort of guessed that it was the Hoga downstairs, but the guys who spent that night in jail said that it was 2 Arabs who said that they had seen people drinking, smoking hashish and running around naked, and white guys screwing Somali girls in the mouth and in the ass, as well as in the usual spot. If the cops pulled the raid expecting to find that, they must have been really pretty surprised at what they actually found.

To Stay or Go

November 30 journal entry. Leo has applied to Washington for what is called the power to grant termination in the field.[244] This would allow people who feel that their work has been affected by the revolution to terminate here with the assurance that their way home would be paid. This would allow people to travel on their way back to the States rather than making them go directly back in order to see if their trip was going to be paid for.

Assessing my overall state at present: In the past month or so a hell of a lot has happened, which, at the time, has convinced me that the best thing to do is to leave. In the last week, however, things have not been too bad. The basketball, for example, was much less troublesome than I'd expected it to be. The people on the street are friendly enough, and many greet me by name, having seen us play at Centro Sportivo. I know a hell of a lot of people at least on a casual basis, and that helps from day to day.

Until maybe a week ago, things were definitely up in the air. I had even gone so far as to pick December 14 as my departure date. But now it looks like I'll probably be around for a while. Our termination date has been officially changed to August 1, which, I think, gives Leo the power to move it up to July 1. I'm leaving for 2 weeks or so leave to Nairobi and East Africa soon, and when I come back the PE program at the Ministry of Education should be back in operation after the Ramadan layoff. As of January 1, I'll only have 6 months until termination, with a month of vacation included. If the PE program keeps working, I'll almost certainly stay around.

But who knows? A week ago, I said that the only thing keeping me here was Fadumo. There hasn't been any real trouble in the last week. If … we continue to be discreet in our behavior around the house, and we get no more hassle from the state, things could look pretty rosy. If, on the other hand, they begin to harass us again, it could be really bad—and who knows what could happen then, especially if the field termination thing is approved. In addition, the lottery for the draft has started, although there are so many unexplained details that no one actually has the vaguest idea what's going on or who's to be affected.

> Complicating my feelings was the fact that in early December the National Commissioner of Sport asked me to coach the men's national basketball team in the Inter-African Basketball Tournament in Cairo in March. It was exactly what I'd been looking forward to.

[I've] started collecting books and films and [am] excited to get started.[245] [I've] been talking to the players about what we [are] going to work on and they [seem] to be excited, too. Six months earlier the reception would have been very cold, but after 6 months [I've] gotten to be pretty good friends with several of them.

I'm no super-whiz kid, but it seems like I'll be able to teach them a lot since, despite tremendous potential in the small group of guys who have been at the game for a while, there has never been any coaching whatsoever.[246] There is also frequently the tendency (very typically Somali) to think that there is very little for anyone to teach them. If this feeling of knowing it all ever breaks down, the players produced as a result will be something to watch. If they want my help they've got it.

For some reason we stay.[247] I've been asked why I play basketball here when the officiating is so partial to the locals and the crowd is so frequently hostile (rock-throwing, booing, etc). I can't say why. The same holds true about staying here in general. From one day to the next, I go from making definite plans to get on a plane on a certain date to deciding that things here aren't that bad after all. I think now, though, that, if the law backs off just a bit (who knows whether they will or not—they're still watching our house like hawks), I'll probably be here for a while longer.

    ✎   *I wrote to a high school friend who was in Peace Corps/ Sierra Leone.*

Glad to hear that things are still going fine.[248] I'm envious as hell, needless to say. I wonder what it's like to have a PC experience that one can look at with any sort of positive attitude. Now I'm exaggerating. There are things here that do provide some small sort of reward.

… Things here are so incredibly up in the air, with the new government, all the rumors, etc. There's no telling where I am going to end up. Our termination date has been changed to August 1, but it's possible that we'll get out July 1. If the draft lottery works to our advantage (another bit of news we just haven't gotten here in the Land of Punt), I may be hot to get home and go to law school. But, like I say, I don't have any idea what's going to happen.

December 16 letter. Let me wish you all the season's best.[249] I've already received my season's greetings: my number in the draft lottery is 213, and, if things work as best we've been able to figure from the one sketchy State Department telegram we've received at this end of the earth, it doesn't look like I'll have to fulfill my patriotic duty to God and country after all—as much as I'd like to.

Nabad [Peace]

Also: I suggest that you send any mail to James A. Douglas c/o American Embassy, Mogadishu, Somalia. We have reason to believe that not all the mail is getting through. Omitting Peace Corps from the address might help.

Kicked Out—Our Last Few Weeks in Mog and Our Conflicted Departure

> ✎ *The Supreme Revolutionary Council abruptly decided it was time for the Peace Corps to go. We left the country on December 26. A week later, I wrote the following from Nairobi to a friend from college.*

January 3, 1970 letter. Here's something that's probably more a letter to myself than to you.[250] I conscientiously kept a journal of my time in the Peace Corps, and I felt I should come up with a last chapter. As I say in the letter itself, I'm kind of confused concerning how I feel about having been in the Land of Punt. Hopefully, my opinions will eventually work themselves out.

Right now, all I want to do is get away from quiet Nairobi with the eventual goal of getting to New York in fairly good time.

Now, turn the page and settle back to the last chapter of my time in Somalia.

December 31, 1969. The last week has really been something. Things for me had just started to go very well. My kids had gotten to the point where they didn't need supervision as much as they needed practice. I had been pretty down during the last 2 weeks of Ramadan, because of having absolutely no work to do and because of the pressure of competing in a black man's basketball tournament. But, like I say, things had started to pick up.

... Then, one Wednesday morning [December 17] we were called to an "extremely important" meeting at the PC office, attendance required. We guessed before the talking even started that we were out. At that time, there weren't many tears—just the opposite. Everybody was pretty excited. But the next 9 days were to be pretty grim.

Everyone was just busy as hell trying to get things organized. The staff was racing around organizing things and each PCV had stuff to do. We sold our houseful of furniture (almost all of which was owned by Peace Corps) for a profit of something like $125 apiece. Jimison did a hell of a job dickering with the dozens of people who came to look at the stuff.

Originally, we were told by the ambassador not to talk to anyone about our having been booted until it came out in the local media. It wasn't to come out until Friday [December 19], and, needless to say, we couldn't keep it from the girls for very long. There was a house full of pretty gloomy people from then on. In the last week, we said our goodbyes and shed more than a few tears when alone with our girls. Things were pretty shitty in general. It was good in one respect, though, which was that it was not our fault that we were leaving. We couldn't do anything about it. The government had decided for us. If we'd finished our tour in August, I'm afraid the fact that we were leaving without being required to do so would have been even more upsetting to the girls.

Except for Fadumo, saying goodbye was actually pretty easy. No one was too upset at our having been given the ax. It was interesting to note, though, that people who had seen us play ball would come up and ask "Is number 4 staying? I heard that he's staying." Others, without ever having had any experience with anyone else, would say, "The rest of the Peace Corps are very bad people but you are a very good person. You're going to stay here and continue working with us, aren't you?"

🖎 *I said goodbye to the basketball players.*

Other people that I'd worked with for months just asked what I was going to give them. Ismail Kamil, with whom I'd worked very closely, was typical. The first time I saw him after the news was released, the first words out of his mouth were "What is the PC basketball team going to do with their shirts?" I had a lot of other people ask me for stuff; I gave stuff to some of them and to others I didn't. There were also people who did not come by to say goodbye at all, including Iman and the Russians, with whom some of us had spent quite a bit of time.

Yusuf, one of the basketball players, was one guy I was genuinely sorry to be leaving. [I think he was the one Somali on Internazionale, the first team I played with after moving into Mog.] Also, Ali Hamari [probably the same as Ali Omar]. I'd done a lot of work with Yusuf, and, although we weren't buddies like Ali and I were, we'd gotten along well and shared a lot of similar ideas concerning what was needed for basketball here.* I didn't get a chance to say goodbye to Ali, because he was laid up with hemorrhoids.

---

* Later, Yusuf sent me a letter about how the national team had done at the Inter-African Basketball Tournament in Cairo. They lost to Central African Republic, 107-43, "Palestine (Gaza)," 104-54, and UAR, 104-71 [by this, he probably meant Egypt, since the short-lived United Arab Republic, consisting of Egypt and Syria, broke up in 1961] . He said that other teams were "all toller [sic] and stronger than us and we were fauling [sic] too much ... Jim, you can't imagine how we became surprised because

I did ask Yusuf to come over to pick up some stuff I had for Ali. He did come, although he didn't stay very long. He was pretty pleased when I gave him a real good book, a ball, and my pair of shoes. I told him that the ball was for Ali and the shoes, for Adamo, but I don't think he listened too well. He had promised me one of their jerseys but had forgotten it. When he came back with it, it was interesting to see this nattily-dressed Somali wearing a filthy pair of low-cut black Converse to complement his outfit. And I'm now probably the only guy in the entire US with a Somalia Police basketball shirt.

Yusuf told me something that really made me feel good. He is going to quit Indipendenza and start his own team composed of guys who have never played before. I was moved, because what I'd always thought was a major thing wrong with the basketball program here is the fact that all of the best players are on only 2 teams. Spreading them out will make for a much faster rate of education.

   ✍   *I felt that I had made a definite contribution.*

For whatever it's worth, I can look back and definitely see progress that happened while I was in Mogadishu. Certainly, it wasn't all my doing, but I played a part and I can definitely take some gratification from knowing that. In the year I was in Somalia I saw the Group A players improve tremendously, and I can't help but believe that I, personally, and especially the PC team in the last tournament, served as examples that were eventually followed, even if begrudgingly.

I saw an interscholastic basketball program started where there had been absolutely nothing. The last day I went to my classes, I saw 250 school kids yelling like idiots as they watched a Mog school and one from a nearby town [probably Afgoi] "battle it out." I took satisfaction from knowing that I had finished constructing

---

we were expecting more than we had but gained a great experience." The entire letter is in Appendix F.

the court the game was being played on and constructed the court that the visiting team practices on. I had also arranged the game between the 2.

But 2 things made me the happiest. One was seeing the visiting coach and a captain from another school in Mog settling on a time for a game between their two schools. I also saw Yusuf, who refereed, do a fantastic job of calling fouls—something the referees for the Group A games never can do competently. Again—it was not all my doing, but I know that my being involved had some effect. I was lucky in having a completely unique position for PC/Somalia, a position where maybe I was able to accomplish a little.

Despite how well things were going with my work and despite any disappointment over having to leave without having had the chance to work with the national team, I don't think I actually minded leaving as far as my work was concerned. The entire experience here was so complex, ranging from absolute disgust and rage with the place and its people to amazing contentment with everything and the country's totally unique quality. I'm not sure how long it's going to take me to work out in my mind anything like a total evaluation of the experience.

✎ *All the 8s had conflicted feelings about our experience in Somalia.*

My feelings during the last week in country and the week since arriving in Nairobi serve as a perfect analogy to the experience in general. All any of us can talk about is fucking Somalia. The place was such a total part of our lives. Living there was such a 24-hour a day job that it has to be difficult to leave the place for whatever reason. After 14 months in the country, we had things pretty well figured out. We'd figured out our relationship with the culture and were getting along fairly well with it within the allowable limits. (Exceptions were the police and the military. We weren't getting along with the new government at all.) And then we were abruptly uprooted. It makes for a pretty psychologically confused little guy.

Like I said, the last week in Mog was very hectic because of having so much stuff to take care of.

The most disturbing matter of all was saying goodbye to Fadumo. Old Fadumo was really something, and I don't think I'll ever completely forget her. When she was good, she was fantastic—unbeatable—and when she was bad she was amazing. My relationship with her was like that with the country as a whole, though. Things had been figured out. I knew when to ignore her; I knew when to fly into a rage; I knew when to sweet-talk her into a better mood. And we got along extremely well about 98% of the time. The only exceptions were when she drank, when she turned into a mad-woman (just like every other Somali girl).

A few days before we left, she drank a bunch of beer in the morning, I guess in preparation for my coming home for lunch. She definitely scared me. She was saying that she loved me so much that she couldn't bear the thought of me screwing anyone else—so she was going to kill me the next time I went to sleep. The only person able to understand the significant amount of fear I felt would have been another guy with a Somali girlfriend. Who knows what she would have done. And then she went into another bit about cutting my dick off and putting it in the refrigerator. I'm just glad she didn't, is all.

The fact we were leaving was very confusing for the group of girls who lived with us. They'd taken shit for so long about being whores and spies simply because they really dug us. It certainly wasn't because of all our money. And then, bingo, overnight we're off—just like that. They'd all been disowned by their families, and, except for the money we left for them (I left Fadumo about 1100 shillings), they were completely on their own—at the mercy of the wolves in Mogadishu who were certainly dying to give them untold amounts of trouble after the PC was gone. They were all planning to go back to Hargeisa, which we all agreed was a good idea. They should have left by now.

Just sitting here, thinking about Fadumo and the 5 months we lived together, I realize that I'm just as confused about my relationship with her as I am about my experience in Somalia as a whole. The last month or so, I knew I really dug her, but also saw the episodes when she gave me a bad time. I told myself that to spend my life with a wild woman like that would be impossible. Despite her tremendous intelligence, curiosity, and very pleasing personality, I told myself that she would never be able to get along in the context of a culture foreign to her own. The Somalis are just too different to ever get along any place else.

But now, after having been away for a little while, the whole experience of Somalia, and especially my relationship with Fadumo, has taken on a dream-like quality. It's difficult to remember what it was actually like, since all I can think of are the good times—and I can't even imagine them exactly. It's very confusing ...

Arriving in Nairobi was something. We spent much of the night before our 7:00 AM departure at the Lido, came home for one last night together and were awakened by the alarm at 5:00. That last goodbye was really unhappy, but at least it had to be fast, and Fadumo and I were both so tired and hung over that we were kind of numb to the whole situation. Anyway, after champagne at the Mog airport, we arrived in Nairobi pretty well whipped out. Tim, who had been up all night and feeling the fact we were being kicked out, sort of wigged out at the airport, but it was later diagnosed as being physical in origin rather than psychological. [We learned later that he'd eaten a chunk of hash.] Anyway, it was a scary way to arrive in Nairobi.

✎ *Nairobi and Mog were very different.*

Nairobi is such a contrast to Mog. There are so many tall buildings that I felt like counting them. There are wide streets, parks, golf courses, modern theaters, and more than 2 restaurants where you are assured of not coming down with dysentery. Everything is different from Somalia: hot water showers; fresh, soft water; a toilet that always flushes. The people seem so much friendlier with each other and with us. Men and women are seen together in public—even drinking. There are more than 2 things on a menu.

But after 2 or 3 days most of us were bored stiff. Living in Somalia had been such a hectic proposition that Nairobi began to seem very dull. In contrast to the Somali women, the women here seem much too big and not attractive at all. The city closes down almost completely at 11:00 PM—the Lido doesn't even start until 11:00! In addition, we had to wait around for a week to get our separation money from PC, which only contributed to our ennui.

The Peace Corps has not been very impressive in the way they've handled us. They paid for our hotel rooms and gave us 20 shillings per day, but that's been about it. Volunteers in Kenya have been discouraged from having anything to do with us—after all we were thrown out of the country and couldn't possibly have anything nice to say about anything. (As an aside, interestingly enough, we recently found out that Somalia was officially ranked by PC/Washington as the least desirable PC country, tied with Chad. [And we later met volunteers from Chad, and they had it much better than we did. People in Chad liked them!])

Right now, we just want to get out. A bunch of us are going to Mombasa tomorrow and see how that works out. I'm still not sure what I'm going to do. In Mombasa, I'm going to talk to shipping lines about going around Africa to Europe, as well as going to Australia. I should come back in a week or so having pretty well decided what I'm going to do next. At any rate, I'll be back in New York by May 1 at the absolute latest.

Somalia 8s irreverent goodbye from Nairobi to Somalia and the Supreme Revolutionary Council. Front row from left: Bill Clumpner, Bob Bonnewell, John Marks, and the author; Back row: Phil Lovdal, John Jimison, Randy Meyers, Dave Zwink, Rich Gallagher, and Gilles Stockton; Missing, Tim Gaudio. Photo by John Jimison.

Fadumo in Nairobi—photo by Randy Meyers

I ended up flying home, stopping in Addis Ababa, Cairo (where several of us were detained for taking pictures of a picturesque bridge), Ankara, Athens, and numerous stops in Europe. I landed in Boston on April Fools' Day.

Fadumo, Shukri, and Zenab (two other PC girlfriends) appeared in Nairobi a few days after I wrote this. They had snuck or bribed their way across the border, gotten to Nairobi, figured out where we were staying, and completely surprised us by popping up from behind the registration desk. After another several weeks, we again said our goodbyes.

Fadumo later lived with and eventually married a PCV in Kenya, and they have lived together for years in Santa Barbara. I've spoken with her occasionally and saw her and her grown daughter in person about fifteen years ago when Fadumo came to Seattle for her daughter's graduation from the University of Washington. Fadumo has had a remarkable life. She's the one that ought to write everything down.

Appendix A

Advice About Joining the Peace Corps

🖎 *One of my friends still in college asked for my advice about going into the Peace Corps. I wrote to him while still in Gorisane.*

April 1, 1969 letter to friend still in college (JR). My particular complaints about my PC experience (that by now are becoming significant in number) are caused by my particular set-up. To better organize my thoughts, I'll start by answering your questions and the points that you make—all good ones.

It sounds like you've thought about things as thoroughly as one could be expected to. You mentioned your experience in Korea, specifically conversations with PCVs who talked about apathy on the part of the local population, the inability to communicate with the locals on any level above that of a precocious 4-year old, the acute lack of privacy, and the lack of government support. I think that all of these would vary from one country to another and even from post to post within one country. I think the choice of country likely affects the entire experience, and I've regretted more than once the fact that I turned down an assignment to Kenya. There are PCVs, not all of whom have been duped by Peace Corps/Washington, who come back from 2 or 3 years in a country and absolutely rave about their experience. I think that the matter of enthusiasm by local people is more or less a matter of luck, affected by such things as the presence of a great PCV. This would certainly affect the experience. Some people have good experiences. The exact percentage is impossible to know, which doesn't help you a bit.

The matter of government support depends on the government of the host country. Kenya, for example, pays the vols from its own budget. Many countries pay a certain share of the PC expense in their country. Some countries have more on the ball than others. African countries that I have heard good things about in this way are Kenya, Tanzania and Malawi—all supposed to provide a pretty decent experience.

The matter of privacy depends on the post and the type of house you live in. There are PCVs here who live in larger towns and have compounds that make for as much privacy as one wants. My situation is an absolute farce, making for minimal peace of mind. The whole experience is an endless rendition of life in a fishbowl. And it really sucks.

The thing about inability to communicate is not necessarily true. In countries like Kenya (where Swahili is spoken) and the countries of Latin America, for example, the language can be learned. If one has any particular aptitude for language, in a couple years he can get pretty fluent. Your point about not being able to have any intellectual conversations (even if one were able to attain fluency) is dependent on what I think has been the most important factor affecting my relatively unsatisfactory experience—that being the impossibly low level of development of the people with whom you've got to work in a lot of the underdeveloped cultures of the world. It gets so frustrating dealing with people who don't know anything beyond their village. Especially when they think they know everything there is to know about everything. It drives me nuts. Fluency wouldn't mean anything when you're talking about dealing with people who don't even know to "plug the hole" when they're cut and bleeding. What are you going to talk about? This place is a zoo, with the level of the present culture precluding any possible over-all impact we might have.

But, again, other countries, with cultures closer to those of the western world, would make for a much easier experience, a more rewarding experience. It's my guess that the countries of South America, especially if one were not in rural development, would be more enjoyable in that respect. Maybe I'm just applying the "grass is always greener" philosophy, but maybe not. When I'm asked for advice concerning my experience and how it has affected my attitudes toward the PC, I guess that my overall conclusion is that Somalia sucks. (It has been anything but an enjoyable experience living out here with Stone Age Man.) But there are probably quite a few places where I could be having a pretty enjoyable, semi-rewarding and partially-fulfilling experience. I think that the host country makes all the difference in the world. I'm convinced of it.

In commenting on your comparisons between PC and VISTA: 1-year versus 2-year commitment is up to you personally, as is your point about being in touch with the revolution at home. Especially about the latter, I'm unable to say. It's been a real surprise to see how quickly all the stuff at home becomes very far away and seemingly unrelated to me. In my conversations with Steve [another college friend who is in VISTA] before leaving the US, we touched on interesting points about his VISTA experience. He's working in rural development and has experienced a reaction similar to mine, because of the very primitive and slow-moving nature of the people with whom he's working. It seems to be a feeling of frustration having to do with the seemingly impossible task that one is attempting to tackle. And in his case, too, the people are from a completely different and un-understanding culture. Like the Somalis, the poor black people he's working with are at such a low level that it's all very confusing to them.

I think that's enough. Something that is very important to remember, though, is that—at least speaking personally—lofty ideals have a way of getting buried as time slowly rolls by. The romantic idea of the super-vol or the magna-VISTA means no more to me than some of the conversations that go on in this village. It's just a long way away, that's all. Time just slips away, and the mind gets more and more time to rest.

Appendix B

My Advice to the Next Peace Corps/ Somalia Group—March 17, 1969

March 17, 1969 cover letter to assistant director Bill Thompson. The following represents the fulfillment of my duty as I saw it … We received pretty shoddy, only quasi-organized advice before hitting these friendly shores, so I thought I'd take the time to draw up the following. It was tough, believe me, to find time in my tremendously cramped schedule, but somehow I managed to do it. If the list looks good, why don't you make additions and corrections, have someone run off some copies and send them without passing go to Baker, LA, wherever the hell that is—probably a suburb of Fort Yates, ND [where my group had its training].

Advice

Our group (your immediate predecessors, Somalia 8) received very little in the way of organized advice concerning what to bring overseas with us, and, in an effort to rectify that faux pas of history, I've compiled the following list. I imagine that my tastes are only somewhat applicable, being in rural development rather than teaching, and I doubt, because of my particular sex, whether the females will be able to benefit from some of the suggestions. But perhaps the following tidbits gleaned from my experience will be of some help as you get ready to come over here.

Point one—don't come anywhere near this country ... This point is strictly for your personal benefit, Thompson, and should probably be deleted. The rest of this has been compiled in all seriousness and with sufficient consideration.

I strongly suggest bringing a tape recorder and a sufficient number of recorded tapes, since a recorder and good sounds provide a lot of enjoyment. Although pretty poor in quality, batteries are very cheap and easy to obtain. Blank tapes of all sizes are available in Mog. You can most cheaply purchase a recorder at a free port en route (e.g., Amsterdam, Rome, Asmara), but remember to bring sufficient travelers' checks to make the purchase. Nothing else but green American dollars can be expected to work. [This was before the proliferation of credit cards.]

I have found a typewriter to be completely indispensable, although this is no doubt affected by the fact that I like to type my letters and by the fact that our group is supposed to file monthly reports concerning our monumental achievements in agriculture. Typewriters are almost totally unavailable here.

You can buy very adequate radios in Mog. Some people with good international radios might disagree, but, personally, my $40 Somali special has worked out very well, pulling in all the basics like VOA, BBC, Armed Forces Radio, etc. The make is Phillips, and all the other vols with similar models are as satisfied as I am.

I suggest you bring a cheap sleeping bag (practically indispensable when travelling). Also, if you anticipate doing much heavy work, a pair of work boots and a pair of gloves are good to have. Excellent and inexpensive desert boots are available, however. I am glad that I brought a hat for working outside, although straw hats are available from the sweet little old lady crooks on the beach in Mog. If you want a good pair of dark glasses, you should bring them with you from the US. Cheesy to adequate models are available in Mog, but they are expensive. A good small-sized travel bag (for 3-day to 3-week journeys) is another good thing to bring. Good ones are available in Mog, but they are not available other places as far as I can tell. I bought one which now has no handles, no zipper, and an infinite number of rips.

Depending on what situation you anticipate, a hammer, ax, pair of pliers, and a cold chisel might be good to bring, although they are almost certainly available in Mog. (A lot of things available in Mog can probably be more easily brought from the US if weight is no consideration.) Speaking from personal experience, other tools, like vice grips, channel locks, and other exotic pieces of mechanica, will never get used.

Things like wire, nails, flashlights, and string are readily available here, but I would have liked to have brought a roll or two of scotch tape as well as some electrician's tape. Thumb tacks, paper clips, rubber bands are available here, but might be more easily brought from home. Paper and envelopes fall into the same category. Sometimes shopping for small items can be very exasperating, as one finds it necessary to hit every store in town to find that nobody has a thumb tack.

You should buy Petromax lanterns in Mog if you anticipate being assigned to a post without electricity.

Airtight containers and almost everything else you'll need for the most modern in kitchen arrangements are available in Mog. Exceptions are plastic bags and measuring spoons and cups. I don't think cook books are available, although they may be. The Fanny Farmer Boston Cooking School Cook Book in paperback has long been a PC best-seller.

Locally obtainable tennis shoes are extremely weak excuses. I advise that you bring a pair or even two if you anticipate much athletic activity (i.e., if you're a jock). That brings up another point: a jock and a pair of gym shorts may also be nice to have, also a swimming suit.

Da'as, sturdier than flip-flops, are worn as shoes by most volunteers, as well as by most Somalis. It is easy to purchase sandals in Mog. One would not seem to need too many pairs of socks, considering the few occasions on which most volunteers wear shoes. (It must be noted, however, that local socks ain't too stylish.)

Odds and ends: Aerosol shave cream is available in Mog. Refills for techmatic razors are not. Bring enough. I shave with a brush and a shaving mug I brought from the US and it works fine. I'm glad I thought to bring a colored washcloth and a heavy colored towel, since they should last and don't show the dirt. It's good to bring a wind-up clock from the US. Film is available in Mog, apparently adequate in nature. If any of you use instamatic cameras, it might be advisable to pick up a healthy initial supply of film at a free port on the way (processing pre-paid), since its availability in Mog is pretty limited and it's completely unavailable other places, as far as I know.

Things I brought that I should have left behind:

Levis—where I am stationed (near Baidoa) they are too uncomfortable. I think this would be the case at most posts. I wear nothing but locally-made shorts, which are excellent in every respect. I think teachers are forced by the system to wear long pants, but I think, in my situation, I would have gotten along beautifully with about 2 pairs of stay-pressed long pants.

Sports coat—I'll never wear it in this country, since things are incredibly informal. The most dressed-up anyone ever gets is to put on a clean shirt, a pair of long pants, and a pair of shoes to go to the Lido. Wearing a sports coat on leave in another country might be a different story.

An abundance of jackets and sweaters is not necessary, although this certainly would vary with location. Apparently it gets pretty cool at night in the north. Having spent time in Mog and Baidoa, I've never worn a sweater and have worn a jacket once. However, a jacket will be nice to have for the rains.

Guys don't seem to wear pajamas, wearing boxer shorts or the local *ma'awiis* instead.

You can realistically get by with few clothes brought from the

States. Stay-pressed shirts are great, but I think about 7 or 8 would do very nicely. Locally-made shirts and long pants are not as good as those from home, but are passable. My overly-abundant supply of underpants, in preparation for 2 years, has been packed away never to be heard from again. It sounds a little savage at first, but the majority of male volunteers find them too uncomfortable. The more loosely clothing fits, the more comfortable you'll be.

To repeat—you don't need to bring a tremendous amount of clothing over here. (My 10 colored t-shirts, 6 work shirts, 8 or so other shirts, 4 or 5 pair of Levis are ridiculous excess.) I was surprised at how few clothes I needed to get by. I am stationed in a town that is small enough to eliminate the need to have a lot of clothes, but I don't think anyone would need too many, especially if laundry facilities or a hard-working *boyessa* is available.

After considering all the fantastic foregoing advice, if there is space left in your trunk, I advise filling the spaces with books. While actually pretty passable, the book lockers are not perfect and are not always available. Our group, as an example, has yet to receive ours. No doubt you've been warned against falling into the "book locker syndrome," but, depending on the post, a good selection of books can be invaluable in warding off both boredom and the debilitating effects of insanity.

I hope the above list is of some assistance in giving you an idea what you might want to bring and what you might want to leave behind.

Bye. See some of you some time in the future.

Appendix C

Report On Agriculture from Khansadere

Kansahdere

June 1, 1969

**Periodic report of work in agriculture by Peace Corps
Volunteers James Douglas and John Marks**

As of June 1, 1969, five demonstration plots are being cared for:

A 25 x 15-meter plot of peanuts, planted on the farm of Alio Buro, is faring poorly, reportedly because of an insect problem.

A 30 x 25-meter plot of sorghum (mixed American-panelated and local variety), planted on the farm of Mohammed Shurie, was meeting with only minimal success because of a breakdown in communication between the volunteers and the farmer, which resulted in the latter's thinning in the manner dictated by local tradition—leaving clumps of three plants approximately every meter. We had planted in thirty-inch rows and had intended to thin to one foot or fifteen inches within the row.

A plot of peanuts, approximately one-half acre in size, planted at the home of Warsama Jama, is attracting considerable local attention because of its success. Due to its having been planted with proper thirty-inch spacing between rows and six inches between plants within the row, the plot seems to be serving as a fine lesson in the importance of proper plant population. The fact that the plot is located in town has certainly contributed to its demonstration value.

A 30 x 30-meter plot of peanuts, planted on the farm of Abdi Noor, also planted to achieve optimum plant population, is also doing very well.

On the farm of Haji Ali Aden, our work being done with his son Abdulkadir, plots of peanuts and local sorghum are doing well. The sorghum has been thinned to one-foot spacing; the peanuts were planted utilizing six-inch spacing—both in thirty-inch rows. The total area of both plots is approximately 40 x 40 meters.

Plots 3), 4), and 5) were planted approximately April 1, in anticipation of the coming rain. The other two were planted two weeks later. Work then ceased because of an increasing general hesitation to plant when it looked as though rain might never arrive.

The factor, basic to success of local agriculture this season, and one which seems to be lacking, is sufficient rainfall. We measured less than one-half inch in April, approximately 4 ½ inches in May. But the last significant rainfall was recorded on May 13. The residents feel that the rains for this season have ended and we are inclined to agree. Needless to say, such an abbreviated rainy season is expected to detrimentally affect the local agricultural effort.

In the upcoming dry months, it is our intention to work with oxen training, beginning on a small scale but with hopes of expanding as the inhabitants become convinced of the advantages of utilizing animal power. We have made arrangements to begin the program with Abdulkadir Haji Ali Aden and Abdi Noor. These men will provide teams of oxen and we will provide instruction in the techniques involved with training and using oxen to plow, plant, and cultivate. It is hoped that the ministry and/or BONKA can be of assistance in making implements available.

Original: District Agricultural Office, Baidoa
Carbon copies: Ministry of Agriculture, Mogadishu
BONKA Experimental Farm, Baidoa
Peace Corps, Mogadishu

Appendix D

Peace Corps/Somalia
II WARRAN [literally "Tell Me News"]

August 12, 1969

One morning not long ago a wild-eyed young man burst into our Galcaio offices crying, "The Mog Scene! Always the Mog Scene! Fools! Don't you know where the real action is?" We locked him in a room with a typewriter, and presently the following was pushed out under the door.

THE UPPER JUBA SCENE
By Bob Bonnewell

The Eights' Conference

The Eights' conference was scheduled for July 2 and 3rd. As a basis for discussion the Eights filled out a Completion of Service form. When the conference opened at Leo's home on the 2nd, these tabulated results and a paper written by Jim Douglas became the basis for the discussions.

The main complaints were aimed at the original programming of the group along with choice of posting sites, lack of support by the Ministry of Agriculture, the attitudes of the farmers towards agriculture, and the attitudes of the Rahanweyn towards the white man in general. Faced with a combination of an unpleasant living situation plus no opportunities to make what they felt would be a meaningful contribution to agriculture in the next two years, four of the Eights decided to leave their original posts.

In the other cases, with three exceptions, the Eights felt that, although their work was not particularly significant, they would return to their posts, as they had a comfortable living situation and hoped to find some other areas of work to augment their efforts in agriculture. The three exceptions felt that they were making a meaningful contribution to agriculture in their areas.

As all the issues seemed to have been talked out on the 2nd, the Eights spent the next day resting up for the party they threw in honor of leaving volunteers Reimers and Malvey. Thirteen cases of beer later (and 8 hours of sleep for Reimers) a small hard core made it to the airport to see them off.

Where the Eights Are

John Marks has been in Bur Hacaba with Diane Guido, observing classes and doing a little teaching himself after two weeks of brainwashing in TEFL [Teaching English as a Foreign Language] methods in Mogadishu. He most probably will be stationed in Belet Weyn and should leave for there shortly.

Jim Douglas is now working in Mogadishu with "sports." He is organizing and instructing recreation at the boys reformatory, completing work on a basketball court in the Ministry of Education's backyard, working on a couple of other basketball courts, and helping the police to build a playground for younger children. For your enjoyment he hopes to have a volleyball court finished at the Beach Club by the next time you hit Mog.

On many afternoons you'll also find Jama [that's me] organizing the schedule at the dart board. According to the recently departed doctor and Jerry Kriss, it's wise to throw about 1 out of every 4 games to Douglas and Thompson, if you want to keep them at the dart board.

Gilles Stockton returned to Brava following the conference, but has also taken a trip to Itala responding to a request from a local deputy, who accompanied Gilles for the inspection tour.

Baker Morrow is again letting blood, this time however it is his own. While driving between Afgoi and Mog, Baker discovered that parked HOGA trucks with no lights or reflectors should indeed be considered immovable objects, and should be avoided at all costs. Unfortunately, due to an oncoming car, Baker was not able to avoid it. He received several lacerations about his head, but they are healing quickly, no thanks to seamstress Shirrar, and lots of thanks to Eve McAllister's TLC.

Meanwhile his roommate, Randy Myers, is handling Baker's teaching duties at the Vet school along with his own responsibilities there, which are rather vaguely described as "Special Projects." From all appearances it looks as though the rinderpest campaign, in which Randy would have occupied a prominent position, will never get off the ground.

Dan Krall, Duane Nosbisch, Tim Gaudio, and Phil Lovdal recently went on leave to East Africa. After a short visit to Nairobi, they planned to proceed to Kampala to visit the Eights' training director, Conn Price. Dan and Duane have returned, and Dan has gone back to his old post at Lugh. Duane is returning to the U.S. Crazy Tim and Nutty Phil were at last report heading towards the Ruwenzori Range with da'as [flip flops], shorts, and one overcoat between them. They had learned three phrases of Swahili: "I don't have any money," "I want to eat," and "I want to sleep." Thus prepared, they expected to complete the frigid climb in 7 days (average time is 10 days) and proceed on to conquer Mt. Kilimanjaro and Mt. Kenya. Phil will then probably return to Somalia, while Tim goes on to Dar es Salaam to visit former Somalia volunteer Mary Wilkins (ex-Guinea).

Eventually Phil and Tim plan to return to their posts in the

Upper Juba. Duane, however, has decided to leave the Upper Juba, but has not yet decided what he will do after returning from leave. Hopefully Tim's hemorrhoids will have cleared up and Scab (his horse) will have put on enough weight to smooth out its protruding backbone, so that once again they may be seen riding off across the plains of Gorisane, telling all the little children that the horse will eat them if they get too close.

Somehow Dave Zwink sweet-talked Shirrar into giving him his second med evac in five months. Someone pointed out that Dave also managed to get scheduled on the same flight to Nairobi as the Good Doctor; just what do we have going on here anyway?

Don Gregg should be back in Texas now, much to his enjoyment. He left on "Baksheesh" Airlines early one Friday morning after an 18-hour stint during which he and 5 or 6 companions made a supreme effort to dispose of every last shilling of Don's through the medium of liquid refreshment. Don then made his departure, downing an "Orange-boom" beer as he walked through the gate, his termination physical scheduled for 4 hours later in Nairobi.

Bob Bonnewell returned to Hoddur for two days following the Ag conference, and then accompanied Leo and Dale Fritz on their tour of the Upper Juba. We've noted that Hoddur is often the butt of many jokes and would like to suggest that it may well be the armpit of the Upper Juba. Of course if you confront him with this, Bonnewell will say it isn't true and feed you a pun based on the name of a nearby town: "Wedgit — Up your ____." On the positive side, most recent visitors indicate that the best entertainment this side of Nairobi is provided by his cook, a real grande dame.

Bill Clumpner continues to pull off the unbelievable. Last February it was a pet monkey which he bought, which bit him and which died all in a 24 hour span. Rabies treatment naturally followed. This time it was a red international pickup (vehicular type, for a change), which, through his efforts and those of Bob Love, received the most all-pervasive carwash yet seen on the beach at Chisimaio. Upon hearing the news, Thompson immediately signed

Bill's extension papers for a third year. Looks like the Nines will have a steady stream of entertainment for the duration of their stay.

News filtering back from Giamama about John Jimison is slim indeed. As a matter of fact, the only report comes from the Nines' Chisimaio training staff who say that John now has three beds in his home. "This one is too hard; this one is too soft; ahh, this one is just right." Good night, Goldylocks.

Appendix E

Peace Corps Goings On

May 12 journal entry. We talked to Giumali after he got back from Mog. He had nothing but the absolute worst news. Omar had taken over from Abby and Nick [as the person in charge of training the Somalia 9's group], hired his own tribesmen from the north to teach language, etc ... But then Denny came from Mog, bringing the latest skinny. At someone's instigation, T-group sessions [a term from the '60s, meaning open and honest discussions] were organized for those who would be training the 9's: the 7's, in-country staff, VTSI [the people who ran our training, including Abby and Nick], language staff. Apparently, the results were fantastic; wish I could have been there. Leo [the new director], or so Denny said, was very eager to have everyone lay it on him and reacted very well to honest criticism. And somebody really leaned on Omar good, because the latest word is that a bunch of southern replacements are to take over language instruction, that the trainees are learning southern dialogues, the whole bit. Tremendous improvements ...

Also at the T-groups, Kelley Coleman was given a lot of shit about his attitudes toward Somali-white American relations. [Curiously, none of us remember who he was.] "You guys don't like Somalis because your white middle class backgrounds can't stand it when these black people won't kowtow." Oh, that's close. A lot of things that needed to be said were finally said. Hopefully, someone listened. If they did, it could be the first time.

... We also got a letter from Zak when Denny came up. He's gone [left Somalia]. He just couldn't wait to get out of here ... When we heard the news, we wished we were with him. He said that he, Bakes and Randy had been doing a good job of counteracting Harvey's BS during training of the 9's. I sure as hell hope so. The chances of the 9's being significantly happier than we are at the end of 6 months are not that great. The trainees will be coming to Baidoa the end of May, and, with luck, we'll be able to get in to talk to them. The more people we can convince to bag it and try some other country, the better off everyone will be. Maybe PC would wise up and pull us all out of Somalia.

August 1 journal entry. When Shirrar [Bill Shirrar, one of the PC doctors] and Kriss [Jerry Kriss, PCV transfer from Niger] were warming up to leave we put in the most incredible 10 or 12 days. We were at the Lido just about every night until 3 or 4 or 5:00. Those 2 idiots were trying to get rid of shillings and talk about generosity! Man— how much beer was drunk! We had a particularly memorable night at the Lido after the ambassador's Apollo party.

The last night of the gruesome twosome was really a classic. Table for 25. Things were slow about 3–5:00, but when it started to get light outside, when it got right down to the real nitty gritty, things got going. By then we were down to Kriss, Shirrar, Thompson, Marks (who turned in a classic performance), Sam Worthington [I don't remember who he was], me, Lul and about 4 Lido girls. "Champagne," said Shirrar. Four bottles, one of which should have been bronzed, having been given us free by the Lido. Lul presented the two with *ma'awiises*, which they promptly put on, with Shirrar deciding to remove his trousers to authenticate the change. There were toasts to everyone: north, south, Somalia, Lido, etc. By now, needless to say, we were the stars of the show, as all other activity at the Lido had stopped so that [people could check us out]. Most people thought we were celebrating Apollo.

During one of the toasts, Shirrar fell off his chair, crushing John. The good doctor, as he attempted to gain his feet (much in the fashion of a beached whale) managed to alternate exposure of his genitalia and his derriere—the view being made possible by the fact that his skirt had slipped. The order of the next steps is fuzzy, but they involved dousing everyone with the champagne. Marks presenting both guys with a beach ball and the "watchman of the cars" patch [worn by the guy who watched the car at the Lido] to Dr. Bill.

Since it was time to head for the plane, the party moved outside, Thompson being supported on each side by [the two guests of honor]. Of course, the entire bunch of people inside followed us to see what was going to happen next. And they were not disappointed as the crazy *gaals* did it again—tossing each other in the fountain, wrestling around on the ground, making a general spectacle for about 15 minutes before making our exit. After stopping to get the guys' stuff we were off to the Mogadishu International Airport.

Checking in, the players looked like this: Shirrar had changed into his green tropical suit, but had his soaking wet *ma'awiis* draped over his head, was dragging his laundry bag and dribbling his newly-acquired beach ball, laughing hysterically. Kriss had on dark glasses, his pineapple shirt (having decided not to change clothes for the flight), his *ma'awiis* (already torn!) on over his white Levis, carrying his ridiculous binder. In such garb, the latter was congratulated by the head of USIS [US Information Service] for his "dedication and contribution." And Kriss kept a straight face.

Despite the [best efforts] by Marks and me—using wit and fluency in 3 languages—we were not allowed into the departure area. I don't know why. So we passed around a few bottles of Oranjeboom, and the boys took off. Everyone had had a good time, although the story is that, once in the air, the boys sped to the bathroom and stayed there until the plane landed.

August 19 letter. Fritz went home just about a month ago.[251] He was genuinely tired of the place and of the experience he was having, although he left in good shape psychologically (after an all-nighter at the bar-on-the-beach). Duane left about 2 or 3 weeks ago for the same reasons. Fritz thought he would go back to school if the draft will allow, and Duane, being draft-exempt, was not quite sure what he was going to do.

Baker left maybe 10 days ago [after his accident] … The Land Rover he was driving was incredibly screwed, and people who saw Bakes after the accident said he was pretty lucky to still be alive. As it turned out, very fortunately, Dr. Shirrar had just gotten in from the north about 2 days earlier and, after about 6 or 7 hours of work, had done a fine job sewing up a dandy laceration clear across Baker's forehead and another one across the back of his neck. Anyway, Baker is gone, perhaps to try to transfer into another program. Hopes were not too high, since Bakes was one of the few who did have an actual job set-up, rather than just stumbling around trying to teach the bushies how to do something with sorghum seed other than stuff it up their nostrils.

September 10 letter. There's a new deputy director named Bob Siegel, who was going to go to the north [Hargeisa] but will almost certainly stay in Mog.[252] He was an associate director in Kenya before, is about 30, say, and seems to be a pretty good guy. Unlike the new doctor, who is quite the twiff when you get right down to it, he hasn't got his head up in the clouds. He's talked to Somalia volunteers in Kenya and has a pretty good idea what's liable to go on. He's attacking the place in beautiful style, I think.

There are two very conflicting rumors about Thompson. I talked to Leo out at Charley's Bar maybe a week ago, and he said that Thompson had decided to stay through early next summer. It was kind of "Well, it's not official, but it's pretty official" … Everyone's betting that he will actually go. He's eating himself up these days, and I'm sorry to see it happen. Every single thing gets him just pissed off as hell …

Jimison is in town, working in the library and museum and looking for a house. Randy just spent a week in Brava with Gilles and enjoyed the vacation. It doesn't look like he'll be taking off for Kenya. They wanted 2 years starting in December, and he wasn't too hot for that idea. I got a letter from Merry Clune, who's working in London at least until the end of September. She's just as loony as she always was and seems to be getting the itch to get to California. Jim Weeks may very well leave Bardera and switch to a place called Genale, which is near Merca. There's an orphanage that can use all the help it can get, and he says that "it's just time to move." It would sure seem like a hell of a hassle this close to the end of his 2 years.

September 14 letter. Thompson is scheduled to blow out of here in about 6 weeks ...[253] We talked about it a few times, and he admits that the place has gotten to him again. Apparently, he was in pretty much the same state of mind when he left for our training program a year ago ...

Marks is in Beled Uen, enjoying the town and teaching quite a bit. I got a letter from him asking me to send him some crab powder, so I'd guess he's generally enjoying himself ...

The new doctor [Sampson] is Negro, over 50, with an attractive wife and 2 pre-adolescent daughters who are going to be real fine women in a few years. He has worked 20-some years in the Philadelphia ghetto. Noble and all that, but his head is too high up in the clouds. He may straighten around as he learns a little more about the place. All that I know is that I don't want to be the first guy to report to him with what is politely referred to as a social disease.

Baker has gone home. He was never the same after the accident. Pissed all the time. Randy got a letter from him, and he's in fine shape psychologically now. Duane's gone home. I heard from him that he's heading for Colorado to work ... I have a new bedroom companion, who has become a very regular thing. That is, her clothes are here, the whole bit. Fadumo is a friend of Gilles's girl, Strother's girl, and Clumpner's girl and is pretty cool ... I'm just about her sole means of support, which, if she had her way, would involve damn near every kumi [$^1/_{10}$ of a shilling] I have. We get along OK, although there's not as much beer-drinking or Lido as there used to be. There aren't that many guys that dig that sort of thing anyway. Not like in ages past.

... Randy is kind of wasting his time here, as far as I can see. He wants to go back to vet school, which is draft exempt, so I don't see why he stays ...

September 16 letter. Rich Gallagher [of the legendary 5's, the school construction team] will get into this lovely maxi-sandbox any day now.[254] Thompson had to walk his ass off and talk with silly locals until he was hoarse, but he finally got Rich a place in the Ministry of Self-Help (of what?) and Rural Development. Ministries said yes, then reneged until dear old Capt. Thompson was a psychotic wreck ... Don Gregg's physical in Nairobi revealed high blood pressure, which wasn't present before the Somali Republic got its licks in. So he doesn't think that he'll have to have his tailor whip up something sporty in olive green khaki just yet. The PC paid his way home, so he figured he could buy a motorcycle and go back to school ...

October 16 letter. Rich Gallagher is back.[255] Poor insane bastard. Just never felt like digging the States. Truly a hell of a guy in all respects and a god damn welcome addition to the matronly group of Mog vols.

... Thompson just got back from a 2 ½ week trip to the Lower Juba, where he was hunting for elephant and lion. That's right. Just like Tarzan or Ramar of the Jungle or someone. Of course, he didn't even see either a lion or elephant, but he had a hell of a relaxing time. It looks like he'll be here for the next 8 or 10 months. They gave him a raise, and the vacation did him some good. He's even talking about giving Lulabelle the old heave-ho, which would do everyone some good. He would like to, but I think that the possible final result of his trying could be a fatal knife wound inflicted by the old witch upon the weakened body of our fearless leader ...

I made a rather disparaging remark about the Mog volunteers in the opening section of this letter, but I actually have to qualify that statement a bit. A couple guys are coming around (if I may be so presumptuous as to believe that my lifestyle is worthy of commendation). They're all more or less waking up to the realities of living from day to day with the psychopaths who inhabit this Horn of East Africa. But a few of the most enlightened are actually engaging in such nefarious activities as drinking assorted nectars and engaging in titillating social intercourse with indigenous members of the opposite sex. It's actually gotten to the point where you can find someone to drink with these days. (Gallagher sees to that, anyway.) Guys like Rich Green and Abbott are working out admirably—when judged by my own prejudiced standards, of course.

Appendix F

Letter From Yusuf Mohamed Osman

Mogadishu
March 22nd, 1970

Dear Jim;

I have received your letter and became really happy. Jim, I think I have much to tell you about the Inter-African championship of Basketball which was held in Alexandria (U.A.R.) We left Mogadishu on the 4th of March and as soon we arrived Cairo we proceeded to Alexandria. Our Coach was Mr. Jack Swank who did his best for us, training us in NTEC for a period of one month. On our way to Alexandria the only things we could see were Military posts and you can immagine the reason. The games started on the 9th and the participant states were SOMALIA, U.A.R., CENTRAL REPUBLIC OF AFRICA, TUNISIA, SENEGAL, LIBYA, PALESTINE (Gaza) and GUINEA (not present). We were put in the first Group together with U.A.R., CENTRAL AFRICA and PALESTINE.

We had the first game with Central Africa and we lost with 107-43. Second game with Palestine—lost with 104-54. Third game with U.A.R.—lost with 104-71. The main factor which caused us the loss was that the other team members were all toller and stronger than us and we were fauling too much, immagine, the first game seven of us were sent out of the court for faults. The Cup was won by the U.A.R.

Jim, you can't imagine how we became surprised because we were expecting more than we had but gained a great experience. In Mogadishu is going on the competions between Schools and it will last sometime in April. I have nothing to say than good bye.

Sincerely yours,
Yusuf Mohamed Osman
Best wishes to you from Ali

Endnotes

[1] December 13, 1968 letter to high school friend eventually in Peace Corps/Sierra Leone (CV).
[2] Undated letter to family.
[3] December 13, 1968 letter to CV.
[4] December 14, 1968 letter to college friend in PC/Nepal (SG).
[5] December 11, 1968 letter to college friend in VISTA in North Carolina (SB).
[6] December 7, 1968 letter to family.
[7] December 11, 1968 letter to SB.
[8] December 13, 1968 letter to CV.
[9] December 14, 1968 letter to SG.
[10] December 15, 1969 letter to married friends from high school (G & LZ).
[11] December 24, 1968 letter to family.
[12] January 4, 1969 letter to 2 friends still in college (RY and DH).
[13] January 11, 1969 letter to SB.
[14] February 6, 1969 letter to SG.
[15] January 11, 1969 letter to SB.
[16] January 11, 1969 letter to family.
[17] January 17, 1969 letter to college friend, my roommate in Italy (CN).
[18] January 17, 1969 letter to the sister of a college friend (DB).
[19] January 14, 1969 journal entry.
[20] April 10, 1969 letter to DH.

21 January 14, 1969 journal entry.
22 January 24, 1969 letter to college friend (LW).
23 January 26, 1969 letter to college friends (FM, MB).
24 January 25, 1969 journal entry.
25 February 3, 1969 journal entry.
26 January 26, 1969 letter to FM and MB.
27 January 27, 1969 journal entry.
28 February 3, 1969 journal entry.
29 February 6, 1969 letter to SG.
30 February 6, 1969 journal entry.
31 February 7, 1969 journal entry.
32 February 7, 1969 letter to family.
33 February 7, 1969 letter to SB.
34 February 6, 1969 letter to SG.
35 February 6, 1969 journal entry.
36 February 7, 1969 letter to SB.
37 February 7, 1969 journal entry.
38 February 17, 1969 journal entry.
39 February 18, 1969 letter to G & LZ.
40 February 17, 1969 journal entry.
41 February 8, 1969 letter to associate director (BT).
42 February 17, 1969 journal entry.
43 February 19, 1969 journal entry.
44 February 23, 1969 letter to DB
45 February 19, 1969 journal entry.
46 February 23, 1969 letter to DB.
47 February 25, 1969 journal entry.
48 February 18, 1969 letter to G & LZ.
49 February 23, 1969 letter to DB.
50 February 25, 1969 journal entry.
51 February 23, 1969 letter to DB.
52 February 24, 1969 letter to friend still in college ("Crasher"?).
53 February 25, 1969 journal entry.
54 February 23, 1969 letter to DB.

55   February 23, 1969 letter to DB.
56   February 25, 1969 journal entry.
57   March 16, 1969 journal entry.
58   February 24, 1969 letter to"Crasher".
59   March 16, 1969 journal entry.
60   March 18, 1969 letter to friend from college in Navy (MB).
61   March 16, 1969 journal entry.
62   March 17, 1969 journal entry.
63   March 18, 1979 journal entry.
64   March 18, 1969 letter to MB.
65   March 18, 1969 letter to family.
66   March 20, 1969 journal entry.
67   April 4, 1969 journal entry.
68   April 5, 1969 journal entry.
69   April 6, 1969 journal entry.
70   April 8, 1969 journal entry.
71   April 10, 1969 letter to DH.
72   March 17, 1969 journal entry.
73   March 18, 1969 letter to MB.
74   March 18, 1969 letter to family.
75   April 2, 1969 journal entry.
76   April 4, 1969 journal entry.
77   March 18, 1969 letter to family.
78   March 16, 1969 journal entry.
79   March 18, 1969 letter to family.
80   March 20, 1969 journal entry
81   April 4, 1969 journal entry.
82   April 5, 1969 journal entry.
83   April 7, 1969 journal entry.
84   April 8, 1969 journal entry.
85   April 10, 1969 journal entry.
86   April 10, 1969 letter to DH.
87   April 8, 1969 journal entry.
88   April 5, 1969 journal entry.

89   April 10, 1969 letter to DH.
90   April 20, 1969 journal entry.
91   April 23, 1969 letter to college friend, a VISTA in the Mission District of San Francisco (FM).
92   April 21, 1969 letter to family.
93   May 18, 1969 letter to SG.
94   April 21, 1969 letter to family.
95   April 20, 1969 journal entry.
96   April 23, 1969 letter to FM.
97   April 20, 1969 journal entry.
98   April 23, 1969 letter to FM.
99   April 20, 1969 journal entry.
100 April 29, 1969 letter to SB.
101 April 23, 1969 letter to FM.
102 April 20, 1969 journal entry.
103 April 21, 1969 letter to family.
104 April 25, 1969 journal entry.
105 April 26, 1969 journal entry.
106 April 28, 1969 journal entry.
107 April 29, 1969 letter to parents of college friend (D & JB).
108 April 28, 1969 journal entry.
109 April 29, 1969 letter to SB.
110 April 28, 1969 letter to CV.
111 May 19, 1969 letter to SB.
112 April 23, 1969 letter to FM.
113 April 28, 1969 letter to CV.
114 May 19, 1969 letter to SB.
115 May 5, 1969 journal entry.
116 May 19, 1969 letter to SB.
117 May 9, 1969 journal entry.
118 May 19, 1969 letter to SB.
119 May 9, 1969 journal entry.
120 May 19, 1969 letter to SB.
121 May 16, 1969 journal entry.

122 May 9, 1969 journal entry.
123 May 19, 1969 letter to SB.
124 May 9, 1969 journal entry.
125 May 16, 1969 journal entry.
126 May 19, 1969 letter to SB.
127 May 9, 1969 journal entry.
128 May 19, 1969 letter to SB.
129 May 9, 1969 journal entry.
130 April 21, 1969 letter to family.
131 April 25, 1969 journal entry.
132 May 19, 1969 letter to SB.
133 May 18, 1969 letter to SG.
134 June 1, 1969 letter to MB.
135 May 19, 1969 letter to SB.
136 May 18, 1969 letter to SG.
137 May 23, 1969 letter to man in charge of our training (CP).
138 June 1, 1969 letter to MB.
139 April 25, 1969 journal entry.
140 May 19, 1969 letter to SB.
141 June 1, 1969 letter to MB.
142 April 29, 1969 letter to SB.
143 June 1, 1969 letter to family.
144 August 30, 1969 letter SG.
145 August 16, 1969 letter to FM and LW.
146 August 30, 1969 letter to SG.
147 July 22, 1969 letter to family.
148 September 16, 1969 letter to my grandmother (LB).
149 August 17, 1969 letter to family.
150 August 16, 1969 letter to FM and LW.
151 August 30, 1969 letter to SG.
152 September 14, 1969 letter to FM and LW.
153 August 16, 1969 letter to FM and LW.
154 August 31, 1969 letter to CV.
155 August 17, 1969 letter to family.

[156] August 31, 1969 letter to CV.

[157] August 31, 1969 letter to CV.

[158] August 30, 1969 letter to SG.

[159] August 16, 1969 letter to FM and LW.

[160] August 17, 1969 letter to family.

[161] September 16, 1969 letter to family.

[162] October 2, 1969 letter to G & LZ.

[163] August 16, 1969 letter to FM and LW.

[164] August 30, 1969 letter to SG.

[165] August 31, 1969 letter CV.

[166] August 17, 1969 letter to family.

[167] August 17, 1969 letter to family.

[168] August 17, 1969 letter to family.

[169] July 20, 1969 journal entry.

[170] August 17, 1969 letter to family.

[171] August 1, 1969 journal entry.

[172] August 17, 1969 letter to family.

[173] August 16, 1969 letter to FM and LW.

[174] August 16, 1969 letter to FM and LW.

[175] August 17, 1969 letter to family.

[176] August 30, 1969 letter to friend still in college (MF).

[177] August 31, 1969 letter to CV.

[178] September 14, 1969 letter to FM and LW.

[179] August 16, 1969 letter to FM and LW.

[180] September 14, 1969 letter to Somalia 8 who went home early (DG).

[181] September 14, 1969 letter to FM and LW.

[182] September 22, 1969 letter to SB.

[183] September 29, 1969 letter to DB.

[184] December 16, 1969 group holiday letter (GHL).

[185] September 22, 1969 letter to SB.

[186] October 2, 1969 letter to G and LZ.

[187] October 16, 1969 letter to LB.

188   August 19, 1969 letter to Somalia PCV who finished his term (illegible, probably PS).
189   August 16, 1969 letter to FM and LW.
190   August 31, 1969 letter to CV.
191   September 29, 1969 letter DB.
192   August 17, 1969 letter to family.
193   August 30, 1969 letter to MF.
194   September 10, 1969 letter to John (posted with him in Kansahdere, now in Beled Uen) (JM).
195   September 14, 1969 letter to FM and LW.
196   September 16, 1969 letter to family.
197   September 22, 1969 letter to SB.
198 October 2, 1969 letter to G and LZ.
199   August 30, 1969 letter to MF.
200   September 16, 1969 letter to PCV who had finished her term (MC).
201   August 30, 1969 letter to MF.
202   September 16, 1969 letter to family.
203   November 5, 1969 journal entry.
204   September 16, 1969 letter to MC.
205   October 16, 1969 letter to LB.
206   October 20, 1969 letter to DH.
207   August 19, 1969 letter probably to PS.
208   September 10, 1969 letter to JM.
209   September 14, 1969 letter to DG.
210   September 16, 1969 letter to MC.
211   October 16, 1969 letter to MC.
212   October 16, 1969 letter to LB.
213   November 5, 1969 journal entry.
214   October 22, 1969 letter to CV.
215   November 5, 1969 journal entry.
216   October 22, 1969 letter to CV.
217   November 5, 1969 journal entry.
218   November 5, 1969 journal entry.

219 December 16, 1969 group holiday letter (GHL).

220 November 5, 1969 journal entry.

221 November 17, 1969 journal entry.

222 November 16, 1969 journal entry.

223 December 16, 1969 GHL.

224 November 7, 1969 journal entry.

225 December 3, 1969 letter to FM and LW.

226 November 13, 1969 journal entry.

227 November 15, 1969 journal entry.

228 November 15, 1969 journal entry.

229 November 16, 1969 journal entry.

230 November 16, 1969 journal entry.

231 December 16, 1969 GHL.

232 December 6, 1969 journal entry.

233 November 16, 1969 journal entry.

234 December 16, 1969 GHL.

235 November 22, 1969 journal entry.

236 November 7 1969 journal entry.

237 November 16, 1969 journal entry.

238 November 30, 1969 journal entry.

239 December 16, 1969 GHL.

240 November 30, 1969 journal entry.

241 November 30, 1969 journal entry.

242 December 16, 1969 GHL.

243 November 30, 1969 journal entry.

244 November 30, 1969 journal entry.

245 December 31, 1969 letter to SB.

246 December 16, 1969 GHL.

247 December 3, 1969 letter to FM and LW.

248 December 6, 1969 letter to CV.

249 December 16, 1969 GHL.

250 January 3, 1970 letter to SB.

251 August 19, 1969 letter to PCV whose term had ended (illegible, probably PS).

252 September 10, 1969 letter to John Marks, now in Beled Uen.

253 September 14, 1969 letter to Somalia 8 who left early (DG).

254 September 16, 1969 letter to Somalia PCV whose term ended (MC).

255 October 16, 1969 letter to Somalia PCV whose term ended (MC).

CPSIA information can be obtained at www.ICGtesting.com
Printed in the USA
LVOW07s0537110116

469976LV00001B/1/P